Handbook of Suicidology

Principles, Problems, and Practice

by

LOUIS WEKSTEIN

Director of Psychological Services,
St. Elizabeth's Hospital,
Boston, Massachusetts;
Associate Clinical Professor of Psychiatry,
Tufts University School of Medicine

BRUNNER/MAZEL, *Publishers* • **New York**

Library of Congress Cataloging in Publication Data

Wekstein, Louis, 1917-
    Handbook of suicidology.

    Bibliography: p.
    Includes index.
    1. Suicide.   2. Suicide—Prevention.
I. Title.
RC569.W44   616.8'5844   79-19221
ISBN 0-87630-211-8

Published by
BRUNNER/MAZEL, INC.
19 Union Square
New York, New York 10003

MANUFACTURED IN THE UNITED STATES OF AMERICA

THIS BOOK IS
DEDICATED TO
THE MEMORY
OF JANIS

FOREWORD

What makes Dr. Wekstein's book especially welcome is, first, that, as a treatise by a single author, it is a somewhat rare event on the current scene of suicide studies. It has, therefore, a cohesion of style, content and approach, making for good reading and great common sense. Second, Wekstein's approach is gratifyingly eclectic. Though writing as an analytic psychotherapist, the author pays far more than lip service to the role of social factors in the widest sense. The medical model which equates suicide with depression as a "disease" and its solution as a matter for medical doctors is on the retreat. Whatever intrapsychic events and personal vulnerabilities may exist, the role of social factors and significant life events seems to be increasingly regarded as crucial in the evaluation of any suicidal person. Wekstein's determination to see behind the presenting "symptom-syndrome" is a splendid reply to the simplistic views of some psychiatrists, and we cannot be reminded too often that anti-depressant drug treatment, naively begun for the suicidal depressive, can increase lethality.

In his sensitive evaluation of the multidisciplinary approach, however, Dr. Wekstein does not underestimate the use of physical treatments in patients properly diagnosed as "psychotic" or "endogenous," which seem to be concepts in the process of being redis-covered in some centers. Analytic psychotherapy certainly has a place, but it is but one place alongside others. Another lesson that cannot too often be repeated is that people in suicidal crises need *time*. The therapist may need to put aside two or three hours for a suicidal patient and be available for follow-up calls or interviews at short notice.

Dr. Wekstein, who combines a lifetime of clinical experience with a vast knowledge of academic background, points to suicidology as a subspeciality every bit as valid as cardiology to internal medicine. Mental health professionals, as he points out, should seek the advice of and share responsibility with suicidologists in the management of particular cases, and in training programs.

Of particular value is a down-to-earth description and critique of the 14 workshops from the American Association of Suicidology training manual. Of the many books on suicide that have lately appeared, precious few offer much to help us cope, constructively, with suicidal people. Dr. Wekstein's book is a happy exception.

RICHARD FOX, M.D.

Senior Consultant Psychiatrist, Severalls Hospital, Colchester, England

Hon. Psychiatric Consultant: The Samaritans

Vice-President & U.K. Representative: The International Association for Suicide Prevention & Crisis Intervention.

PREFACE

This book is an effort to explore and critically appraise a multidisciplinary approach to suicidology. The author has tried to integrate the multiple aspects of the subject and has perceived life-threatening and self-destructive behavior as a gestalt. An attempt has been made to relate the major contributions of the past both to recent studies and to proposed research.

Influences and forces that determined moral, legal, religious, and cultural attitudes that persisted for centuries and still exist in subtle forms are reviewed. Since the etiology of self-destruction is unknown, the variety of causal relationships are evaluated and discussed. Theoretical constructs and formulations are considered in perspective. The emphasis is on the most recent clinical studies—their empirical findings, their implementation, and their efficacy in contending with life-threatening behavior. The relationship of psychopathology and suicide is examined in the light of the symptom syndromes and their functions as defensive armamentaria against suicide. The dynamics of prophylaxis, intervention, and postvention are discussed, and current procedures and techniques, as well as others that are in the offing, for dealing with the suicide and the victim-survivors are examined. A major section of one chapter is based upon the *Suicide Prevention Training Manual,* which is the product of the combined efforts of leading figures of the American Association of Suicidology. The last two chapters are specifically directed to management.

My main purpose is to incorporate the basic principles of and some of the vast problems inherent in the practice of suicidology into one dynamically oriented text that is, above all else, functional. Considerable attention has been devoted to illustrative case material.

The book is aimed at a diverse audience that includes not only the professionals—physicians, psychiatrists, psychologists, sociologists, etc.—but also lay people who seek to acquire a realistic view of the vast panorama of suicide and life-threatening behavior.

Louis Wekstein

June, 1979

ACKNOWLEDGMENTS

Writing a book is a self-imposed endeavor. Assumption of such an undertaking implies that the author believes he possesses the knowledge, experience and skill to accomplish the project. However, it is virtually impossible for even a multifaceted author to rely solely on his own resources. Although a bibliography may reflect some of a writer's orientation, a myriad of significant figures are consciously and unconsciously woven into his orchestration. It would require an autobiography to identify and to enumerate these influences. The acknowledgments below list only a few of the individuals who were instrumental in making this book a reality.

Everyone who writes about suicidology is indebted to Dr. Edwin S. Shneidman, Professor of Thanatology at the University of California; he originated the word "suicidology," and his work spurred many productive research and clinical endeavors in the area of self-destructive behavior.

Past associations are indelibly imprinted: Dr. Erich Lindemann, who was Chairman of the Department of Psychiatry, Harvard Medical School, and Director of Psychiatry at Massachusetts General Hospital, prolific and inspiring, first stimulated my interest in grief reactions more than 30 years ago. Dr. Theodor Reik, founder of the International Psychological Association of Psychoanalysis, transmitted some of his astute dynamic echoes from the third ear that still resound. Dr. Paul G. Myerson, Chairman of the Department of Psychiatry, Tufts University School of Medicine, and Psychiatrist-in-Chief, New England Medical Center, has broadened my perspectives for more than three decades.

Appreciation is also expressed to Dr. Philip Quinn, Chief of Psychiatry at St. Elizabeth's Hospital, lifelong friend, realist to the core, who encouraged my effort and whose indomitable tenacity epitomizes the forces for life; to Pamela C. Cantor of the Radcliffe

Institute of Harvard University and the Boston University faculty for her generous contributions and comments; to Dr. Lawrence E. Abt; and to Dr. Peter B. Field of the International Graduate School of Behavioral Science, Florida Institute of Technology, whose penetrating criticism of the manuscript was positive and encouraging; to David Goldstein of Tufts University Graduate School, who reviewed portions of the manuscript relative to public health and sociology; to Evelyn Geffen, who was infinitely patient and dedicated in deciphering illegible handwritten notations and transcribing taped dictation that was hardly audible; to Clem Hallquist, Chairman of Public Relations for the American Association of Suicidology, for his gracious support and interest.

Expressions of particular thanks and gratitude are extended to Mr. Louis Rains who was indefatigable and dedicated to the infinite complexities that ensued in editing and copyreading.

Ms. Deborah T. Almquist, Medical Librarian at St. Elizabeth's Hospital, truly proved her expertise and ingenuity in providing resource material; and Ms. Christine Umana was dedicated in verifying the bibliography.

The 14 workshop problems as they appear in the *Suicide Prevention Training Manual* were used with the permission of The American Association of Suicidology and of the Health Information Services, Merck, Sharp and Dohme Division of Merck and Co., Inc.

Harper and Row, Publishers, gave permission to use excerpts from *Suicide*, Jack P. Gibbs, editor.

Excerpts from "Recent Decline of Suicide in Britain: Role of the Samaritan Prevention Movement in Suicidology," by Richard Fox, in: *Suicidology: Contemporary Development*, E. S. Shneidman (ed.) 1976, were quoted by permission of Grune and Stratton, Inc. Approval was also given by E. S. Shneidman and Richard Fox.

Permission to quote from "The Visual Arts Today" by Felix Deutsch, which appeared in *Daedalus*, Winter, 1960, has been given by the American Academy of Arts and Sciences, Boston, Massachusetts.

Times Books granted permission to include an excerpt from *Splitting: A Case of Female Masculinity*, by Robert Stoller.

CONTENTS

HANDBOOK OF SUICIDOLOGY

Principles, Problems and Practice

CHAPTER 1

INTRODUCTION TO SUICIDOLOGY

An enigma that has confronted and haunted mankind for eons is the realization that not all people wish to live. Life is precious above all else, and once rooted there is a tenacious attempt to hold on to it and to maintain it at all costs. This clinging to life in the face of tragedy, adversity, torture, anguish, humiliation, the ravages of old age—even interminable pain when death is manifestly imminent—is characteristic of the overwhelming majority of humanity. There are, however, those who elect to terminate their existence. These individuals, on a seemingly volitional basis, make a drastic, irrevocable decision to divest themselves of life. The German word *Selbstvernichtung,* self-destruction, accurately describes this act.

There are, then, individuals who, under varying circumstances, perceive life as so ungratifying, so unfruitful, so futile, and so meaningless as to cause them to end it by murdering themselves. These people choose to execute themselves on the basis of their own rationale and on their own terms rather than wait out the normal course of events that inevitably results in demise as the inexorable force of fate.

Although there is a strong tendency towards denial about such matters, most people have at one point or another encountered gigantic conflictual struggles and crises in their lives and have considered suicide as an option. The vast majority have resolved, averted or diverted these self-destructive temptations, impulses and urges. However, the very facts that such premeditation is so prevalent and that many people merely postpone their suicide only to reinitiate the attempt at a later date emphasize the vast preoccupation with death in human society. On this basis alone, there is ample reason for scientists to investigate this form of lethality.

There is a provocative and intriguing—but elusive and impenetrable—aura of mystery surrounding suicide. In "Thoughts for the Times on War and Death," Freud (1915) wrote:

> Is it not for us to confess that in our civilized attitude towards death we are once more living psychologically beyond our means, and must reform and give truth its due? Will it not be better to give death the place in actuality and in our thoughts which properly belongs to it, and to yield a little more prominence to that unconscious attitude towards death which we have hitherto so carefully suppressed? This hardly seems indeed a greater achievement, but rather a backward step . . . but it has the merit of taking somewhat more into account the true state of affairs . . . (p. 299) .

Freud, the somber realist, bravely attempted to take death into true account, but death remains an impenetrable, intriguing and elusive vale from which no man returns.

For centuries speculation and superstition about suicide were largely interspersed with moral, religious and philosophical dogma. It was not until the twentieth century, when scientific methodology was well on its way, that Emile Durkheim and Sigmund Freud dispersed the archaic cobwebs and opened more objective avenues for the exploration and study of suicide. The panorama that was revealed encompassed every sphere of human relations, including public health and medicine as well as mental health. Epidemiologists, statisticians, sociologists, psychiatrists, psychologists and physicians became increasingly aware of suicide as a leading cause of death.

Since the preliminary work of Durkheim (1897, 1952) and Freud (1917, 1923, 1930, 1950) , their proponents and opponents alike have brought forth a multitude of additions, elaborations, new concepts, hypotheses and constructs. The world's most renowned theorists and mental health practitioners offered their contributions, and the literature is replete with such figures as Adler (1910, 1929, 1937), Jung (1939, 1959), Abraham (1953), Stekel (1910), Rado (1951, 1956), Zilboorg (1935, 1937, 1938), Fenichel (1945), Menninger (1933, 1938), Federn (1918, 1929a), Anna Freud (1937), Glover (1922, 1928, 1956), Sullivan (1953, 1956), Horney (1942, 1945, 1950), Halbwachs (1930), Dublin (1963), Fox (1976, 1978a, b), Henry and Short (1954), Cavan (1926), Maris (1969), Douglas (1967), Gibbs and Martin (1964), Powell (1958), Shneidman (1967), and Stengel (1964).

As early as 1910, suicide was the subject of a meeting of the Vienna Psychoanalytic Society, the minutes of which have been translated by Paul Friedman (1967). Freud's thoughts on suicide were influenced by his clinical experiences, and his theoretical positions changed considerably throughout the years. Litman (1967) documented these progressions that extended from 1881 to 1939, the year of Freud's death.

At the 1910 Symposium, Freud was brief and reserved. He hinted that further elaboration of his thinking was forthcoming. Apparently, he was referring to *Mourning and Melancholia,* published in 1917. Freud's cautious words (Friedman, 1967) are still pertinent:

> I have an impression that, in spite of all the valuable material that has been brought before us in this discussion, we have not reached a decision on the problem that interests us. We were anxious above all to know how it becomes possible for the extraordinarily powerful life instinct to be overcome: whether this can only come about with the help of a disappointed libido or whether the ego can renounce its self-preservation for its own egotistic motives. It may be that we have failed to answer this psychological question because we have no adequate means of approaching it. We can, I think, only take as our starting point the condition of melancholia, which is so familiar to us clinically, and a comparison between it and the affect of mourning. The affective processes in melancholia, however, and the vicissitudes undergone by the libido in that condition, are totally unkown to us. Nor have we arrived at a psychoanalytic understanding of the chronic affect of mourning. Let us suspend our judgment till experience has solved this problem (p. 140).

A new era, in a new Zeitgeist that reflected the growing interest and concern about suicide as a psychologic, psychiatric, sociologic phenomenon, was inaugurated when the Los Angeles Suicide Prevention Center was established in 1958 under the aegis of Edwin S. Shneidman, Norman L. Farberow and Robert E. Litman (*Suicide Prevention Center,* 1960), with the help of a five-year U.S. Public Health grant. Their functional, dynamic and innovative approach became a prototype for others, and their phenomenal literary output, in conjunction with their associates, gave impetus to a new optimism about the growing field now referred to as suicidology.

SUICIDOLOGY AND THE MULTIDISCIPLINARY APPROACH

Every psychotherapist deals directly with suicide or encounters suicidal problems in one form or another in his practice. However, not every psychotherapist is a suicidologist. A comprehensive study of suicide encompasses the entire gamut of psychopathology and it is generally included within the broad spectrum of psychopathology (Hendin, 1967; Shneidman, 1975; Farberow, 1969; Litman, 1965a; Page, 1975). However, the magnitude of the problem is such that it cannot be demarcated and limited to any one province or discipline. The immensity and complexity of the issues involved in the destruction of oneself transcend classical psychiatry. Edwin S. Shneidman et al. (1970, 1975) refer to the psycho-socio-dyadic-existential state and suggests that a configurationistic approach is a prerequisite for providing insights that can lead the suicidologist to more effective intervention techniques.

Although the intrapsychic and interpersonal factors are undoubtedly significant and often predominant in suicidal crises, the relationship between biological, physiological and genetic forces should also be explored and evaluated. Theoretical formulations, investigation, research, intervention, therapy and postvention require a multidisciplinary approach. The interrelationships that exist among anthropology, philosophy, psychology, psychiatry, sociology and demography in implementing the interdisciplinary effort are demonstrated in overall discussions by Hendin (1967), Gibbs (1968), Perlin (1975),

Weisman et al. (1973), and Shneidman et al (1975). Other disciplines, such as medicine, social work, nursing, teaching and law, are influential and contributory. Alvarez (1972) provides a sensitive portrayal of creative artists—particularly poets and writers—who have enriched suicidology with provocative intrapsychic material. Existentialists and philosophers have also addressed themselves to the problem of life's meaninglessness and despair (Camus, 1945).

Paramedical, paraprofessional and ancillary figures cannot be excluded in a totalistic approach. A diverse conglomerate of individuals, such as bartenders, police officers, friends, relatives and acquaintances often see the patient prior to his arrival at the suicide prevention center, before the referral to the psychotherapist is made. Their interaction and participation have proved to be significant. The Samaritans, a group of interested laymen organized in 1966 by Varah, an Anglican priest, have been effective in the British Isles, functioning as nonintrusive friends to people in the throes of suicidal crises. In spite of their modest and seemingly limited role as volunteers, their impact has been considerable—so much so that they have now established centers in the United States. The Samaritans underscore the positive effect of a nonsectarian group of varying backgrounds, occupations and socioeconomic strata in the intervention of suicide (Chowdhury and Kreitman, 1971).

The psychotherapist who is also involved in suicidology cannot rely solely on his classical knowledge and expertise in psychopathology and psychotherapy. He can neither retain his professional isolation nor maintain a stereotyped, structured professional posture. He must be ever ready and alert to amplify and to modify his techniques in order to fully utilize the increasing armamentaria that provide for lifesaving measures. Shneidman, Farberow and Litman (1961) stress the importance of the integration and extension of services, and their implication is that the number of collaborators cannot be predetermined.

Techniques of assessment are not always in accordance with standard psychiatric protocol. For example, the initial evaluation that ordinarily requires the classical hour may in the case of the suicide consist of two or even three hours of interviewing. The suicide's mistress, lover, or homosexual or alcoholic confrere may be required to provide data, cogent background material and support. They may be instrumental in the dyadic relationship with the potential suicide, and they, too, may require evaluation, guidance, counseling, and even therapy. The suicidal crisis represents an event with lethal urgency, and no efforts can be spared for scholastic deliberation and judgmental attitudes. The matter of breaching confidentiality, with its attendant medical, legal and ethical problems, may loom large in the face of an emergency evaluation of a patient who is uncompromisingly death-oriented. The rigid and "ethical" therapist may, under certain circumstances, forfeit his patient's life by preserving confidentiality. Litman and Farberow (1965) allude to this problem. Shneidman (1975) stated:

> Admittedly, this a touchy and complicated point, but the therapist should not ally himself with death. Statements given during the therapy session relating to the patient's overt suicidal, or homicidal plans cannot be treated as a secret between two collusive partners (p. 1782).

The need for responsibility as well as flexibility in coping with such issues necessitates the utilization of a multidisciplinary approach which may require the participation of all available agencies, measures and resources.

While it is not our purpose to examine emergency evaluation and treatment of self-destruction in this section, it becomes manifest that a departure from standardized psychiatric procedure is not atypical and is often mandatory. It is also an oversimplification to ascribe all suicide to mental illness without considering the constellation of other factors and forces.

Multi- and interdisciplinary participation is not the sine qua non of suicidology alone. Over the past half century, medicine has slowly relinquished its role as the sole arbiter in matters relating to health; as cumulative advances have been made, there have been a growing rapprochement and collaboration of the related sciences.

An outstanding example of such cooperation exists in physical medicine and rehabilitation, where much progress has been attributed to the realization that health problems cannot be demarcated by an archaic system of professional stratification. Rusk (1946, 1958) was particularly adept in mobilizing interdisciplinary and paraprofessional resources for purposes of habilitation and rehabilitation. Physical medicine and rehabilitation are related and share innumerable common problems with suicidology. It is not coincidental that many patients who require rehabilitation are or have been suicidal. Numerous victims of physical trauma or accidents give evidence of intentional or subintentional self-destructive motivation. Shneidman (1971a, 1975) strongly suggests that such individuals are inclined to behave in the inimical manner that has been well documented, particularly by Menninger, who has written extensively on this aspect (1935, 1936, 1938). Accidents are often caused by subintentioned or intentioned death wishes which may lead to misuse of drugs, alcohol, refusal to accept reality, and a negative behavior that consciously and unconsciously leads to, or dictates, a suicidal course. Even patients who come to a rehabilitation center because of inherited defects or chronic illnesses may be compounding their diseases and infirmities with a wish to die that aggravates or exacerbates their condition. Menninger (1938) enumerated a large number of partial and focal deaths—maiming, mutilation and inflictions of injuries. These often bring the patient not to a suicidologist or psychotherapist but to an emergency room, to a general hospital, and ultimately to a rehabilitation center.

In the disciplines of suicidology and rehabilitation, there is the necessity for careful assessment, diagnosis, therapy and postvention, in addition to medical care. Even the goals are basically similar, namely to modify and resolve intrapsychic and external forces and pressures in order to enable the patient to derive maximal gratification through realistic coping. This is a creative process that requires the exploration and mobilization of the patient's physical, intellectual, social, emotional and vocational resources in such a way as to bring about an integration—a wholeness of the personality. Neither field can be limited to one discipline, and a multidisciplinary team is required to work in concert.

Wekstein (1964) points out that:

Integration does not mandatorily require agreement or unanimity. Eclecticism, differing terminologies, methodologies with differences of opinion can coexist, and interdisciplinary communication can be facilitated and enhanced if a common frame of reference could be developed that possesses sufficient latitude and meets nonconflicting criteria. Such a frame of reference should: (1) Provide concepts and formulations that transcend skills and fields of specialization and make it possible for the team member to better appreciate his role in the multidisciplinary configuration. (2) Enable the team to perceive the patient dynamically as an adjusting organism responding to multiple forces from within and without. (3) Be subject to clinical and experimental verification of its concepts, principles, formulations and assumptions (pp. 47-48) .

The Problem of Etiology

It is indisputable that the most effective approach in contending with the maladies and the disequilibria attendant to mankind is to isolate and identify the specific causative agents. A barrage of measures currently available could then be mobilized and implemented to counteract and to control them. The formidable contribution of organicists represented a great triumph for the thesis of etiology in the history of medicine (Sigerist, 1943). Alzheimer, Wernicke, Golgi, Babinski, and Broca are merely a representative few whose work on the localization and coordination of voluntary and reflex motions of the brain was considered revolutionary in their day (Wechsler, 1943; Zilboorg and Henry, 1941; Jaspers, 1963) . The discovery of the treponema pallidum by Noguchi as the cause of syphillis of the brain and the establishment of the tubercle bacillus as the cause of tuberculosis by Koch brought further confirmation of the organic viewpoint. The search for specific causes and localization perseverated and gripped science with an obsessive tenacity (Hebb, 1958; Weber, 1939). This preoccupation with etiology has persisted with unabated fervor to the present day.

In the area of human relations, where procedures cannot be carried out with the same elegance of experimental design, exactitude and quantitative measurements as in medicine (Eysenck, 1955; Hebb, 1958), much criticism and dissatisfaction have existed. Prestige bordering on veneration came to be attached to research in areas where breakthroughs resulted in specific findings and where a particular problem could be isolated and ultimately resolved. Such remarkable achievements as the vaccine for poliomyelitis and the synthesis of antibiotics for a wide spectrum of infectious diseases are illustrative. However, an interminable series of intricate variables cannot be easily reduced. Tracking down a microorganism or lesion is a far cry from the analysis and assessment of the myriad stimuli that impinge on the brain, with resultant patterns of divergent and unpredictable behavior.

Apropos of this, Linn in his contribution "Clinical Manifestations of Psychiatric Disorders" (1967) stated:

It used to be said that the best diagnosis is one based on knowledge of etiology (p. 546).

Later in the same article he went on to elaborate:

The life process in health and disease consists of an ongoing series of adaptations. Depending on their effectiveness, an individual may be healthy and functioning with unimpaired efficiency or he may be mortally affected by stress, or he may display a number of intermediate reactive patterns representing disease states that are, in effect, the continuations of life in the face of handicaps. Thus, a symptom or even a complex disease process in its entirety may be viewed as a reaction pattern having adaptational significance.

The clinical manifestations are the outcome of complex interacting forces—biological, sociocultural, and psychological (p. 546).

This general attitude exemplifies the current thinking in suicidology (Shneidman and Farberow, 1957a; Menninger, 1938; Jackson, 1954, 1957; Lennard-Jones and Asher, 1959; Gibbs, 1968; Pokorny, 1964; Stengel, 1964; Litman, 1965a; Hendin, 1967; Perlin, 1975).

In examining the issues and considering the reverberations of the impassioned polemics of those who insist on an organic etiology as a primary consideration, Spitzer and Wilson (1975) jointly concluded:

> (1) More or less distinct human conditions are associated with suffering and disability with more or less distinct causes and natural causes that respond differently to more or less distinct treatments. (2) The study and treatment of these conditions are at least partly the responsibility of the medical profession. This conception of the medical model makes no a priori assumptions as to what etiological factors—physical, social, genetic, psychological, developmental—are responsible for the development of these conditions nor what kind of treatment—somatic, psychological, social, behavioral—will be most effective (p. 827).

Such declarations represent a departure from the strict adherence to the eternal search for finding and treating specific causative agents.

Szasz (1961) adopted the most radical and extreme stance by suggesting that all mental symptoms are manifestations of life problems and that the syndromes seen by psychiatrists are not illnesses but are, rather, representative of conflicts over attempts at achieving social values. Szasz considers the use of terminology as an utterly valueless obfuscation.

A more plausible approach is suggested by Menninger, Mayman and Pruyser in *The Vital Balance* (1963). They propose that as alternatives to nosology and the preoccupation with etiology it would be beneficial to perceive emotional illness as a unitary process and that any differences be considered as merely of degree. Although Menninger et al. are hardly naive and fully appreciate the significance of the diagnostic criteria enumerated in the *American Psychiatric Diagnostic and Statistical Manual* (DSM II), they nevertheless consider that differences in psychic states are far less significant than the level of disorganization that they represent, and that they (the symptom syndromes) are no more than a partial approximation at best.

The intriguing conceptualized system of Menninger et al. involves five stages. In the first, there is minor impairment of adaptive function of coping ability, which might be termed nervousness. In the second, the level of disorganization has increased, and in this category they include the neurotic syndromes. The third is representative of lability, loss of control and aggressivity. In the fourth, the level of disorganization has increased further and intensified, with a resulting regression and denial of reality. In this category they included the traditional psychoses. They regarded the fifth level as the ultimate form of disorganization, with a malignant anxiety and depression which is death-oriented and lethal.

Although the views of Menninger et al. have been subjected to criticism, their perspective has had a neutralizing effect in the interminable search for etiology. They made it abundantly clear that the classification, progress and control need not be impeded or inevitably bound by the idée fixe of specificity.

Accumulated material relative to suicidal behavior has grown immeasurably, and the trend reflects the requirements of modern methodology. Farberow (1969) compiled 1200 titles extending from 1957 to 1967. When this compilation was extended from 1897 through 1967, there were 3400 items enumerated. Choron (1972), in an analysis of Faberow and Shneidman's bibliography (1961a), in which approximately 2100 items were included (1897 through 1957), found that only 25 were listed under a religious or philosophical category. The remaining items were in areas where scientific and objective scrutiny was possible.

Kahne (1966) and Lester (1970) concluded, after an analytic examination of the literature, that there had all too long been a profusion and a proliferation of material that was erroneous and poorly authenticated. The favorable atmosphere and outlook, particularly after the mid-1950s with the establishment of the Los Angeles Suicidal Prevention Center, provided a multitude of avenues and insights that are diametrically opposed to esoteric, metaphysical and pedantic discussion. The emphasis on problems of suicide, rather than on suicide as a problem, has created an optimistic and productive atmosphere.

However, it is undeniable that the etiology of suicide still remains unknown. Research to this date has neither unearthed nor revealed what possesses some individuals to effectuate their own demise and why such a desperate course of action is dictated. Shneidman (1975)

comments that the suicidal person himself is least aware of the complicated motives that impel him. An imaginary slight to a vulnerable
individual can provoke a successful suicidal attempt, and yet other
non-suicidal individuals survive ordeals such as concentration camps
(Bettelheim, 1951, 1967; Frankl, 1929). The multitude of contradictions, exceptions, diverse theories, formulations and speculations
clearly excludes a single solution.

In spite of chiding and scepticism, the suicidologist has no cause
to be defensive about his inability to be definitive. The matter of
etiology has never been established in innumerable human conditions, ranging from war and crime to cancer and the common cold.
The physician's wry quip to the patient who consults him for a
simple respiratory infection that he return with a more serious ailment such as pneumonia, for which the etiology and therapy have
been determined, hardly strikes a responsive chord. It is indeed ironic
that many serious ailments—plagues and scourges for that matter—
have an authenticated etiology, but some of the most prevalent pathological states and causes of death can only be empirically treated at
best. Zubin (Beck et al., 1974) noted:

> The search for etiology in the classification of human behavior
> is similar to the search for evolutionary similarity in the classi-
> fication of animals. However, there is much more known about
> evolution (p. 3).

When Sigmund Freud wrote *Mourning and Melancholia* (1917),
he provided a frame of reference for an examination of the dynamics
of depression. Durkheim (1897) focalized on those forces of society
which influenced the outcome of life. Both of these pioneers, although diametrically opposed in their theoretical conceptualizations,
agreed that there was no panacea and that much work remained to
be done. After a symposium on suicide in Vienna in 1918, Freud
frankly conceded that psychoanalytic approaches had not provided
any solutions. Almost 20 years later, Zilboorg (1936a) reiterated that
clinical psychopathology had failed to find a causal or even a strictly
empirical solution. Many of the investigators who analyzed the exist-

ing barriers proved far more profound in sophistry than in etiological understanding.

Miller (1967) quotes Jung as stating:

> Even if everyone knows how everything in a given person has come about, that person would still be only half understood (p. 589).

May et al. (1958) perceptively and vividly expressed the enormity of meeting and evaluating a fellow human being:

> We may know a great deal about a patient from his case record, let us say, and may have a fairly good idea of how other interviewers have described him. But when the patient himself steps in, we often have a sudden, sometimes powerful experience of here-is-a-new-person, an experience that normally carries with it an element of surprise, not in the sense of perplexity or bewilderment but in its etymological sense of being "taken from above." This is, of course in no sense a criticism of one's colleagues' reports . . . The data we learned about the patient may have been accurate and well worth learning. But the point rather is that the grasping of the being of the other person occurs on a quite different level from our knowledge of specific things about him (pp. 37-38).

In a summary of theories, Jackson (1957) considered the synthesis of sociologic and psychoanalytic data and abstracted a variety of approaches that have served as a frame of reference in the approach to suicide. Miller (1967) emphasized the adaptational, the dynamic, the changing and the integrating functions of personality as the patient deals with his milieu and contends with the multitudinous problems that emerge and eventuate. Bernard (1961), in a comprehensive paper presented before the Third World Congress of Psychiatry, detailed the interrelationships of community psychiatry, mental health programs and research in social psychiatry as a symbiotic function.

In spite of differences in wording and scope, it is the general consensus that the total human being as well as the impact of society must be taken into consideration. The thrust of the Los Angeles Suicidal Prevention Center is in accord with eclectic attitudes: focalization on prophylaxis, public participation, dissemination of information, improving intervention techniques and the development of postvention procedures (Shneidman, Farberow and Litman, 1961).

The lack of an etiology, therefore, need not be considered as an inability or a failure to cope with the problems of suicide. It is a confession neither of ignorance nor of impotence. This is well illustrated by the etiological parallel that exists between suicidology and malignant disease. A constant, persistent flow of data emerges and is collated with efficiency and dispatch. The results of ongoing studies are optimistic. Battle lines are constantly reinforced. The foe is mortality and morbidity. In both areas, diagnosis, assessment, therapeutic intervention, prevention and postvention are defined, refined and enhanced. Both make large utilization of the multidisciplinary approach and the enlistment of educational media, hoping to secure the largest possible public interest and participation. There is now general accord in oncology and in suicidology that no one field has within itself the resources, the manpower or the potential to come forth with the answer and that all professional boundaries must be transcended and breached to attain the desired goal.

SUICIDOLOGY AS A SUBSPECIALITY

According to the medical model, a subspeciality is a speciality within a speciality; e.g., a cardiologist is essentially an internist (already a specialist) who further confines himself to diseases of the heart. He may limit himself exclusively to his subspeciality or practice within the wider sphere of internal medicine. The professional psychotherapist who elects suicidology as a subspeciality, whatever his discipline, needs additional training. He must actively pursue a program of study combined with clinical work and practice, with a close and active participation in a multidisciplinary center. Just as the cardiologist may function as an internist for varying portions of his time, so the suicidologist may be involved with research and a wide

variety of patients in addition to those who present suicidal problems.
It should be emphasized that not everyone involved with suicidology is a psychotherapist. Conversely, not every psychotherapist
is well versed in suicidology. Anthropologists, epidemiologists, sociologists, clergy and others can be suicidologists. They may be involved
in research, education, prevention, intervention, etc. The large
majority of suicides are deterred and averted by humanistic, highly
motivated and dedicated people from all walks of life (Fox, 1978b).
The qualifications for membership of the American Association of
Suicidology state: "Membership in the AAS is open to individuals
from various disciplines and fields of experience who share a common
interest in the advancement of research and training and practice
relating to suicide prevention and life threatening behavior." In
another section: "The AAS is a multidisciplinary organization of
professionals and nonprofessionals who share a conviction that the
advancement of suicidology will contribute to our knowledge how
best to reduce human self-destruction. The objectives sought by the
AAS are represented by the affiliations and training of the membership, reflecting the belief that a combined effort of encouraging
research, education, services, and training is best to advance our
common goals."

Individuals without formal training as therapists—that is, without extensive, highly specialized backgrounds in psychopathology,
dynamics and psychotherapy—have served, and will continue to serve,
the cause against self-destruction. However, motivation and well-
intentioned caring must be implemented and reinforced with training. (Later chapters of this book deal with the training entailed in
acquiring effectiveness in suicidology.)

It must be recognized that the nonprofessional suicidologist may
not be trained or equipped to contend with the complex problems
that emerge or transpire and that management or befriending alone
may be insufficient. In such instances, referral to a professional
is indicated for treatment that may require active psychotherapy,
drug therapy, or electroconvulsive therapy. Professionals and nonprofessionals have no need to compete in the struggle against needless
deaths. Dr. Richard Fox, honorary consultant psychiatrist to the

Samaritans (1976), has provided an in-depth exposition of these unpaid but carefully selected and trained nonprofessional volunteers who are carefully supervised and required to submit regular reports to a leader. Backup services are available, and professionals can be called in or clients can be referred when the process of befriending is insufficient. Fox notes:

> Experience has taught that clients with severely inadequate personalities stand to gain little by befriending and those with aggressive psychopathic traits could actually be harmed. If a relationship were allowed to develop with emotional dependency and a development of unrealistic expectations, there could be negative results when the client felt let down. Training is directed at recognizing those who must not be befriended as well as those who can be. Decisions like this and referral to doctors are made only by branch leaders (p. 517).

It is obvious that lives can be saved by a variety of means, disciplines, and people. However, those who profess expertise in the area of suicidology as professionals—as consultants or therapists—and are engaged in active therapy with self-destructive patients must be willing to undergo a self-imposed, extensive training program. There is, Psychiatric Association or the American Psychological Association in as yet, no subspeciality board accreditation by either the American this field. Suicidology is still in an embryonic state, and it has been estimated that no more than a few hundred psychotherapists are now sufficiently well versed and trained in research, or in primary, secondary and tertiary preventative methods which correspond with prophylaxis, intervention and postvention procedures and techniques.

The therapist who has selected this sphere as a subspeciality is subsequently identified by his colleagues as an individual who can be relied upon to deal effectively with suicidal patients. The professional—the therapist who is also a suicidologist—may provide services on a supportive consultative basis where he evaluates the patient and then provides a treatment program that can be implemented by the referring physician or psychotherapist. In some cases, it may be advisable that both the therapist and the referring source become jointly involved. The suicidologist may suggest that the patient continue under his treatment alone until the high degree of lethality has been decreased (some psychoanalysts prefer such an arrangement), or he may conclude that a hospital milieu, where maximal security measures can be taken, is advisable.

The suicidologist may practice privately or within the structure of a suicide prevention center. There are those who feel that a professional who practices suicidology, like the traumatologist and emergency room physician, should not be in private practice. However, if he is in private practice, one would expect him to be intimately related to a hospital or center where immediate admission of his patients is assured and an array of multidisciplinary facilities is available. In all cases, he should not hesitate to enlist collaboration.

Litman and Farberow (1965) discussed the indications for consultation and the criteria for referral. A disconsolate patient who routinely presents himself to his therapist with suicidal ideation as a result of an identity crisis, a mild depression or transference reaction need not require the services of a consultant when a therapeutic alliance and collaboration exist. However, there are times when the physician or the psychotherapist is called upon to deal with a patient who is overtly lethal and in severe suicidal crisis. Here it is obvious that the risk factor can be decreased by arranging consultation with a suicidologist and that such a course would be in the best interests of the patient.

Psychotherapists who pride themselves on successfully dealing with severely disturbed and suicidal patients should bear in mind that they must be accessible at all times and that unavailability could result in tragedy. Moss and Hamilton (1957), Farberow (1957), and Litman (1956a) call attention to the protean problems of attending to the needs of such patients. In accord with these attitudes, many practitioners place a limit on the number of suicidal patients they treat. One or two highly lethal patients are deemed sufficient in a busy therapeutic practice. The involvement with and treatment of presuicidal individuals are both energy- and time-consuming. Aside from the long initial evaluation, the therapist must be carefully attuned to any shifts in the therapeutic alliance and the transference that might indicate the reactivation of suicidal impulses. He must be fully aware of the nuances, subtleties and abrupt changes that can take place. In order to accomplish this, it may be necessary for him to see the patient every day—perhaps even more frequently. Immediate hospitalization may be required, and staff privileges with direct access to emergency facilities are essential.

There are therapists who play it by ear—a form of denial—and, after superficial assessment, conclude that the patient is not likely to commit suicide. Some have fortuitously emerged from dangerous situations by the skin of their teeth. Others have had to face the grim, harrowing consequences. It is not surprising that psychotherapists as a group are notoriously shy about discussing their failures in the therapy of suicidal patients. Omnipotence and narcissism can be jolted and ruptured when that most tragic of all experiences to a doctor takes place. It is not an accident of fate that the highest rate of suicide in the medical profession exists in the speciality of psychiatry (Blachly et al., 1968; Freeman, 1967).

There are still many psychiatrists who classify every suicidal patient as depressed—a "safe" diagnosis when suicidal ideation exists—and then treat such patients with antidepressant drugs, which may provide paradoxical effects. They then offer support and wait hopefully for a remission. This is a perilous course, and more psychotherapists are becoming aware of the limitations and the dangers inherent in such an approach. Although every psychotherapist is technically entitled to treat the suicidal patient, how well equipped he is to do so is all too often determined by his own opinion of his competence. Referring the determined, death-oriented patient to a colleague or to a specialized center where suicidologists can evaluate, assess and offer therapy during a vulnerable state may be the wisest course. As Shneidman (1975) states:

> The psychiatrist, especially if he practices relatively on his own in private practice, does well not to attempt to bear the entire burden of a patient suicide by himself. Trying to go it all alone can be unnecessarily abrasive (p. 1783).

In summary, a growing subspeciality now exists which enables a psychotherapist with a suicidal patient to request consultation for a more complete assessment of risk—to share the responsibility and/or to facilitate hospitalization for intensive care. The psychotherapist with doubts or reservations may prudently elect not to tempt fate by accepting highly lethal, perturbed and actively suicidal individuals. Similar attitudes have been pervasive in medicine for a long time. A frank self-appraisal enables the practitioner to make a wise decision.

CHAPTER 2

ORIENTATION TO SUICIDOLOGY

HISTORICAL OVERVIEW

The history of suicide reflects the history of mankind. Suicide has existed as a form of behavior since the dawn of civilization. Although the word suicide is of relatively recent origin (Fedden, 1938), research and the investigations of anthropologists over the past century have clearly demonstrated its ubiquity (LaFontaine, 1975). Westermark (1906) presented convincing evidence that there were variations in primitive groups, just as there are in all groups, with regard to suicide. Subsequently, Malinowski (1926) discussed some of the significant forces that influenced primitive peoples and caused them to initiate their own deaths. Choron (1972) postulated that early man had to develop some concepts about death before taking a self-destructive course.

Formerly there was a long-held theory that suicide was a result of the increasing complexity of civilization and that primitive people, uncontaminated by progressive influences, could live out their lives idyllically without the need for self-destruction—an attitude epitomized by Rousseau in the 1770s. Voltaire (1772) satirically suggested that savages have no need to destroy themselves because of any disgust for life and that disillusionment was a negative side effect of civilization. Rousseau and Voltaire were, in fact, making the basic assumption that man is essentially good and that it is the deteriorative influence of society that exacts such tragic consequences.

During the 20th century, there has been no doubt that suicide is a universal phenomenon (LaFontaine, 1975; Rosen, 1971, 1975; Choron, 1972; Zilboorg, 1936b).

Although suicide can be perceived in varying temporal contexts and its significance is subject to differing value systems, a consistency of motives persists throughout the history of civilization. In his list, Westermark (1906) included:

> Disappointed love or jealousy; illness or old age; grief over the death of a child, husband or wife; fear of punishment; slavery or brutal treatment by a husband; remorse, shame or wounded pride; anger or revenge. In various cases the offended person kills himself for the express purpose of taking revenge on the offender. Killing oneself upon the head of another.

Broadly speaking, this compendium differs little from current explanations and ascribed simplistic motives.

There are but five reports of suicide in the Bible—only one is mentioned in the New Testament—and there has been considerable speculation about this paucity of instances of suicide in the Bible. It is conceivable that such occurrences were mentioned only when they were deemed important, or that some suicides may have been perceived as accidents, perhaps natural deaths. The infrequency of suicide among the Jews of the Old Testament period has also been attributed to an emphasis on life and a positive attitude towards the world. The Bible taught that the world was created by an omniscient God and therefore the world was good. There is no evidence of prohibition or condemnation of suicide in either the Hebrew Bible or in the New Testament, and there were no desecrations of the bodies of those who did destroy themselves or sanctions against their survivors.

There is, however, ample documentation of marked shifts and fluctuations about self-destruction in Greece, Rome, Egypt, Persia, India, Japan and, later, in Europe. These attitudinal changes varied widely and were often dependent on religious, medical, legal, philosophical, economic, moral, ethical and other values (Fedden, 1938; Choron, 1972; Perlin, 1975; Gibbs, 1968). The modifications of official reactions and countermeasures were often conflicting and paradoxical, with dissociated precepts existing side by side. Although some dynamics were readily comprehensible, contradictions required elaborate rationalizations (Rosen, 1971, 1975; Stengel, 1962; Leighton and Hughes, 1955; Jeffrey, 1952). It can be categorically stated that even in permissive societies there were guidelines and restrictions (Gibbs, 1968).

TERMINOLOGIES AND DEFINITIONS OF SELF-DESTRUCTION

There were no specific words for self-destruction in any of the early records, and the term suicide was not coined until about the middle of the 17th century. In the Bible it was described with simple, economic use of language as an event that had occurred. There is a statement regarding Judas Iscariot in Matthew 27.5, "He went and hanged himself." The early Romans did not use a specific term, but later a series of euphemisms were employed. Rather than use a single word for self-destruction, they used circumlocutions—they talked around it. Jacques Choron (1972) gives a number of frequently used expressions: *"sua manu cadere"*—indicating that the victim fell by his own hand; *"sibi mortem conscisere"*—signifying that the individual produced his own death; and *"vim sibi inferre"*—that violence was caused to oneself. The English preferred *"felo-de-se"* implying that the the victim was also the felon.

In Germany until the late 18th and the early 19th century, the term *Selbsttötung*—self-killing—was used, and subsequently the word *Selbstmord*, murder of oneself, came into vogue. The philosopher Immanuel Kant insisted that if *Selbstmord* was used, then a crime had been committed.

The linguistically versatile Germans devised other terms, such as *Willkürliche Entleibung*, which implied a volitional factor and suggested that alternatives or options were available. Another word, *Freitod*, voluntary death, was even more empathic about the freedom of choice aspects. A term that eliminates the murderous, hostile and aggressive overtones is *Lebensmüder*. This accents the feelings of tiredness, futility, resignation and despair associated with ending one's life.

The popularity of the word suicide, which was derived from the Latin, may in part be due to its brevity or, perhaps, to the fact that it concisely masked a multitude of ambiguities, and in Germany it came to be adopted as *Suizid*. Durkheim immortalized it in *Le Suicide*.

The Germans derived yet another term which suicidologists tend to consider more meaningful and appropriate, *Selbstvernichtung*— self-destruction. The limitations inherent in the word suicide were criticized by Pokorny (1974) and Eissler (1955), and discredited by Tabachnick and Farberow (1961). Their objections were based primarily on the loss of meaning of the term suicide as a specific concept; its applications were too diverse and that its usage promoted confusion. Pokorny (1974) took exception to the eighth revision of the *International Classification of Disease* (U.S. Department of HEW) for placing "suicide and self-inflicted injuries" into one category. This is tantamount to combining completed suicide (CS) with suicide attempt (SA). Thus, a diagnosis of "suicide and self-inflicted injury by hanging" may have described either death (CS) or lesions to the neck and cervical vertebrae (SA). Ascertaining the outcome would require delving into the record. Suicidologists are inclined to regard the term suicide as best serving a quasi medico-legal function, namely, as a mode of death. They consider self-destruction a construct that lends itself far better to a more comprehensive investigation and appreciation of the conscious and unconscious determinants, as well as to the psychodynamic interplay and the theoretical implications. However, the term suicide has been so deeply imbedded and ensconced in common parlance and in the professional literature that it is unlikely to ever be supplanted. In defining self-destruction, Shneidman (1976) defined suicide as the "human act of self-inflicted, self-intentioned cessation" (p. 5). He then proceeded to elaborate on the diverse conscious and unconscious motives and processes that can lead to such self-inflicted, self-intentioned cessation.

The matter of defining "suicide" raises formidable issues when volition and intentionality are regarded as prerequisites. The Japanese hara-kiri, the Indian suttee, the Junker military code, and other forms of institutional suicide were dictated by strong social pressures. In "heroic" suicides, the victim sacrificed his life to save someone else, or for the sake of honor or revenge. To help clarify the contradictions, Choron (1972) cites the French psychiatrist, G. Deshaies, who defined suicide:

> . . . as an act of killing oneself, usually in a conscious manner, and taking death as a means or as an end (p. 93).

Weisman et al. (1973) went even further to suggest that self-destruction may be required—demanded—by forces from the psychosocial milieu.

Varieties and Classifications of Suicidal Behavior

If any number of individuals were to terminate their lives in exactly the same manner (e.g., shoot themselves in the head), the only conclusion that could be reached would be that they committed suicide. This is not a cause of death but rather a mode of death. The precipitants—the phenomenological, the physiological, the intrapsychic, and the interpersonal factors and numerous other imponderables—would be completely overlooked if the act were described merely on the basis of the mode alone. The constellation of promptings may in some instances be well defined, and in others defy even the most fertile imagination. Inferences, deductions and attempts to arrive at logical explanations of the suicidal act are inadequate. Even postvention with its psychological autopsy, which promotes a scientific approach that is less likely to be misleading, can, like all autopsies, prove to be inadequate (Curphey, 1965).

The motives associated with suicide range from trivial slights to the experiencing of interminable pain, with death from natural causes inevitable and perhaps only a few breaths away. The diverse rationalizations that supposedly resulted in self-inflicted death have included a poor scholastic grade, an insult from a peer or a superior, concern about health despite repeated negative physical examinations, revenge, the wish to escape into a better existence, etc. Suicidologists are likely to be suspicious about such simplistic explanations. If an appreciable number of the abjured, aggrieved or disappointed of this world sought a better life to ensure freedom from pain through the expedience of self-cessation, then we would most assuredly not have an overpopulation problem. Since most of humanity elects to stay on as long as possible, it is clear that an understanding of lethality must take into account deeper issues and multiple forces. Menninger (1957) stated:

> To anyone who reviews any considerable number of suicides, it is unmistakably clear that the assigning of *the* cause or *the* *causes* for the final act is naively absurd and grossly misleading. But the nature and degree of the internal stress and the external evidence of it—these are a different matter. These can be found if searched for. . . .

Attempts at classification began with Durkheim (1897), who sought to explain suicide as a sociological phenomenon and arrived at three basic types: (1) egoistic suicide, due to lack of or poor social (family, religious, state) integration, (2) altruistic suicide, due to excessive identification and integration, and (3) anomic suicide, attributed to trauma, catastrophe or a loss, with resultant alienation, social isolation and loneliness.

Others have attempted to categorize and describe the spectrum of suicidal behavior, and they often confused ideation, fantasy, intent, vulnerability or the attempt with the completed act. Some classifications are not sufficiently comprehensive and are too segmental. However, for purposes of orientation, a representative few commonly referred to are presented here:

> (1) *Chronic Suicide,* in which the victim masks his death orientation by excessive use of and addiction to drugs or alcohol, initiates multiple surgery on dubitable grounds, etc. This category overlaps
>
> (2) *Neglect Suicide,* in which the victim ignores reality factors. It is exemplified by the diabetic who indulges himself with a harmful diet of his own choosing, the hypertensive who ignores prohibitions against sodium and "forgets" to refill his prescriptions and the coronary patient who continues to maintain an inordinately arduous schedule. This category in turn overlaps

(3) *Sub-Intentional Suicide,* in which the victim engages in dangerous activities such as driving through red lights, disregarding weather conditions to venture forth in a small boat or plane, and generally engages in potentially perilous activities. These individuals deny suicidal intent, but all the while they promote self-destruction. Although some die quickly, others prolong the process for years, arranging for their demise with an exquisite masochistic artistry. Ironically, if they do not suffer a premature death by homicide, their ultimate mode of death is usually ascribed to accident or natural causes. Menninger (1938) has presented an excellent and elaborate account of this group. His comprehensive conceptualization of chronic suicide includes such self-destructive behavior as martyrdom, asceticism and psychogenic invalidism, in addition to addictions, psychophysiological and personality disorders (anti-social behavior) and psychoses. Menninger describes this category dynamically with masterful clinical acumen.

(4) *Surcease Suicide,* discussed by Shneidman (1960), which is predicated on a "logical" conclusion to end life. Choron (1972) referred to it as "Rational Suicide." It might also be referred to as auto-euthanasia (Wekstein, unpublished article), where the individual recognizes that his plight is irremediable, is suffering intractable pain and decides on intellectual grounds to bring his life to an end.

(5) *Psychotic Suicide,* as described by Bergler (1946), which is intended to explain underlying schizophrenic ideation, where the victim does not intend to die but rather attempts to excise, extirpate, in effect to exorcize, his psychic malignancy.

(6) *Focal Suicide,* discussed by Menninger (1938), which theorizes the concept of partial death, where a limited part of the body is killed. Self-mutilation, maiming, multiple surgery, contrived accidents, as well as some types of sexual impairment in the form of impotence and frigidity, are considered to fall into this classification. There may be considerable overlapping of (5) and (6).

(7) *Automatization Suicide,* as defined by Long (1959), depicts a relatively unmotivated suicide when an individual under severe stress proceeds to alleviate tension by the utilization of a barbiturate, achieves little or no relief and continues to ingest more. His ability to perceive is progressively diminished—con-

stricted—and a hypnogogic state ensues in which he ingests even more of the same drug or adds others, perhaps alcohol, in a robot-like fashion, with resultant death. Dorpat (1975) stated:

> I reviewed a number of reports of patients who initially denied making suicide attempts and who mistakenly ascribed their intentionally self-destructive actions to supposed accidental causes such as "drug automatism" (p. 251).

It has been hypothesized that the actress Marilyn Monroe may have died in this way. Psychological autopsy revealed that prior to her death she had been taking three kinds of drugs and may have died accidentally (Curphy, 1969).

(8) *Accidental Suicide,* which may be due to misinformation, ignorance (Datsun and Sakheim, 1960), or poor timing. A manipulative venture may boomerang. This type of suicide is basically a miscalculation or a blunder. The Russian Roulette category, differentiated by Shneidman and Farberow (1961), can be included here. They described a victim who carefully identified the empty chamber of his revolver before pretending to commit suicide. However, at a party, he was handed a revolver that rotated clockwise, unlike his own revolver that he had previously used at such parties. His death was ascribed to an accident.

(9) *Existential Suicide,* also described as "Victim Precipitated Homicide," which was exemplified by Camus (1945), who emphasized the burden of enduring hypocrisy, the meaninglessness of life, the ennui, and the lack of motivation to continue to exist. Camus was paradoxical, perhaps ironic, when he stated, "Life will be lived better if it has no meaning" (p. 46). Siegmund (1961, 1963), a Catholic priest, disagreed and felt strongly that it was the lack of meaning to life that impelled individuals to suicide.

(10) *Suicide by Murder,* which is a fascinating classification resulting from studies by Wolfgang (1959). The victim considers suicide as a nonvirile and cowardly act. In order to promote his own death, he selects a superior adversary, provokes him and thus brings about his own demise. Such a death is most likely to be termed a homicide.

(11) *Suicidal Threats,* (12) *Suicidal Thinking,* and last, (13)

Test Suicides, which are all vague classifications. Neuringer (1974) suggests that an individual should be regarded as suicidal if, "he gives suicidal or depressive responses on psychological tests, especially projective personality tests."

The classification of Dorpat and Boswell (1963) is based on the degree of intent: (1) suicide gesture, (2) ambivalent suicide attempt, (3) serious suicide attempt and (4) completed suicide.

Porterfield (1968) differentiated between honor suicides, misery suicides, suicides of affection, sacrificial or patriotic suicides of exhibitionists. Fedden (1938) considered the major historical types of suicide to be institutional and personal. Suttee was the custom that called for the Hindu widow to immolate herself on her husband's funeral pyre, until forbidden by the British in 1829. Another familiar form of institutional suicide is hara-kiri, which was restricted to aristocrats. Hara-kiri in its dramatic form has been succinctly described by Porterfield (1968) :

> It takes place in a garden facing a residence. A cotton curtain forms an enclosure around three sides of a blue mattress on which the act is performed. Seated on this mattress, the actor uses a short sword, handed him by an assistant, with which he slashes his abdomen from left to right before witnesses. Then, the assistant beheads the dying man to speed his release from misery.

Junshi is a variant form used by those who wish to join a leader or a master in death. Shinju was an option available to the lower classes, as in the case of lovesick people who tie themselves together dyadically and jump from a cliff.

The vexing question about institutional suicides is whether they were truly voluntary and intentional. One can conjecture that these "volunteers" submitted to the rites and ceremonies that eventuated in self-termination, but that their compliance was in fact tantamount to a verdict and a sentence by a particular society that they were required to carry out. The pressure to destroy oneself may be so intense and coercive that Weisman (1973) has concluded that it is possible to be driven to suicide. This may be exemplified by the

mass suicide at Jonestown, Guyana (*Time,* March 26, 1979, p. 27).
In a tape reportedly found by a U.S. consular employee, Jones was
insistent and emphatic, and said, "So you be kind to the children and
be kind to seniors, and take the potion like they used to take in
ancient Greece, and step over quietly, because we are not committing
suicide—it's a revolutionary act."

OVERVIEW OF TERMINOLOGY AND CLASSIFICATION

Terminology and classification in suicidology leave much to be
desired. Terminology has suffered from vagueness, ambiguity and
even basic disagreement about nuclear words that are as imperative
to suicidology as anatomy is to medicine. All too frequently, classifications and compilations have consisted of static data that offered
little or no substantive dynamic input or leverage. The stereotyped
information that abounds in the literature has little or no clinical
usefulness beyond the enhancement of the author's ego or perhaps
to serve as an antidote for self-destruction—to publish rather than to
perish. Even the prolific contributors have periodically lapsed into
an abstract or philosophical realm that merely adds new terminology
to compound and to complicate an enigma that does not require
further confusion. Similar criticism can be made about classification.

In 1970, a conference of major importance was held in Phoenix
for which the staff of the Center for Studies of Suicide Prevention
of the National Institute of Mental Health (NIMH) and invited
suicidologists were asked to prepare an agenda of topics that they
considered most crucial in this area. It is interesting to note that 60
years after the 1910 conference in Vienna, described by Friedman
(1967), the matter of terminology and classification was still unresolved and considered to be of paramount importance. Beck (1972)
forcefully pointed up the ill-defined boundaries that required demar-
cation and called for an effort to help resolve semantic confusion
and imprecision about definitions and terms. He demonstrated that
even the same author was often inconsistent and contradictory in
his terminology. Pokorny (1974) noted:

> Writers on suicidal behavior seem to assume they are talking about the same phenomenon when using the same word, even though careful reading shows this to be untrue (p. 30).

The committee in Phoenix found it expedient to compromise rather than to create further cleavages with resultant disharmony. There was agreement that suicidal behaviors should be classified into three broad categories: (1) *Completed Suicide* (CS) would include all deaths that resulted from self-intentioned, self-inflicted cessation as the result of a life-threatening act. (2) *Suicide Attempt* (SA) would include any act that appears to have life-threatening potential or does in fact carry such a potential and such an intent, but which has not resulted in death. Unfortunately, this category tends to be nonspecific because it would include suicidal gestures—histrionic and ambivalent attempts—as well. It might be perceived as a waste-basket classification because it includes virtually any attempt short of completed suicide. The term SA is therefore imprecise because it is impossible to determine the degree of intent or lethality, and/or the mitigating circumstances, on the basis of the uncompleted act. (3) *Suicide Ideas* (SI) would include a category in which the individual may give indication, either directly or indirectly, that he is preoccupied with self-cessation. On this basis it may be possible to infer that plans to end his life are being formulated. Verbal and nonverbal communications can reveal SI. Writing a farewell note, counting the number of capsules in a bottle of tranquilizing agents, and even loading a gun would be circumstantial or inferential examples of SI. However, if several of the pills were ingested or the individual pulled the trigger with self-cessation as the intent, it would be termed SA. In the latter situation, pulling the trigger, the lethality is high, but unless death ensued, it would still be SA. Obsessive patients who are preoccupied with self-destruction and are terrified of any instrument that might cause death to themselves, who cut themselves accidentally, would also fall under this category (SA), in spite of the fact that the degree of suicidal intent is zero.

Five other dimensions were added in order to refine these categories: (1) *Certainty* refers to the clinician's certainty expressed in percentages as to whether an act is or is not suicidal. While this provides clinical subjective impressions, it can not be used officially. (2) *Lethality* is rated in terms of the deadliness of the suicide act or the contemplated act according to medical standards. Even if an individual did not appreciate or was unaware of the jeopardousness of an act—the deadliness of its consequences—the rating as to its lethality would still be based on medical standards. A high degree of lethality is also manifested when, due to the irreversibility of the means selected to self-destruct, there is little possibility for medical rescue. Degrees of lethality are rated zero, low, medium, or high. (3) *Intent* may be determined in part from self-reports, but it must be recognized that such reports can be exaggerated or understated and are not always genuine. Judgment of intent may be based on inference and circumstantial evidence. Again, this approach is unsatisfactory. We may perceive an individual's inability to contend or to cope with life, we may note his poor adjustment and lack of resiliency, we may appreciate the low frustration-tolerance—but to assume or to deduce that such factors are directly responsible for self-destruction is too simplistic. It is extremely difficult to differentiate among the variables or the disequilibria and traumata that transpire in the normal course of living in order to justify the taking of one's life. The intensity of the determination of the individual to self-destruct may give some index of his intent. The same act with high lethality may differ in terms of intent—an individual who overdoses while alone shows a higher degree of intent than one who performs the same act within easy notice or access of others. There is also the possibility that an individual who does indeed have a high degree of intent may not, because of his naiveté or ignorance, take into account the body's capacity to mobilize in its own defense. A factor of unpredictability may therefore arise from his act. Intent is rated on the same basis as lethality: zero, low, medium or high. (4) *Mitigating Circumstances* would suggest that specific factors precipitated the act. Examples are infirmity, old age, organic or functional disease, drug states, etc. Conditions that interfere with awareness, particularly drugs such as alcohol, may play a large role. In some instances, the mitigating circumstances can be identified and contended with, modified by treatment or reduced by other means. Recidivism can thus be decreased. The same scale is used for rating mitigating circumstances. (5) *Method of injury* is significant because it may reflect on the degree of intent, lethality and the mitigating circumstances. The bizarreness of the modus operandi that an individual selects for self-destruction may cast light on his psychopathological state. Self-immolation is a far cry from a suicide attempt with aspirin. Pokorny (1974) stated, " . . . the frequent sedative overdoses encountered in clinical practice are not frequently associated with deep-seated psychoses as compared with suicides by fire, where a severe psychotic illness is usually present" (p. 40).

Although the Phoenix committee's guidelines, designed to bring some measure of conformity and consistency to terminology and classification, are helpful, suicidology does not lend itself to concise, circumscribed definitions. Exceptions, disagreements and disappointments have been frequently voiced by the participants. The committee has also considered the addition of a secondary classification of suicidal intent in deaths that did not carry a suicide label—or in self-destructive life-styles not falling into the category of suicide attempts.

In a personal communication to the writer, Richard Fox, Honorary Consultant Psychiatrist to the Samaritans and the United Kingdom representative to the International Association for Suicide Prevention, points out that the term "parasuicide" is rapidly replacing "attempted suicide" in Europe and is a more comprehensible term to indicate a deliberate but nonfatal self-injury.

Pokorny (1974) suggested that the one-word term "suicidality" was more appropriate when referring to the risk of future suicide or suicide probability, and that combinations of the hyphenated word—e.g., high- low-, or highest-suicidality, etc.—would be more meaningful to the reader.

Every student of suicidology must learn to accept the fact that a unanimous concordance of opinion about the mystery of self-destruction is highly unlikely, if not impossible. When we listen to the last strains of Pagliacci, we hear the somber line, "La commedia e finita." We understand these ominous words—they are unmistakable

—it is over. But, if we have heard only those words or seen only the gruesome end, we can only surmise or guess about *the course of events* that has been sardonically referred to as the termination of a play—an act—the final result of a piece of behavior. Zubin (1974) stated it simply:

> Suicide is the end result of a process, not the process itself. In most behavior disorders we have at least part of the process at hand for examination. In suicide all we usually have is the end result, arrived at by a variety of paths. Unravelling the causes after the fact is well nigh impossible (p. 4).

Suicidologists must feel free to continue to find acceptable, applicable terms and to explore the common denominators that can provide for categorization. However, this does not necessarily provide information concerning dynamics, nor does it cast significant light on the multiplicity of variables that must be considered in order to provide leverage for the implementation of prevention, intervention techniques and therapy.

ATTITUDES TOWARD SUICIDE

The major disciplines—medicine, law, theology, philosophy, etc. —have been directly or indirectly involved with and affected by suicidal behavior. Some have given opinions, others have delivered sermons, dicta, admonitions and regulations. Existing attitudes have been based on issues of morals, ethics and values as well as on such practical considerations as economics and depletion of population. Tolerance and acceptance in a given period, culture or milieu have fluctuated (Williams, 1957; Dublin and Bunzel, 1933; Fedden, 1938), but self-destruction has never been regarded by society without reservations and restrictions. Perhaps the act reactivates and kindles inner, dormant anxieties. At one time or another, we have all contemplated the possibility of terminating our lives. The realization that there are those who follow through with this purpose has had— and can have—a profound effect, particularly on those whose ego controls are labile and shaky. Seiden (1969) wrote:

> Suicide troubles and appalls us because it so intransigently rejects our deeply held conviction that life must be worth living (p. 1).

One means of contending with the fait accompli, that self-destruction is an available escape from coping, has been through reaction formation. Perceiving suicide as sinful, profane, cowardly or criminal and responding to the perpetrators of such an act with disdain, ostensibly served to dissuade others from such an unsanctioned deed. Farberow and Shneidman (1961a) note:

> Yet society, perhaps because of the very nature of the phenomenon and the kinds of feelings evoked by suicidal activity, have tended to deny its very existence (p. xi).

The Zeitgeist—the prevailing cultural, philosophical and religious concepts—was frequently translated into the law, and the harsh evidences of this have been depicted by Silving (1961), Williams (1957) and Alvarez (1971). If man was the creature of God and man chose to destroy that which God had created, then man was a murderer, a felon; although he had escaped conviction by his death, his goods and his lands were still subject to confiscation and his reputation was destroyed. Many governments benefited from expropriation, and abolition of confiscatory and punitive laws was unduly slow in coming. Old customs relating to magic and fear were frequently combined with religion and law. Economic factors were always important criteria; slaves, soldiers, and commoners were expressly forbidden to kill themselves.

The macabre treatment of the cadaver of the suicide can be traced to ancient superstitions, and a variety of measures were used to prevent the "ghost" of the suicide from seeking vengeance on the survivors. In many cases, this probably afforded some comfort and a sense of protection to those who felt that they had been responsible for the suicide. An ingenious countermeasure often invoked in England and in other European countries was to hang the corpse in the nude, after which the body was dragged through the streets and ultimately buried at a crossroad during the night with a stake driven through the heart. Presumably, the additional precaution of the burial at the crossroad was to impair the corpse's sense of direction. Rosen (1975) noted that a suicide was interred at the corner of Commercial Road and Cannon Street in East London under edict as late as 1811, and the practice was not formally banned until 1823.

The three most significant penalties for self-inflicted death were the confiscation of property, degradation of the corpse—symbolic of dishonor—and the denial of burial in consecrated ground. Although these attitudes prevailed from the Middle Ages through the 18th century, the grotesque rituals were not rigidly enforced, and how they were applied varied from time to time and place to place. Distaste has been voiced by a humanistic segment throughout every period of history. Consideration was also given to the social status of the suicide and his family, as well as to the circumstances that precipitated the act. Self-destruction due to chronic illness or mental disorder was regarded as more justifiable, and therefore the corpse and the family of these suicides were not subjected to severe penalties. On the other hand, the body and family of an individual who was impoverished or indebted were more harshly treated because he was considered to have flouted the civil law.

Subsequent to the Renaissance, the upper, educated classes increasingly disagreed about absolute condemnation, but it was not until 1961 that the Suicide Act in England was finally changed. Today, survivors of the suicide are no longer liable to prosecution. However, aiding and abetting a suicidal act is still technically punishable in England by imprisonment of up to 14 years.

Although society professes to be less moralistic and has somewhat relaxed its rigid, archaic posture towards ending one's life, repugnance persists in an effort to counteract the anxiety engendered by and attendant to the suicidal act—a reaction that often takes the form of denial. It is apropos to quote Freud (1915), who wrote:

> In the unconscious everyone of us in convinced of his own immortality . . . whenever we attempt to do so (conceive of our own demise) we can perceive that we are in fact still present as spectators (p. 289).

Equally as poignant is the comment that society does not wish to be reminded that death is a built-in reality and that man can be his own catalyst.

CHAPTER 3

DIMENSION OF THE PROBLEM OF SUICIDAL BEHAVIOR

STATISTICS

Statistics on suicide are synthetic; that is, they are concocted products, and their inaccuracy and unreliability are an open secret. They are contrived by necessity; and variations from country or region may reflect overt or covert underrepresentation. The great variations in ascertaining and reporting the cause of death are obvious (Monk, 1975; Curphey, 1961).

Analyzing statistics of suicide is not unlike interpreting dreams (except that we do not know the dreamer). The raw data must be accepted at face value, for better or for worse, with their distortions and secondary elaborations. The conclusions that are drawn often reflect the frame of reference and theoretical predisposition of the interpreter. Nevertheless, some information can be gleaned or inferred from statistics. Differences in sex, age, group, race, marital status, religion, occupation and historical period can provide data for investigation and research.

There are only four modes of death: natural, accidental, homicidal or suicidal. However, the stigma of death by suicide is so pervasive that it is avoided or denied whenever possible. A death labeled by a mode other than suicide is more acceptable both to the bereaved and to society. Suicide casts a pall that far exceeds other modes of death. Long after a suicide's departure, his presence lingers on, festering, and hounding the life of the family and others associated with him.

Death can be equivocal so that the physician or pathologist may find it extremely difficult, and at times impossible, to determine the exact cause. A victim may so cleverly contrive a death that it appears to be accidental or natural. Accidents lend themselves to such a purpose and probably represent an appreciable number of suicides. Curphey (1961), a pathologist, illustrates the problems that the coroner faces when the evidence is superficial, incomplete, or preconceived rather than factual and objective. As a result, certification is often ambiguous, with the notation "accident-suicide, undetermined." Whenever a doubt exists, there has all too often been the tendency to label a death as accidental or due to natural causes. When postvention procedures and the psychological autopsy are employed, the accuracy of the finding—the mode of death—is markedly increased. However, Moriyama and Israel (1968) discuss the complications that affect the postvention process. The medicolegal officer may be a physician without specialized training in pathology or forensic medicine. He may function as a coroner with no medical training whatsoever, and in some jurisdictions may be appointed or elected. It becomes obvious that such conditions make investigative procedures dubious at best.

Bennett (1957) suggested that there are as many as 50,000 suicides a year in the United States, which is more than double the number of suicides recorded in official vital statistics. It was Dublin's (1963) opinion that the understatement of recorded suicides is between 25 and 33 percent.

Aside from their admitted inadequacies, there are a number of sources of suicidal statistics, such as Dublin (1963) and the booklets of the World Health Organization on the Prevention of Suicide (1968). *Suicide in the United States from 1950 to 1964* (1965) and *The Facts of Life and Death* (1970), published by the United States Department of Health, Education and Welfare, are helpful references.

Unreliable statistics and even lack of statistics may carry political connotations. Although Russia is a member of the World Health Organization, it will not reveal its suicide statistics. Choron (1972) implies that this is an image-saving device. Perhaps it is one area in which the Russians elect not to surpass the Western World.

Gorwitz (1975) voiced his discontent about the dubiousness of statistics and also expressed his pessimism on this score. He doubted that a completely accurate count would ever be attainable—some cases would either not be recognized or deliberately covered up. He suggested that regional data banks on suicide and suicidal attempts be established, with case registers that could be computerized so that linkage with comparable data from other case registers would provide more accurate information.

In the United States, suicide is considered to be one of the ten leading causes of death. According to the most recent *Monthly Vital Statistics Report* (Summary Report, 1973, Final Mortality Statistics) of the U.S. Department of Health, Education and Welfare, Supplement 2, dated February, 1975, the suicide rate in the United States is 12.6 per 100,000. (More recent estimates put the rate at 14 per 100,000.) However, the rate for males is 18.0 per 100,000, appreciably higher than for females, which is 6.6 per 100,000.

The ratio of men to women who commit suicide is three to one. There is a reverse ratio of about three to one for women who attempt suicide. There is, however, statistical evidence which would indicate that the ratio for women is rising. A similar increase has been noted for nonwhites. Whether this rise is due to changes in life-style, pressures related to urbanization, or improved postmortem procedures in ascertaining the cause of death has not yet been determined.

Suicide as a mode of death may at first appear to be alarming. For whites male aged 15 to 19, it ranks second. Shneidman (1975) explains this on the basis of the fact that youngsters of that age are unlikely to die from organic diseases. White males aged 10 to 15 significantly rank fifth in death from suicide. There tends to be a steady increase in the statistics with advancing age, except for the 65 to 74 age group (Massey, 1967). The statistics would skyrocket if masked, disguised forms and more equivocal deaths were attributed to the proper mode.

It is difficult to comprehend how frequently suicide takes place. Menninger (1957) noted:

> Once every minute, or even more often, someone in the United States either kills himself or tries to kill himself with conscious intent. Sixty or seventy times every day these attempts succeed. In many instances they could have been prevented by some of the rest of us (p. vii).

Attempted suicides, where the potential victim survived, are far more numerous than completed suicides. Stengel (1964) and Parkin and Stengel (1965) estimated that the annual number of attempted suicides was two million. Stengel (1967) reported that one to five percent of individuals who had attempted self-destruction completed the act within the following five to ten years. A higher estimate of at least five million attempted suicides per year was made by Mintz (1970).

Although such astronomical projections are bewildering, they were derived from a series of studies that indicated an approximate ratio of eight to ten attempts for every completed suicide (Shneidman and Farberow, 1961; Parkin and Stengel, 1965). Even these estimates were considered to be low by suicidologists; and in some groups, attempts are much higher. Jacobziner (1965) arrived at a ratio of 100 attempts to one completed suicide in adolescents. Whitehead (IASP Proceedings, Mexico, 1971) provided the highest ratio of suicide to attempted suicide with a ratio of 700 per 100,000.

When these combined data are extrapolated, an approximation can be made. The actual number of suicides in the United States is estimated conservatively as 25,000-30,000 annually. When this figure is multiplied by ten, the total number of survivors is in excess of one quarter of a million. One must next consider that this population is comprised of relatively young people, and if their life expectancy extends for 30 or more years, and the total of a quarter of a million is multiplied by 30 plus, the estimated grand total of survivors of suicidal attempts well exceeds five million. Many epidemiologists and suicidologists would be inclined to consider even this figure as modest.

The present official suicide rate of 12.6 per 100,000 for a general population exceeding 200 million may not appear unduly high, but it should be repeated that these figures do not include individuals who present themselves for help or who are in the process of receiving help. Laymen and even physicians are lulled by the low base-rate of suicide. Silverman (1968) points out how deceptive this thinking can be. Successful suicides occur in the ratio of one to 5,500 for current mental hospital patients and one to 2,000 for former patients. A study by Wilkins (1970) of callers who were willing to give their names to the Chicago Suicide Prevention Clinic revealed that the ratio for this group was one to 400. McCulloch and Philip (1972) reported that at least 25 percent of completed suicides had made previous attempts. Wollersheim (1974) appropriately stressed the base-rate aspect:

> However, taking assurance in the low base-rate phenomena of successful suicide can be misleading, for the clients that the practicing clinician is apt to see are a more select group than the general population and have a much higher base-rate of successful suicide.

STATISTICAL VARIATIONS IN WORLD NATIONS

According to the Scientific and Technical Information Branch of the Department of Health, Education and Welfare, suicide statistics of other countries are not compiled by the United States. However, the most recent abstract from the 1970 Demographic Yearbook of the United Nations (Table 19), which is based on rates per 100,000 from selected countries, provides some perspective. The table was limited to sovereign countries with "reliable" estimated populations of one million or more and with "complete" counts of death-by-cause lists that include suicide. The table indicates that countries with the highest rates of suicide are Switzerland (17.0), Denmark (20.5), Federal Republic of Germany (21.3), Sweden (21.5), Finland (21.6), Austria (22.3), Czechoslovakia (23.9), Hungary (33.1). Countries with low rates of suicides are Greece (3.5), Italy (5.4), Israel (6.4), the Netherlands (7.4), Norway (8.1) and Portugal

(8.2). All current tables place the United States in a median position—the 15th rank of the 30 countries listed.

The data supplied by the World Health Statistics Annuals in Geneva, Volume 21, No. 6, 1968 (compiled by the World Health Organization) give comparable rates.

The large differences enumerated above give good cause for reflection, skepticism and puzzlement. Attempts to explain them are essentially tautological, and the only conclusion that can be drawn is that differences do indeed exist. Labovitz (1968), a sociologist, summarized this state of affairs:

> No social status or condition generates a constant rate in all populations. For example, an occupation with a high suicide rate in one community may have a low rate in another; and rates for countries or religious groups change substantially over time. Therefore, no theory can adequately explain variation in the suicide rate in terms of single classification like marital status, urbanization, religion, occupation, age, etc. A general and parsimonious theory of suicide must postulate a common denominator or factor that distinguishes all populations with high rates (pp. 72-73).

Those two omnipresent words, "reliability" and "paradoxical," are literally and figuratively worked to death when writing about self-destruction, but they persist for good reason. Two small examples help to illustrate: According to Farberow and Shneidman (1961a), the attempted suicide rate for Los Angeles County in 1957 was 111.4 per 100,000, with a completed suicide rate of 14.5 per 100,000. But in the year 1957, the United States suicide rate was 9.8 per 100,000. Labovitz (1968) cited a low rate for firemen in the United States, but a high rate for them in Los Angeles.

On the basis of his analysis, Douglas (1967) concluded that there were five major forms of unreliability that were manifest in official statistics on suicide:

> (1) unreliability resulting from the choice of the official statistics to be used in making the tests of the sociological theories;
> (2) unreliability resulting from subcultural differences in the

attempts to hide suicide; (3) unreliability resulting from the effects of different degrees of social integration on the official statistic keeping; (4) unreliability resulting from significant variations in the social imputations of motives; (5) unreliability resulting from the more extensive and professionalized collection of statistics among certain populations (p. 203).

Multiple approaches can be taken in the interpretation and extrapolation of statistics. Some are profound, others are absurdly simple, and yet the smorgasbord—the conglomerate that results—does illuminate the panorama of suicide. Unfortunately, the paradoxes do not lend themselves to neat categorization.

The matter of suicide in Scandinavia is a case in point. These countries all have extensive economic planning and social welfare benefits, with governments that demonstrate deep concern for the citizenry. However, statistics indicate that Denmark and Sweden have almost three times as many suicides as their neighbor, Norway.

A sophisticated and perceptive psychosocial analysis of this enigma was offered by Hendin, a psychoanalyst (1960, 1962, 1964). He suggested that in each of the three Scandinavian countries there were discrete, highly individual cultural attitudes and pressures that influenced self-destruction. He perceived the Swedes as having rigid performance standards and low capacity for dealing with frustration and failure. Failure for them was equated with death and concomitant with feelings of detachment and repressed hostility. In the case of females, he postulated an inability to achieve the feminine identification necessary for the maintenance of heterosexual relationships. It was his thesis that the inculcation of early independence resulted in manifestations of anger and detachment. He attributed a great deal of significance to a behavior epitomized by silence—a withdrawal. Hendin perceived this silence, which in Sweden is referred to as *tiga ihjäl*, as an unconscious manifestation of the wish to kill. This seemingly abstract thesis is corroborated by Gordon et al. (1950), who considered that hypereridism, a pathological aggressivity, can persist and that after a long, festering incubation may, as a result of reinforcement, ultimately be turned inward and induce an attempted or a completed suicide. This is, in effect, an extension of

Auenbruggers' theory (Rosen, 1971) that self-destruction is the end result of psychic pathology manifested by a silent rage that ultimately culminates in depression followed by suicide.

Hendin's rationale for the high suicide rate in Denmark was predicated on the inculcation of strong dependency and submission, attendant to frustration. When a dependent person suffers the loss of a meaningful relationship, suicide may result. Hendin considered that postpartum suicides were caused by the rupture of a woman's dependency needs. It was his observation that dependency was fostered, then utilized as a weapon, and the passive dependent was expected to inhibit anger as the price for having received unlimited gratification. Guilt was used as leverage to maintain a state of inhibition, with resultant aggression toward the self.

Hendin believed the Norwegian socialization techniques were more realistic in that they taught children better coping mechanisms and permitted the expression of hostility. He felt that Norwegians were less doting and more open than the Danes and not so detached and overly serious as the Swedish. The Norwegians could therefore externalize their feelings of anger and had less need to destroy themselves.

In comparing the Norwegians with the Danes, Farber (1968) also concluded that the Norwegians were less dependent, less concerned about the manifestation of affect, and better oriented for autonomous behavior.

In examining cultural determinants of suicide in Sweden, Rudestom (1970) additionally related the Swedish tendency to inhibit anger to a long indoctrination of pacifism as a life-style. He confirmed Hendin's view that a contributory factor was uncertainty about sexual identity.

The wide variation of suicide rates in Scandinavia has been explained on other than sociological and psychological grounds. Crucial questions emerged as to whether many suicides in Norway had inadvertently been attributed to accident rather than to self-inflicted death. Norway is a country with remote areas, where people live under rigorous conditions and medical facilities are not so readily available as those in Denmark and Sweden. Documentation of equi-vocal deaths is therefore likely to be inaccurate.

A fascinating and cogent bit of information emerged from the World Health Statistics Report (1972) : The reported death rate for accidents, exclusive of motor vehicle accidents, was 36 per 100,000 for Norway, 24 for Denmark, and 28 for Sweden. If the accident rate in each of these countries is combined with their reported suicide rate, then the results are 44 per 100,000 for Norway, 45 for Den-mark, and 50 for Sweden. There is very little disparity here, and this fact lends considerable credence to the possibility that accident and suicide may not be well differentiated in Norway. Another interest-ing statistic is that the homicide rates in all three countries are low, and the differences in this mode of death are of small significance.

SUICIDE AMONG PHYSICIANS AND MEDICAL STUDENTS

The average individual finds incomprehensible the high suicide rate of physicians, psychiatrists, and medical students. Our stereo-typed image of caretakers is that they are effective; imbued with pro-tecting life, and impervious to such foibles as inflicting death upon themselves. The fact that doctors do take their own lives is disquiet-ing at best, but the fact they do so in larger numbers than the general population (Freeman, 1967; Thomas, 1974) brings forth reactions ranging from anxiety to consternation. How can we trust the experts whom we rely upon to maintain and prolong our lives if they are so callous with their own? Perhaps their medical knowledge and know-how have provided them with a faster, more expedient solution —the doctor is reputed to know what is best.

According to Ross (1975), the death rate for physicians reported in the 1965 to 1967 period was 33 per 100,000, about double that for white American males. Ross estimated that the number of male physicians who commit suicide every year is equal to the graduating class of an average American medical school. Although Steppacher and Mausner (1974) questioned the accuracy of these high rates and were somewhat critical of previous studies which they felt contained some systematic biases, they limited their own studies to data supplied by the American Medical Association and admitted:

We do not know what proportion of deaths among physicians are unknown to the AMA, or whether suicides are reported to them proportionately less often than deaths from other causes. Furthermore, published U.S. suicide rates come from compilations of statements about cause of death given on death certificates submitted from the more than 3,000 counties in the United States. The quality of information on the death certificate varies widely. This is particularly true for suicide, where accurate diagnosis may be precluded by inadequate toxicologic and other investigation, or by dissembling in order to protect the deceased or his family. As a result, the published suicide figures are a poor reflection of the actual numbers. The true level of occurrence is probably grossly understated (p. 327).

Although suicide among male physicians is considered high, Ross (1971) and Notman (1975) indicate that death by suicide of female physicians is even higher, with a rate of 40.5 per 100,000. This would place them in the highest suicidal category for all groups of females (Craig and Pitts, 1968). The closest female subgroup, with a rate half that of the female physicians, consists of divorced women over age 70.

The mortality rate from suicide attempts among medical students is also extremely high, and according to Simon (1966), it is regarded as the second most common mode of death for this subgroup and is reported to be rising.

The decision to apply for admission to medical school is initially one of self-selection, but it is presumed that acceptance is predicated on careful screening. Nevertheless, it has been common knowledge that the number of medical students who suffer from psychiatric problems is large. While the exact number will probably never be known or determined, there have been some studies in this area. Almost 50 percent of senior medical students at the University of Pennsylvania were found to be struggling with major emotional disorders (Strecker, Appel, Palmer and Braceland, 1937). Psychiatric difficulties are by no means restricted to any one school, and numerous studies indicate that comparatively large numbers of medical students required treatment (Pitts et al., 1961; Brosin and Early, 1952). According to Bojar (1961), his six-year study of Harvard

Medical School students indicated that 13 percent required psychiatric intervention. The criteria for "psychiatric intervention" are often subjective and variable.

It should be stressed that psychiatric disorders per se do not necessarily result in suicidal behavior. It is, however, generally agreed that severe emotional disturbances make for vulnerability and that in combination with other factors this may increase the risk of self-destruction.

Ross (1975), who has been chairman of the American Psychiatric Association Task Force on Suicide Prevention and is an acknowledged authority in this area, has constructed a composite picture— or profile—of the physician who is most likely to commit suicide:

> Statistically, he is a 48-year-old doctor graduated at or near the top of his high prestige medical school class, now practicing a peripheral speciality associated with chronic problems, where satisfactions are difficult and laggard. Because he is active, aggressive, ambitious, competitive, compulsive, enthusiastic and individualistic, he is apt to be frustrated easily in his need for achievement and recognition, and in meeting his goals. Unable to tolerate delay in gratification, he may prescribe large amounts of anesthetics or psychoactive drugs in his practice. Add a non-lethal annoying physical illness, mood swings, personal problems with drugs and alcohol—itself a reflection of suicide proneness— in one who may feel a lack of restraints by society, and one who has a likely enough combination to induce significant anxiety and depression, symptoms which not only may require psychiatric treatment, but which also often hamper a worthwhile relationship with a psychiatrist. Self-seeking and self-indulgent, versatile and resourceful, lacking control, he may often resort to hasty, impulsive or immature behavior—possibly suicide (pp. 16-17)!

It is easier to rationalize and to account for suicides of physicians who had already been exposed to the terrible daily frustrations of confrontation and ministration to human suffering. However, the large incidence of self-destruction among medical students is more difficult to explain. They have not yet embarked on their chosen vocation and are still in the preparatory process. Perhaps an orientation towards death is a factor in choosing medicine as a career, since denial and reaction-formation mask unconscious preoccupation and subintention. If so, the initial attrition may be due to poor selection and screening.

On the basis of the Minnesota Multiphasic Personality Inventory administered to first- and third-year medical students, Schofield (1953) found a pattern that indicated poor capacity to cope under severe stress. Presumably, this would predispose such individuals to great anxiety, low frustration-tolerance, and, subsequently, self-destruction. It is possible to presume further that some individuals would not be vulnerable until later in their lives when other variables that had a cumulative negative effect impinged upon them.

The matter of denial which has been alluded to above may take the form of refusal to seek help or an inability to face intrapsychic pathology. Many physicians are therefore inclined either to treat themsleves or to ignore their prodromal morbidity (Ross, 1975; Blachly, Disher and Roduner, 1968).

A hypothesis suggests itself that many aspirants for medical careers seek and attempt to achieve omniscience, omnipotence and virility by identifying themselves with the esteemed and exalted role of the physician. The attempt to achieve such goals is incompatible with reality and is doomed to failure. Healthy self-actualization emerges from a resolution of inner conflicting forces, and an integration of the personality results in the capacity for flexibility and compromise. The motivation to practice medicine in order to obtain magical powers that do not exist and are not inherent in any profession can lead to death-oriented behavior when the narcissistic bubble bursts.

It is a plausible thesis that for some the realization that their venture is an exercise in futility strikes home early, while they are still medical students. Others graduate, retain their pathological posture reinforced in part by a suggestible society, and continue their eternal search for the mirage with ever-mounting frustrations until they achieve the requirements for the composite—the profile that Ross (1975) delineated so accurately.

SUICIDE AMONG PSYCHIATRISTS

A paradoxical statistic is that psychiatrists have the highest suicide rates in the medical profession. In a study of the suicide rate of 16 medical specialities, Blachly et al. (1968) found that psychiatrists had a rate of 61 per 100,000. Blachly's study revealed that pediatricians had the lowest rate—10 per 100,000. The highest rates were for opthalmology, anesthesiology and, at the head of the list, psychiatry. Freeman (1967) and Blachly et al. (1968) were inclined to explain this ironic situation on the basis of the preselection that brings the psychiatrist into a more intense, involved and prolonged relation with the patient.

Self-selection implies that the psychiatrist is attracted to a particular aspect of human suffering, a realm that is unrelated to and divorced from his many years of training (Braun, 1973). It is often puzzling to his colleagues that one who has shared their long, arduous educational experience and apprenticeship should make such a drastic move from the mainstream of medicine.

After his medical training is completed, the psychiatrist no longer treats patients for physical problems or ailments. If they give indication of being physically ill, he refers them to another physician. His link with medicine is tenuous and largely maintained by his use of psychotropic drugs or electroconvulsive therapy in conjunction with psychotherapy. Some psychiatrists even abstain from utilization of all drugs and confine themselves solely to psychotherapy. Although the psychiatrist continues to regard himself as a physician, he does not use the instruments that are associated with the practice of medicine. It is he, the pyschiatrist, who becomes both the diagnostic and therapeutic instrument in contending with highly variegated and diverse affective states.

This complex process, oriented to achieve a progressive, meaningful, ameliorative and remedial relationship, is referred to as psychotherapy. When death-orientation predominates, the sensitivity, compassion, insight and expertise of the psychiatrist may determine whether life forces will triumph.

The psychiatrist is at a distinct disadvantage during critical periods compared to his medical colleagues. The expectations, demands and impositions that are made upon him are often excessive when due consideration is given to such matters as the accessibility of backup services at a given time; the problem of arranging for immediate consultation/hospitalization; contending with inadequate therapeutic collaboration; concern about splitting the transference; dealing with a lack or refusal of cooperation from the family or friends who ignore the gravity of the situation; unpredictability of the patient; paradoxical reactions to pharmacotherapy; sudden shifts due to reactive factors; indifferent compliance with instructions, which can later be used to promote lawsuits; etc.—all of which make for a corrosive existence.

In the practice of medicine, the physician can generally justify a fatal outcome. He makes a diagnosis and his therapeutic procedures are based on physical findings, authenticated by comprehensive data gathered from an array of instruments and laboratory tests. Even in sudden death, an autopsy is likely to disclose the cause on anatomical and physiological grounds, and subsequently the clinical pathological conference provides a clearly stated scientific explanation.

On the other hand, the postmortem does not vindicate the psychiatrist, nor does it offer him much solace. He has cause only for reflection, guilt and anxiety. Self-destruction by whatever euphemism still spells out self-inflicted cessation.

Suicide by a patient represents the greatest threat to the psychiatrist. Even if he saw a patient once and could not elicit any overt manifestations of death-orientation or high lethality, he is in a defensive position. If the patient commits suicide during treatment, the psychiatrist is even more vulnerable—and secretive. In addition to his own guilt, he may suffer recrimination from hostile relatives of the deceased and even be faced with the prospect of a lawsuit. He has no x-rays, no lab reports, no EKGs, and only his notes, recollections, and reflections to justify the treatment and precautions that he had taken.

Subjected to a daily routine of awesome responsibility, the psychiatrist cannot long rely on his own previous treatment or analysis to serve him as a shield and to maintain his self-image.

Not all psychiatrists face the same risks, and those who work in a hospital setting have more backup services available, and there is less reluctance to utilize consultants and staff meetings to share decisions.

Although some investigators consider the incidence of suicide among pyschiatrists to be underestimated, others insist that it has been exaggerated. Shneidman (1975) adopts a humanistic approach in which he deemphasized the matter of numbers:

> At present, data seem equivocal, but whatever the rate for psy-chiatrists in this grizzly sibling rivalry among the professions and among the medical specialties, any suicide by a psychiatrist involves an unspeakable waste and an enormous tragedy—and a searing trauma for his patients (p. 1777).

Baffling though it may be, perhaps we must learn to accept that profession, prestige and intellect do not prevent individuals from ending their lives.

CHAPTER 4

THEORETICAL CONSTRUCTS, FORMULATIONS AND DATA RELATING TO SELF-DESTRUCTION

PRODROMAL SIGNS AND CUES

It is a cardinal principle of psychodynamics that man cannot contain the manifestations of his strivings and his plans, in spite of his best efforts to mask or deny them.

Freud's life and work were dedicated to unraveling the panoramic skein of those subtle, disguised manifestations of urges and impulses. Whatever their myriad flux, or form, he attempted to penetrate their hidden recesses until they disclosed themselves to his probing. Throughout his life he translated these motives and their symbolic representations with ascetic endurance. As the founder of psychoanalysis, Freud conceived of it as a research method, a psychodiagnostic instrument and a therapeutic technique. Freud's labors, gathered together in the *Standard Edition of Psychoanalysis* (1935-1965) illuminated the boundaries and cast a searching glow over a vast, uncharted psychic hinterland with a prolific account of man's eternal struggle with his promptings—their morphology, their outlets, their distortions, and attempts at subjugation, defense and resolution.

In his "Psychopathology of Everyday Life," Freud (Vol. 6, 1938) gave many specific examples of the parapraxes—the self-revelations through somatic or symbolic representation, such as lapsus linguae, fantasies, dreams, symptoms, and patterns of reaction. He also indicated his awareness of an instinct for self-destruction on the basis of his clinical findings.

Utilizing Freud's basic premise that man is impelled to disclose himself, it would be logical to assume that his plans or motives would be subject to overt, covert or subvert betrayal. In *The Compulsion to Confess,* Reik (1959) examined the necessity to reveal oneself in such other areas and disciplines as religion, art, language, teaching and criminology.

Since self-destruction is such a cataclysmic act, it is logical to assume that before the act is carried out there is a ferment of intrapsychic havoc; that during such a time there would be a period of incubation and uncertainty; that preparatory steps would be required to complete the suicidal act, and this phase could provide an opportunity for intervention.

Freud in 1901 (Vol. 6, 1938), stated:

> . . . and even when suicide actually results, the inclination to suicide will have been present for a long time before in less strength or in the form of an unconscious or suppressed trend . . . Even a conscious intention of committing suicide chooses its time, means and opportunity; and it is quite in keeping with this that an unconscious intention should wait for a precipitating occasion, which can take over a part of the causation and by engaging the subject's defensive forces, can liberate the intention from their pressure (p. 181).

The studies of Shneidman et al. (1961), Stengel and Cook (1958), Dorpat et al. (1959a; 1959b), Jensen and Petty (1958) and Robins et al. (1957) confirm the existence of a prodromal phase and that such a state can be regarded as presuicidal.

Provocative questions about the presuicidal population abound. The size, the course and the fate of this category are not known. Since a presuicidal or prodromal state is even less likely to be reported than attempted or actual suicides, it is difficult to determine how frequently this phase occurs, how many seek the help of a physician or a psychiatrist, how many have a spontaneous remission or exacerbate later, and how many attempt or complete suicide. However, careful investigation of attempted suicides and postvention of actual suicides have yielded significant data. The work of Robins et al. (1957) corroborates that suicide is not the sudden phenomenon that it is perceived to be or alleged to be by shocked outsiders and that the victim communicates his intentions through a variety of behavior and responses. The prompt interpretation of these signals is vital.

It cannot be sufficiently stressed how imperative it is to listen, to observe, and to act decisively when individuals mention, hint of or even jest about self-destruction. Shneidman et al. (1961) reported that in one group of individuals who had completed suicide, 75 percent had given overt indication of their plans, had made a preliminary suicide attempt, or had done both. However, in spite of the overlapping of suicide attempts and completed suicide, it is presumptuous to conclude that a suicide attempt constitutes the basic model for successful self-destruction (Zubin, 1974).

An individual may appear to be in a presuicidal state, but it would be difficult indeed to predict whether such a prodromal phase will result in an attempt or a successful suicide. About eight attempts result in one suicide—so the ratio is eight to one (Shneidman, 1975). Erwin Stengel (1964) postulated that those who make the attempt(s) and those who succeed may represent different populations, although, admittedly, the two groups overlap. Shneidman (1969) and Weisman (1972) place the greatest emphasis on the degree of lethality. Nevertheless, the implications of a presuicidal, prodromal state are ominous and it behooves us not to disregard any pleas for help.

Anyone threatening suicide—anyone making even a halfhearted attempt, such as scratching his wrists or overdosing with a nonprescription drug—should be taken seriously and should be carefully evaluated. Individuals who feel it necessary to contact a suicide prevention center may be revealing a presuicidal state. Sawyer et al. (1972) arrived at a completed suicide rate of 288 per 100,000 during the first four years of the operation of the Cleveland Suicide Prevention Center. This clearly indicates that persons contacting the center represent a high suicide risk.

Although depression is an important prodromal sign and the great majority of suicides exhibit depression, it should not be considered an absolute. Individuals in other diagnostic categories may commit suicide (Pokorny et al., 1964). The most decisive indicator, regardless of the diagnostic label of affective state, is a high degree of lethality. The concept that only the mentally ill are likely to be self-destructive is erroneous. An individual who is considered to be sane should therefore not be precluded, and due credence should be given to his threats of suicidal intention (Shneidman and Farberow, 1961; Shneidman, 1975). In intractable pain or stricken with irremediable illness or disease, the suicide may be well-oriented, with a clear sensorium.

SUICIDAL FANTASIES AND IDEATION

Although everyone has thoughts and fantasies of self-destruction at some time, the clinician must take account of their content, their bizarreness, sudden onset, frequency, intensity and duration. There are individuals of an obsessive melancholic pessimistic predisposition who are inclined to chronically dwell on suicide without ever harming themselves. However, they should not be dismissed lightly, and they deserve careful assessment and evaluation.

Fenichel (1945) emphasized the dynamics of the wish fulfillment aspects of suicide. The unconscious motivations include such diverse hopes and fantasies as to be loved again (Bender and Schilder, 1937), a longing to rejoin a deceased person with whom there was still a libidinous identification and attachment (Zilboorg, 1937), a longing for an incestuous union (Garma, 1937), attempting to punish introjects of a sadistic superego (Bernfeld, 1929), or seeking orgasm through death (Reich, 1935).

The motifs that may be elicited or spontaneously expressed involve preoccupation with such fantasies and ideas as accidents, afterlife, killing, being revived or saved just prior to death, worthlessness, helplessness, despair and anguish. Those individuals whose capabilities for coping are poor or lacking must be seriously considered as presuicidal. A life-style involving high risk increases the hazard. However, a test pilot, a motorcyclist, or a mountain climber may be no more or less dangerous to himself than a telephone linesman or a physician (Menninger, 1936, 1938). Fantasies and ideation provide a valuable indication of death-orientation and they warrant investigation, but, as Shneidman (1969, 1971a, 1971b, 1975) pointed out explicitly, they should not be equated or confused with lethality. Thoughts, fantasies and perturbation do not kill per se.

There are people who are monotopically preoccupied with death —some appear to be death-intoxicated—and yet they do not constitute a suicidal hazard. A 34-year-old physician in analysis revealed his fantasies, ideation and death-orientation as follows:

> When I drive to my office in the morning, I pass two funeral homes, and I slow down to check whether there are any preparations being made or whether the hearse is already there. When an ambulance passes the hospital zone, I try to get closer to ascertain if there is a body inside. One of my office windows faced a large undertaking establishment some years ago, and I spent the day peeking compulsively, peering, looking at the windows which were always curtained, trying to determine which room they used for embalming. I would look out periodically to count the deliveries, take time from a patient to watch the hearse enter the loading zone.
>
> I read every name in the death columns, and if the name was even remotely familiar, I would check on the funeral arrangements. Sometimes I even looked for my own name, or a name that resembled mine. I was particularly interested in the age of the deceased. I had a few patients who were embalmers, and I was both fascinated and repulsed by them. I was afraid they would discuss their work, and yet I provoked them to do so. All my corny jokes are about death. Did you hear about the widow who insisted her husband be buried face down? He had threatened to dig his way up after his death.
>
> Every time I walked through the coronary care unit, I glanced toward the pathology laboratories, which were on the same floor. If a sheeted patient was wheeled in, I would stand there rooted and horrified. The thought would linger all day.
>
> To this day I have great difficulty in giving a patient an injection. The drugs I use are fairly innocuous, but I'm scared

to death of causing a anaphylactoid reaction. When I prescribe pills I use homeopathic doses.

I love to sleep and often make believe that it simulates death. It's so tranquil, so calm, so safe, so enticing. Sleep is my greatest pleasure.

Since adolescence I have had thoughts of killing myself. During rough periods I have the fantasy of putting on dirty clothes, going into the garage with some new spark plugs, getting my hands greasy to look like I have been working on the motor, shutting the garage doors and turning the motor on. My death would appear to be an accident and there would be no disgrace. Never a knife or a gun. I have seen some people who blew the tops of their heads off. They haunt me.

This man never made a suicidal attempt. He proved to be a severe obsessive who had been subjected to a sadistic socialization. The resolution of his archaic problems, after many years of psychoanalysis, ameliorated his vast preoccupation with death.

Normal Suicidal Ideation

The process of life constitutes an infinite number of intra- and extrapsychic changes and adjustments. All adaptations initially represent a compromise which presupposes an expansive ego development and which is inextricably a function of ego flexibility.

Erikson (1950, 1958, 1968), in his epigenetic theory, expanded on the function of the ego and laid great emphasis on it as the instrument whereby healthy organization and integration are effected. In postulating eight stages, which begin with birth and continue until death, Erikson elaborated and added another dimension and extension to correlate with Freud's thesis of psychosexual development.

Personality structure cannot be isolated from those demands of culture and society that have a positive as well as a negative effect— the admixture of destructive and constructive influences that coexist. Erikson perceived the eight stages as a continuity rather than as discrete steps and subject to modification throughout the life cycle.

We are all too often taught to live out one life-style, and many individuals come to believe that any modification is utterly alien, anathema and impossible. At every stage of life the individual may be thrust into situations that are intolerable to the ego. Intense anxiety and regression may ensue, with subsequent disequilibria and turbulence. The outcome may or may not be serious, depending on the ego state—its capacity to weather the storm, to find new avenues and to improvise rather than to retreat and succumb.

All questionnaires and suicide profiles advertently and inadvertently stress identity crises and confusion as periods during which the suicidal individual is particularly vulnerable. The death of a parent in early life, loss of a spouse, illness, infirmity, aging, loss of a job, drug addiction, confusion, etc. predispose an individual toward rumination about death and suicide. All the forces and events mentioned above can contribute to an identity crisis and confusion. It is perfectly logical to assume that any disruption in an individual's life can cause an upheaval and that the ability of the ego to mediate may prove inadequate. However painful, this process does not necessarily lead to lethal consequences.

Felix Deutsch (1960) noted:

> Psychoanalytic studies of adults and children have shown that real and imagined losses are significant emotional events of early childhood. They often lead to an attempt to regain the lost object either in fact or in fantasy. This seems to occur even in the case of the loss involved in the separation of the self-image from the image of the outside world. The primitive experience that the world was once a part of the self and that gradually it was taken away or became externalized is never completely accepted. The unconscious wish to regain it, along with the sense of timelessness and omnipotence that goes with it, leads to highly charged emotional attitudes (p. 38).

Later in the same article Deutsch wrote:

> Any loss of an object calls upon the ego to retrieve it with new means, or find a substitute object. The loss revives the ambivalent conflict and reawakens the early infantile hostility to objects, the loss of which had either been threatened, desired, shared or experienced—a hostility which has to be repressed or gratified.

Feelings of revenge and grief caused by the loss can hardly be harmonized to give a satisfactory result. Loss means "having been abandoned." Revenge means to leave this object and turn to others more dependable. The first step may lead to isolation, the preoccupation with the self as an object one can love or hate, exalt or devaluate, which can be revived and enjoyed as an alter ego, and for which one can mourn . . . (p. 42) .

In identity crises, the subsequent continuation, attentuation and heightening of anxiety are a response to the loss and the blow that the ego is unable to tolerate flexibly. If other avenues are closed off, recourse to self-destructive options may be consciously or unconsciously dictated. Even if the ego is functioning well, transient suicidal fantasies and ideation can be expected. Whenever an individual must relinquish a pattern of behavior, outmoded and unsatisfactory though it be, symbolic death is involved. An archaic part of oneself —and its introjects—is perceived as the victim, and the new, emergent self is perceived as the murderer.

Psychoanalysis is probably the most sophisticated technique for enabling changes in identity to occur by emancipating the analysand from the archaic, punitive superego by a controlled regression wherein the past can be relived and placed in proper perspective, resulting in better integration and expansion of ego functions. However, every analysand, regardless of his determination to get well, demonstrates his ambivalence with a tenacious resistance. During such periods, death fantasies and suicidal ideation may predominate as the infantile forces and their introjects struggle to prevent the emergence of more mature attitudes and their integration into a higher level or epigenetic phase.

It is, therefore, normal to experience suicidal thoughts and affect when an individual feels required to initiate, to undergo and to implement intrapsychic change. There is a conflagration, and a battle is waged against primitive surges to punish, expel, excise, extirpate, eradicate and to "kill" the resisting infantile forces that impede the ego from accepting the new, ostensibly desirable state of affairs.

Perhaps it was not coincidental that so many of the world's creative giants endured deep depression and suffered suicidal ideation in escalating to a higher form—one that required even further change or sublimation.

In spite of our sophistication, we are all too often amazed and perhaps startled when we learn that an idolized or an idealized figure is preoccupied with, fantasies about or longs for death. This is all the more puzzling and disconcerting when such a person has shown great valor and energy in coping with life's adversities and has faced the inevitability of death realistically, honestly and with dignity. There is no better example than Freud. If we accept the statement of his devoted disciple, Ernest Jones (*The Life and Work of Sigmund Freud*, Vol. I, p. 5, 1953) : "He (Freud) once said he thought of it (death) every day of his life, which is certainly unusual." Perhaps it appeared so unusual to Jones, the psychoanalyst, because it involved the heroic and unflinchingly ascetic conquistador, Freud.

Every dynamic psychotherapist has seen individuals who frequently present suicidal fantasies and ideation. These fantasies are most common during the course of a transition from one phase to another. A typical illustration is a dream or dream fragment in which a child has died or has been murdered. The patient is able to recall that either directly or indirectly it was he who was responsible for the death. His associations soon establish that the child is indeed an early image of himself, and it becomes evident dynamically that he destroyed an aspect of himself that was impeding him from attaining his goal. In the dream, he committed both suicide and homicide. The author has found that such patients show little anxiety or remorse if they are truly well motivated and that the dream lacks the terror of pavor nocturnus. The revelation is often acknowledged with relief, and even a trace of amusement. Such insights can be helpful in crossing the bridge that is essential for working-through and resolution.

The conclusions that death fantasies and ideation can be normal, benign attempts to effectuate emancipation, growth and integration should never be lightly drawn. The same careful assessment and analysis that enable the physician to differentiate hyperventilation from dyspnea and attendant congestive failure are required.

In determining whether morbid thoughts and feelings are growth attempts, the clinician should give careful consideration to the patient's mental status—his orientation, sensorium and controls. He should assess lethality with great caution. He should decide whether the transference is stable; whether he (the therapist) has a good grasp of the psychodynamics; whether the suicidal material has logical relevance to the current problem under discussion; whether the patient has made any previous suicide attempts; whether the morbidity is due to reactive forces. He should examine the content of the fantasies and ideation in great detail. He should see the patient frequently enough to be aware of any sudden shifts or changes. Above all, he should not hesitate to change his mind or to ask for consultation.

Communication of Intent

There may be many indications of preparation to depart this life —or there may be few. However, even the secretive person or the individual who is unaware of his lethality will impart some cues of his self-destructive plans. Shneidman and Farberow (1961) found that eight out of any ten people who destroy themselves have given evidence of their intention to do so.

A simple, matter-of-fact, verbal announcement may be the precursor for suicide: "I've decided to kill myself"; "I've had it"; "I'm through"; "I've lived long enough"; "I'm calling it quits—living is useless"; "There's a better way."

Declarations of intent may be vague, nonspecific, philosophical or abstract. The content may reflect seething rage, a motive for revenge, quiet resignation, contemplativeness, happy anticipation and even humor. Some examples: "I hate my life. I hate everyone, everything"; "It was good at times, and I can't complain, but we must all say good-bye"; "Now they won't have me to kick around anymore"; "I won't need another appointment, doctor. Don't take it as an insult. You were very helpful"; "Do you believe in reincarnation?"; "I'd like to come back someday. Maybe things will be better then"; "If I don't see you again, thanks for everything"; "I'll be back to haunt them all"; "Really, you won't have to worry about me anymore— that's for sure"; "I have a premonition—I'm going far away on a long

trip"; "What's wrong with cremation?"; "I've been seriously thinking of making out my will" (this from a pregnant woman of 24 with
two children) ; "Do you know the procedure in donating your eyes
after death?"; "How do they preserve kidneys for transplantation if
you die suddenly?"; "I wish I could tell you how important you've
been. You've helped me to see things clearly. Now I know the only
road that's open for me"; "Life is like a short circuit. There's a sput-
ter, then the lights go out."

Communications of intent can be in writing, with the same morbid
content or suggestions. Anyone who receives a note or letter that
carries direct, indirect or even symbolic connotation of death-orientation and lethality should waste no time attempting to determine its
authenticity but, rather, should act. The potential victim may still
harbor ambivalence, with some hope or wish for rescue. If received in
time, the distress signal of the suicide note can be lifesaving.

Shneidman and Farberow (1957b) conceded that their study of
suicide notes was limited to a relatively small number of samples—
suicide notes are usually destroyed. It is understandable that relatives
of the deceased are loath to make such personal documents available.
On the basis of 721 notes examined over a nine-year period, they
suggest that such material be analyzed from the perspective of a
projective technique such as the Thematic Apperception Test
(TAT). They considered personal communications to be extremely
important and hoped that their studies could be expanded with a
broader base. Shneidman and Farberow (1961) reported that 35
percent of males and 30 percent of females wrote notes before
completing suicide. These figures were higher than those submitted
by Stengel and Cook (1958).

The findings of Shneidman and Farberow suggest that the genuine
suicide note carried imperious overtones. Although omnipotence is
reflected, confusion coexists. The nuclear aspect of the note is the
reality of intended departure, and yet the directions and demands
that the suicide insists be complied with presume that the writer may
still be around, that he is immortal, that he is living by killing himself (O'Connor, 1948), that he will supervise his survivors so that his
dictates are carried out scrupulously. The confusion and contradiction

are implicit in the concern that others must serve as his extensions after death. Why should anything matter if one is forever gone? Death-oriented or determined though it be, the suicide note often reflects ambivalence and denial (Weisman, 1972).

It is also important to appreciate the fact that suicidal notes often reflect terrible unhappiness, distress and pathology. However, as Shneidman (1976, 1975) reiterates, they are by no means conclusive, nor are they pathognomonic of mental illness.

Allport (1942) in his monograph provided a detailed list of the rationales that motivate individuals to write personal documents, e.g., exhibitionism, desire for order, special pleading, securing personal perspective, redemption, public service, immortality, literary delight, scientific interest, etc.

BEHAVIORAL PREDICTORS

An individual may frankly disclose his intention to kill himself by going through what is tantamount to a dress rehearsal. Such a dry run may backfire because of miscalculation and result in a completed suicide; or it may appear on the surface as a relatively minor, unimportant or halfhearted venture—a gesture. A nonlethal overdose, five or six tablets of an over-the-counter sleeping pill or aspirin, may be regarded as a bid for attention rather than a cry for help. A cut on the wrists may be ascribed to an accident. In a busy emergency room, the harried physician, intern or resident may suture the wound and complacently accept such an explanation. Physicians particularly should make a thorough inquiry into the circumstances of every accident, injury or inappropriate drug ingestion. Alertness and awareness will help the clinician to detect suicidal maneuvers.

An adolescent presented herself for evaluation because of "drug addiction." She wore a shirt with long sleeves, but every time she raised her cigarette to take a puff, her sleeve slipped and disclosed skin lesions. At first she denied they existed and refused to roll up her sleeve. After some persuasion she agreed. Her right arm was covered from wrist to mid-elbow with multiple superficial cuts. She insisted she had scratched herself in her sleep—then that someone scratched her. Finally she admitted, "I did it with a razor. I kept going deeper and deeper to see if it would hurt. The bleeding didn't frighten me." Further questioning revealed that she had been contemplating suicide for two months. Although initially hostile and belligerent, she accepted the recommendation of hospitalization with a sigh of relief. Then she admitted that it was not drug-taking that had motivated her to seek help but, rather, her wish to die. It is highly questionable whether she would have brought up her suicidal preoccupation spontaneously.

There is a large, growing literature that provides significant cues, prodromal signs and features as well as useful insights to help identify potential suicides. Farberow (1950) summarized a number of cogent signs and findings. Menninger (1938), Motto and Greene (1958), Pokorny (1960, 1974), Robins et al. (1959), Bachrach (1951), Dorpat and Boswell (1959) have written extensively in this sector.

THE ROLE OF THE PHYSICIAN IN PRESUICIDAL STATES

If we accept Shneidman's findings (1961) that 75 percent of all suicides consult with a physician at least four months before they complete suicide, we are confronted by a provocative statistic. Dorpat and Ripley (1960) corroborated Shneidman's study that 75 percent of completed suicides had indeed sought medical attention, but within 12 months prior to their deaths. However, Barraclough et al.'s (1968) study in England indicated that an even larger number had sought medical help within a shorter period of time prior to when they terminated their lives. What impels people to see a physician if they are planning to kill themselves? If they have decided to end their lives, why should they be concerned about any ailment or disease, real or fancied? Only uncertainty, ambivalence and the hope of an alternative could impel the majority of presuicidal individuals to seek out a physician.

These individuals are most likely to present themselves with a somatic complaint—a gastric disturbance, chest discomfort, headache, anorexia, insomnia, malaise, psychomotor retardation compounded by anxiety and depression. They are less likely to bring up futility, inability to cope and suicidal intent. The competent physician who focalizes on the presenting problem quickly rules out organic disease, reassures the patient and treats him for a functional disorder on an empirical basis. If he is perceptive and recognizes excessive anxiety or a masked depression, he prescribes a tranquilizer. In most instances, he has neither the time nor the inclination to probe more deeply—nor does he feel the necessity. He considers that he has performed his medical obligation. These deductions are corroborated by the overwhelming evidence of the studies by Shneidman (1961), Dorpat and Ripley (1960), and Barraclough et al. (1968), that the presuicides' call for help was not answered effectively.

The patient who is contemplating suicide may, like a child, endow the physician with god-like omniscience and omnipotence. Unconsciously he hopes that his somatic concern will be translated by the physician, that his anguish and despair will be revealed and that the doctor will take care of him. On the other hand, he may be deluded and misconstrue the symptoms or syndrome as the direct cause of his suicidal preoccupation. The physician's reassurance that his physical examination is negative may destroy and obliterate this defense. He is now even worse off in that he can no longer displace his concern to an organic etiology.

The utilization of tranquilizers in attempting to calm or ameliorate functional problems in the presence of a presuicidal, lethal state that has not been uncovered by the physician may be termed empirical, or it may be termed blind therapy. The antidepressants are notoriously paradoxical. Depression, anxiety, agitation, or the entire gamut may become intensified and act as a catalyst in the presuicidal state.

Some individuals consult a physician to secure drugs which they accumulate until they have a lethal dose. Prescribing even small doses and renewing the prescription periodically are unwise unless the physician has a good grasp of his patient's affective state.

All physicians should be made aware of the necessity to go beneath the surface when the patient is emotionally distressed, distraught or depressed. It requires very little investment of time to inquire in a tactful and direct manner: "Have you thought of taking your own life?" or "Have you felt that you want to kill yourself?" or "Have you ever thought of suicide in the past?" The old myth that talking about taking one's life might provoke the patient or precipitate a suicide has long been disproved. On the contrary, it may well be that the patient's confidence in his doctor is increased and for the first time he can voice intentions and plans to kill himself to someone who had the perceptiveness and discernment to inquire—one who is listening thoughtfully and taking the matter seriously (MacKinnon and Michels, 1971). After he has elicited this disclosure, the physician can express his concern about the patient. It can be unequivocally and dogmatically stated that such an approach would save countless lives.

An article in the *Journal of the American Medical Association* (Rockwell and O'Brien, 1973) takes issue with the ineffectiveness of physicians in contending with suicide prevention because of gaps in their background and knowledge. The article reiterates that 75 percent of suicides seek out a physician prior to completion, and the implication that many physicians are ill prepared was underscored. Ninety-one percent of physicians polled thought that their knowledge was insufficient. An optimistic aspect was reflected in the fact that 70 percent were interested in embarking on a program to further acquaint themselves with this leading cause of death. Graduate and post-graduate courses were recommended and, in the light of our litigous Zeitgeist, would probably be well attended.

Ross (1965, 1967), a psychiatrist, suggested that in addition to a careful history and physical examination the physician should look for the following clues that he has included in a profile of presuicidal individuals:

> One's first observation may be of a palefaced, sallow person sitting huddled in a waiting room chair, evidencing little or no spontaneous activity. Further inspection reveals an accentuation of the facial wrinkles and eyelid folds, a lackluster to the hair, some evidence of weight and sleep loss. Carelessness or even unkempt grooming also may be noted.
>
> When one shakes hands with the patient, he may become aware of the various stigmata of underlying emotional tone through psychophysiologic communications: warmth, dryness,

dampness, cold, clammy, firm, listless, forceful, weak and the like.

The patient's chief complaint may be a generalized feeling that "something is wrong," an apprehensiveness or a generally alarmed state. This may be linked to an expressed fear of a dread disease or to complaints of regional aches and pains and, frequently, to various complaints of gastrointestinal dysfunction.

Characteristically and commonly, there is a reported change of bodily feeling expressed as a decrease or loss of the feeling of wellbeing. Tiredness, fatigue, "heaviness" are presented in various degrees . . . sleep patterns are apt to be altered in quite characteristic, almost pathogenic, ways of depression. Most often the patient complains of awakening early in the morning, unable to return to sleep, but still too fatigued to face the new day.

Loss of appetite is apt to be marked and sustained. But in order cases food may be used as a tranquilizer, leading to overeating and obesity. But no matter which, increased or decreased intake, there is no true pleasure in eating because food seems to have lost its taste.

Women patients may report various menstrual disorders and libidinal loss.

Some persons will indicate they are committing what can best be described as "social suicide" through their behavior. This may be apparent in a history of alcoholism, sexual escapades or business failure (1967, p. 1096).

OVERVIEW OF DYNAMIC CONTRIBUTIONS

Every student of suicidology has eagerly sought meaningful hypotheses, formulations, principles, and protocols that are logical, cogent and also prognostically optimistic. In a scientific era, optimism requires some structure based on a relevance that is predicated on the collection of data pertinent to the problem and conclusions that are carefully drawn with statistical backup. Unfortunately, many investigations and conclusions have yielded tons of verbiage and little else.

Suicidologists have been faced not only with the mystery of self-inflicted death, but with many fallacies—hunches, guesses, conjectures and inferences that have often proved to be counter-productive, sometimes farcical and pathetic, sometimes exercises in futility—and sometimes fatuous in their simplistic naivete.

The Eight Myths

In 1961, Shneidman and Farberow wrote about the misconceptions of suicide—the myths of suicide. The misconceptions that they listed in the form of a concise, concrete, one sentence fable followed by an answer have become what is tantamount to the eight commandments of suicidology. Although they have been repeated ad infinitum, and for good cause, any overview of dynamic contributions would be remiss without their inclusion. These eight fables and the authenticated facts provide an optimistic frame of reference that helps clear the path for prevention and intervention:

(1) *People who talk about suicide are unlikely to commit suicide*: Eight out of ten individuals manifest their intention to kill themselves. It is sheer folly and dereliction to disregard their ideation, their warnings, their threats or their gestures.

(2) *Suicide occurs precipitously*: Many signals of distress are sent out. If they are heeded, death can be averted.

(3) *Suicidal individuals are fully committed to self-cessation*: The large numbers that seek medical help clearly indicate that there is indecision, ambivalence and a wish to be dissuaded from self-destruction.

(4) *Suicide is a problem of lifelong duration*: Periods of vulnerability represent crises that are of short duration. Intervention and therapy may reduce the vulnerability and enable the individual to readjust and learn to cope.

(5) *Improvement after a crisis indicates that the risk factor is over*: Remobilization of morbidity can ensue during an apparent remission. The individual should be considered vulnerable for a period of three months.

(6) *The rich or the poor are most likely to destroy themselves*: All socioeconomic strata are proportionately represented.

(7) *The propensity to suicide is inherited*: There is no evidence that a self-destructive potential is inherited.

(8) *All suicides are victims of mental illness and demonstrate psychopathology*: Individuals who commit suicide are distraught, distressed and unhappy, but they are not necessarily mentally ill.

Subintentioned Deaths

Although the international classification of diseases lists about 140 different causes for death, there are only four modes of death—natural, accident, suicide and homicide. This rather static conception does not take into consideration the possibilities for overlapping. For example, when is an accident really suicide? When is an apparent homicide a suicide, or vice versa? What is a natural death? Is there such a death? Death from coronary disease—a myocardial infarct—is generally considered to be a natural death. Death from malignant disease is considered "natural." However, the work of Karl Menninger (1936, 1938) suggested that man may be instrumental in his own death even though the cause is chronic or organic. This attitude is now well supported throughout the literature. Friedman and Rosenman (1974) clearly demonstrate a life history pattern in the development of heart disease. For that matter, many investigators are of the opinion that predisposing psychological factors will be found in the development of all disease. LeShan (1959, 1961, 1966) has written well over a dozen articles on the emotional life history pattern that is associated with neoplastic disease. Although the possibility that malignant disease may be associated with destructive life-styles and patterns has been conjectured about for the past quarter century, it is only now coming into focus. LeShan and Worthington (1959) wrote a preliminary report on the psychological correlates of neoplastic disease in 1955. There are those theorists who maintain that the only natural cause of death would be a catabolic process that is due to the exhaustion of old age—a function of cellular degeneration. Even this theory has been subjected to raised eyebrows by gerontologists who are becoming increasingly optimistic about reversing catabolic and degenerative processes.

Shneidman (1973) felt that the large majority of all deaths are subintentioned. He suggested that in addition to the classification of natural, accident, suicide and homicide all deaths should also be considered as intentioned, subintentioned and unintentioned. In the intentioned death, the individual is playing a direct role in self-cessaton. An unintentional death would be defined as one in which the individual was not overtly involved. In such instances, the death is due to physical forces or trauma external to the individual or from a biological pathology or failure from within that could not be correlated with a psychic factor.

Shneidman (1975) defined subintentioned deaths:

> . . . deaths in which the decedent plays some partial, covert, or unconscious role in hastening his own demise. The objective evidences of the presence of these roles lie in such behavioral manifestations as poor judgment, imprudence, excessive risk taking, abuse of alcohol, misuse of drugs, neglect of self, self-destructive style of life, disregard of prescribed lifesaving medical regimen and so on—where the person fosters, facilitates, exacerbates, or hastens the process of his dying (p. 1780).

Shneidman differentiates his concept of subintentioned cessation behaviors from Menninger's chronic, focal, and organic suicides. In Menninger's (1938) concepts, the individual continues to live on in spite of his self-destructive life-style, whereas in the subintentioned behaviors, the lethal goal is more imminent. Subintentioned deaths may fall within any one of the modes. A subintentioned death may therefore appear to be natural, accident, suicide or homicide. It becomes obvious that the NASH categories of death may be convenient for a coroner, but they are, unfortunately, archaic and imprecise.

Lethality, Perturbation and Inimicality as a Measure of Suicidality

One of the largest problems in the confrontation of the presuicidal individual is to evaluate those elements that are prognostically significant—most intimately related to self-cessation—and to determine the degree of intention to self-destruct.

Shneidman (1969, 1971b, 1975) divided the patient's affective state—his emotional struggle, his crisis—into a triad of components that are essentially continuous but that can be examined discretely as well. It is very helpful to separate these components in order to perceive the interrelations.

(1) Lethality, rated on a one to nine scale, reflects the probability of "deathliness"—determination to kill oneself. Hurting, wounding, injuring or even maiming is still a far cry from the irreversibility of death. Broadly speaking, one can categorize lethality as absent, low, medium or high.

(2) Perturbation, which can also be rated and categorized similarly, refers to the degree of psychic upheaval and disorganization. An acute psychotic episode might indicate a high perturbation, but perturbation per se does not result in suicide. Most acutely disturbed individuals do not kill themselves in spite of panic states and divorce from reality. Although lethality and perturbation, or perturbation and lethality, may be synergistic, it is the lethal component that is deadly. The clinician who is faced with a highly perturbed patient may have to contend with a difficult management problem that requires skill and acumen as a therapist and is indeed urgent, but this should not be confused with the urgency of lethality. Perturbability may be minimal, and yet the patient may terminate his life.

(3) Inimicality enters the picture in the sense that a destructive life-style may potentiate suicide. Drug dependency or the refusal to take drugs when necessary to maintain life or good health, self-neglect and risk taking—gambling with one's life and courting failures—can be contributory. The form and degree of inimicality are pertinent.

The clinician's judgment about the immediate hazard of suicide can be significantly improved by the subjective utilization of this triad of components, and the decision about disposition—hospitalization, long- or short-term psychotherapy—can be better defined. Lethality is the key factor in the management of the presuicide. However, the reciprocal function of perturbation and inimicality in this continuous, ever-changing fluctuating process should be assessed and reassessed frequently.

It is self-evident that an individual who is rated high in all three components represents a high risk, and appropriate safeguards should be initiated. On the other hand, low lethality with high perturbation that is related to a history of chronic inimicality may not require nor call for extreme precautions. However, this is not a static situation. Therefore, the clinician should be aware that increased perturbation and inimicality can intensify lethality and the picture can change very quickly.

High-lethality—the crisis of suicide—is relatively brief (Shneidman, 1975, 1976). Its duration can be thought of as short—hours or days rather than months and years as in the case of perturbation and inimicality. This is not to say that an exacerbation or resurgence of lethality is unlikely but, rather, that intervention can avert self-destruction and that subsequent therapy can provide more constructive avenues of coping.

The matter of ambivalence should be underscored because while it represents confusion and uncertainty, it also offers an opportunity for intervention. It is not atypical for an individual to ingest a fatal overdose and immediately call for an ambulance. The call may come too late, but if previous expressions of the cry of help are heeded and answered, lives can be saved.

DYADIC ASPECTS

On the surface, suicide appears to be a solitary, private matter when an individual proceeds to arrange for his demise by his own doing. Most, if not all, suicides are dyadic and, to use the familiar phrase, involve a significant other. There are those theorists who would delete "most" and state categorically that all suicides are dyadic.

At the 1910 conference on suicidology in Vienna (Friedman, 1967), Wilhelm Stekel made the statement that "no one kills himself who has not wanted to kill another or wished the death of another" (p. 87). Out of context, these words probably appeared extreme more than 60 years ago. Later, psychoanalytic theorists (Zilboorg, 1936a; Menninger, 1938) elaborated with more sophisticated theoretical conceptions.

Some dynamically oriented suicidologists and sociologists consider that aggressivity and the hostile introjects of the love object formulation are not the sine qua non and include hopelessness, helplessness and dependency as other important factors in the dyadic interplay (Litman, 1967).

Whether it be hostility or dependency and helplessness, Toynbee (1968) emphasized the dyadic relationship as an integral feature of death—that there are two parties to a death—the individual who dies and the survivors, who are the victims.

Although the intrapsychic forces may incubate and ferment from archaic influences, the displacement is to figures in the present who are interacting with the individual who has elected to terminate his life as a solution. They are closely and intimately related to him— husband, wife, lovers, children, etc. The experienced suicidologist would immediately zero in on the dyadic relation—or significant others in his attempt to intervene and to prevent suicide.

After the fact, it becomes a postvention responsibility to minister and to provide treatment to the bereaved—the victims. The adherence to the philosophy that it is a prerogative to take one's own life and that efforts at intervention are an intrusion might well consider the plight of those who are abruptly left behind to endure a guilt and condemnation that may never be eradicated or resolved.

There is at present a wealth of basic knowledge that provides the suicidologist with a grasp of fundamental issues and principles. Although these are admittedly insufficient, it is pertinent to note that answers to malignant disease and oncology offer little more. We are instructed to observe, watch and heed signs, and consult physicians when the danger signals are manifested. If malignancy—suicidal intent—is detected early, the outlook is far better and there are possibilities of cure and/or remission. There is always the danger of exacerbation, but there is also hope. Formulations, constructs and empirical data have provided guidelines that save lives.

CHAPTER 5

CLINICAL SYNDROMES

PSYCHOPATHOLOGICAL REACTIONS RELATED TO SELF-DESTRUCTION

Linking psychopathological states with suicide suggests that those who wish, plan, or are determined to end their lives are mentally ill and that they therefore fall within the domain of psychopathology or psychiatry. This clearly implies that the self-destructive intent and the motivation are pathognomic of mental illness.

Gibbs (1968), a foremost sociologist, took issue with this attitude and questioned whether the connection between suicide and psychopathology was a manifestation of popular conventional thinking—of circular reasoning—namely, the basic assumption that anyone who took his own life must have been mentally ill. In his critical analysis, Gibbs pointed out how elaborations of such a thesis lead to other conclusions. Since many individuals who have contemplated, attempted or completed suicide give evidence of mental illness, the psychiatrist, who is ostensibly the guardian of the mentally ill, considers himself the sine qua non whenever the matter of self-destruction crops up, and it therefore becomes his obligation to intervene. Gibbs rhetorically asks: (1) Why are psychiatrists contacted or consulted in matters pertaining to suicide? (2) Why do individuals who are intent on self-destruction manifest symptoms that are considered or construed to be indicative of psychopathology? He proceeds to propound on both questions:

75

Though merely speculation, one answer to the first question is that the conditions of the decision lead would-be victims to a psychiatrist, and possibly for reasons unrelated to mental illness per se. Some individuals accept the cultural interpretation of suicide (i.e. the act itself is clearly indicative of mental illness), and particularly when the act is clearly proscribed socially and/ or legally. Even if an individual does not accept the cultural interpretation, he may contact a psychiatrist for sympathetic advice that is not provided by others because the topic is taboo. Finally, if the normative evaluation of suicide is ambiguous or clearly permissive, the would-be victim would seek the opinion of a psychiatrist to ease the burden of what would be otherwise a purely personal decision, and all the more so since he cannot appeal to those who have undergone the agony of making the same choice.

Given the fact that some individuals who are contemplating suicide do come to the attention of a psychiatrist, why do the psychiatrists so often detect symptoms of mental illness? If the patient has accepted the cultural interpretation of suicide, his belief that he is mentally ill could influence the perception of a psychiatrist; and it may be that the psychiatrist himself accepts the cultural interpretation. But still another possibility is not so obvious. The condition of decision undoubtedly produces a considerable amount of psychic strain, which may be manifested in symptoms of mental illness. In other words, the possibility is entertained that some suicides are associated with mental illness not because the latter produced the former but because the conditions of decision produce symptoms of mental illness. In any event, the interest of psychiatrists stems not only from the fact that would-be victims tend to consult them but also because suicidal behavior is likely to be interpretated as indicative of mental illness, the primary concern of psychiatry (p. 6).

Gibbs' comments cannot be taken lightly and deserve an answer. Psychiatrists are not invariably contacted or consulted in matters of suicide. No one can document how many presuicides have been averted from a self-destructive course by the intervention of significant others—or just others, including spouses, lovers, friends, physicians, clergy, teachers, policemen, bartenders, firemen, samaritans, suicide prevention center personnel, or just strangers who were fortuitously there. Presuicides who are likely to consult a psychiatrist are frightened, anxious, ambivalent and in the throes of upheaval. Any cogitation about cultural interpretation is superseded by inner chaos; they are in no condition to intellectualize or to question whether the visit to a psychiatrist is predicated on the prevalent attitude that suicidal inclination is due to mental illness.

On the other hand, a highly determined, highly lethal, death-oriented individual does not require the opinions of psychologists or psychiatrists and is not likely to agree to a consultation. At this point he is even less likely to be influenced by conventional thinking, cultural interpretations of norms, or the perceptions of psychiatry or society about self-termination.

The individual who is considering suicide and does consult with a psychiatrist is still uncertain about his decision, is still wavering, and is hopeful that another avenue may be available. This is what brings him to seek help—not cultural or legal proscriptions. He often welcomes hospitalization as a reprieve that enables him to review his plans and his decisions.

Consulting a psychiatrist merely for sympathetic advice because of the taboo of suicide is equally untenable. A highly lethal individual is not deterred by taboos and restrictive cultural injunctions. The large incidence of self-destruction is mute testimony to that. Sympathetic advice can be secured from a multiplicity of sources (friends, relatives, clergy, etc.) ; the presuicide has no reason to presume that the topic of self-destruction would be less anathema, taboo or more palatable to a psychiatrist than to anyone else. If it is sympathetic advice alone that he seeks, he could find it at far less cost and effort.

In his second question Gibbs asks ". . . why do such persons often exhibit what are construed to be symptoms of mental illness?" The answer may be very simple: Many individuals who come to the psychiatrist contemplating suicide or who have attempted suicide do, indeed, present psychopathology because they are emotionally disturbed. The psychiatrist did not induce these symptoms although Gibbs' use of the word "construed" suggests that the psychiatrist is misinterpreting the significance of overt psychopathology.

Even if we were to accept the possibility of the hypothesis that cultural interpretations of suicide bring the presuicide to a psychiatrist or a psychologist and that such a presuicide presents psychopathological manifestations, how on earth can this individual be categorized? Should special dispensation be granted to presuicides? Should their diagnosis be qualified as mental illness because of "construed psychopathology"?

Gibbs' last possibility is more subtle and suggests that the decision of suicide produced the psychic strain which in turn resulted in the symptomatology of mental illness. No one can deny that planning one's execution would create anxiety and psychic strain and that such manifestations of emotional distress might qualify one for psychiatric evaluation. However, the psychiatrist might still correctly conclude on the basis of his consultation that the individual was indeed suffering from mental illness. It would seem that a more significant question is why the patient was so disturbed before the psychic strain and in such a state of dysphoria—anhedonia—as to justify the wish, intent and determination to end life.

It is dogmatic to insist that suicide is always related to mental illness and it is equally dogmatic to maintain that psychopathology can be divorced from suicide.

Choron (1972) stressed the need for further intensive study of the presuicidal population, but, to date, the results of such studies have been inconclusive. Some investigators have been inclined to perceive mental disorders as a conglomerate, some have limited mental illness to the psychoses, others have included neuroses and personality disorders, and still others rely on their own clinical impressions as to what constitutes mental illness. As a result, the estimates of the frequency of mental disorders in completed suicide from various countries range from a low of 20 percent to a high of 94 percent (Prevention of Suicide, *Public Health Paper No. 35*, Geneva; World Health Organization, 1968).

In two clinical studies of completed suicide (Dorpat and Ripley, 1960; Barraclough et al., 1968), almost all of the suicides, 90 percent, were judged to have been mentally ill on the basis of their clinical history. In a study by Robins et al. (1959a, 1959b), the largest number of completed suicides were considered to be psychiatrically disturbed. In addition to the large incidence of mental illness reported, these studies also revealed that one or two easily identifiable psychiatric conditions existed concomitantly—depression and/or alcoholism.

In 11 studies of attempted suicide (Stengel, 1960), the incidence of mental illness was reported to be 100 percent, and in the remaining seven studies the incidence was still high, with none reporting under 74 percent.

It is particularly alarming that such large numbers of the presuicidal population remain undiagnosed, untreated, or improperly managed. There is ample evidence that relatives of those intimately related to the suicide find it expedient to deny that they had prior knowledge of mental illness. Physicians employ the same rationale.

Many laymen and physicians and some psychiatrists and psychologists are inclined to regard depression as the sole pathological criterion for suicide. In this regard, the findings of Pokorny et al. (1964) are particularly interesting. The suicide rates per 100,000 per year for psychiatric patients in a Texas Veterans Administration hospital calculated over a 15-year period were: neuroses—119, personality disorders—130, alcoholism—133, organic states—78, schizophrenia—167, and depression—566. Although the high incidence of depression is manifest, the variegated distribution of other psychopathological states clearly demonstrates that depression is not the only pathological state that may result in self-destruction.

The symptom-syndrome is a defensive strategy. It should not be a surprise that all symptom-syndromes carry a risk of lethality. They are all defensive systems—maneuvers designed to help the individual cope. It is not the symptom-syndrome that causes lethality but, rather, the inability of the individual to continue to derive sufficient support and positive feedback from techniques that served him in the past. It is invariably puzzling to an objective but naive observer to note the cumbersome, complex strategies that are required for minimal emotional self-sustenance. It is even more amazing that the bubble didn't burst long before. Psycho-economically, the individual may be on the brink of emotional bankruptcy but is still able to survive through an intricate utilization and exploitation of one or a number of psychopathological states.

Litman (1967) extrapolated Freudian dynamics of the breakdown of ego-defenses—the release of primary process with its attendant destructive instinctual energy. Retroflexed aggressivity from the loss of love objects is now directed toward introjects. The combination of narcissistic injury and inundating affect is such that one part of the ego may be at war with other parts. A ferocious and tyrannical superego may attack full force. Although the symptom-syndrome and the type of defenses that are implemented are significant, considera- tion of the dynamics is crucial. The inability to maintain the dyadic relationship, to manipulate it, perhaps to maintain coexisting death wishes, may make it impossible for the individual to sustain himself and continue to exist. Rigidity and inability to modify the milieu and to adapt to new circumstances represent extensions to Freudian doctrine and further exacerbate rage, hopelessness and helplessness. The vengeance against the significant other is accomplished by killing the introject—suicide (Hendin, 1963, 1964; Jackson, 1957; Meerloo, 1962; Zilboorg, 1936a, 1936b) .

Some symptom-syndromes offer better defenses than others. Depres- sive states, with resultant helplessness, hopelessness and inability to cope with loss, are particularly vulnerable (Minkoff et al., 1973). The obsessive-compulsive, on the other hand, is extremely well- equipped and well-organized, constantly on the alert, with a self- imposed vigilance against the archaic forces. However, if such a Maginot line is breached or pierced by adverse intra-/extrapsychic events, a decompensation results; the patient is now depressed, with all the vicissitudes that accompany depression.

It must be emphasized that most depressives do not commit suicide (Christ, Brownsberger and Solomon, 1974). While the number of suicides who are depressed are well represented (Pokorny, 1964), most individuals who are clinically depressed are by no means totally incapacitated and are able to make a minimal adjustment. Many are able to derive sufficient secondary gain, so the majority manage to survive in spite of their anergias, retardations, melancholias, and variegated somatic and masked symptomatology. If there is a loss, or the significant other refuses or is unable to fulfill the dyadic obliga- tions or requirements, then the lethality may be increased and inten- sified (Shneidman, 1975). This holds true for such other symptom-syndromes as, for example, the personality disorders. An individual may continue for a lifetime with an ego-syntonic, characterological disturbance, but it is only when he can no longer manipulate and justify his psychopathy, that anxiety and depression emerge. One sees this frequently in the therapy of personality disorders when the patients improve and their acting-out is finally self-perceived as pathological.

Many suicides have proved to be alcoholics—but most alcoholics do not commit suicide. If alcoholics were deprived of the tranquilizing effect that results from depressing the cortex, the incidence of suicide attempts in this highly oral-dependent category might be far higher (Motto, 1974). It is also conceivable that many depressed individuals might commit suicide if they were unable to tranquilize themselves with ethanol or other drugs. Depression, with its attendant reward from sympathetic, significant others—in many instances even from physicians and psychotherapists—may have an ameliorative and even therapeutic function. Reassurance and support are often necessary (Christ et al., 1974).

It becomes important to reiterate and to emphasize that it is not the psychopathological state that results in self-termination, but, rather, the limitations, inadequacies and inflexibility of the defense system. When the behavior and maneuvers inherent in the psychopathological state become untenable or impossible, a lethal crisis may ensue. It therefore behooves the clinician not to interfere with symptom-syndromes or attempt to eliminate or eradicate systems of defense unless he has a good knowledge of dynamics and can estimate the patient's ego strength. An individual with depression and anxiety may have his lethality intensified in the course of treatment, and under such conditions the hazard of suicide may arise or increase. Psychoanalysts are particularly sensitive about giving premature interpretations and attempting to offer insights indiscriminately (Glover, 1955; Greenson, 1967).

PSYCHOSIS

Psychosis is perceived by Grinker (1975) as a behavioral term that signifies a withdrawal or a concerted effort to compromise reality with primary process and its chaotic, illogical thinking and affect.

Attempts at restitution are manifested by hallucinations, delusions and bizarre thinking. As a consequence, psychotic behavior is unrealistic, adaptation may be severely disrupted, and disorganization of the personality can follow. Because of marked regressive phenomena—delusions and hallucinatory defenses—the psychotic is generally considered to be more vulnerable to suicide. This is not to connote that most psychotics terminate their lives, but, rather, that they are more likely to do so.

The functional psychoses include the schizophrenias, depression and manias. The organic psychoses include the arteriosclerotic, the senile, the alcoholic, the toxic, the infectious and the traumatic. Many psychotics, in an attempt to avert the psychotic break, may demonstrate a neurotic overlay. Menninger et al. (1963) conceptualized a five-phase continuum between the neuroses and the psychoses. As stress increases, mild anxiety and dysphoria progress and intensify to cause more serious disorganization and ultimately self-destruction. The last two phases of the progression are psychoses. Although the suggestion that the neuroses and psychoses differ only in degree may be semantically more palatable, Menninger's schemata do not negate the reality of the psychoses nor do they influence the prognosis or the recalcitrancy to treatment.

Grinker and Holzman (1973) took issue with Menninger et al., and their data indicated that the processes involved mitigate against a continuum. There are adherents to both approaches (Hoch, 1972). Further research in psychopathology may resolve this matter.

It is important for the suicidologist to recognize that psychotics are prone to a self-destructive course. In a paper presented before the *Fourth International Congress of Social Psychiatry,* Miller (1972) discussed 270 patients, divided into three groups—psychotics, personality disorders and reactive disorders—who had attempted suicide. The psychotics were found to have significantly higher scores than the other two groups on conceptual disorganization, hostility, suspiciousness, emotional withdrawal, anxiety, hallucinatory behavior, blunted affect, unusual thought content, excitement, sexual dysfunctioning, disorientation and obsessive thinking. Their ratings on isolation, overall functioning and lethality were also higher.

DEPRESSIVE REACTIONS

The term "depression" is used in a variety of ways: It may refer to symptoms relatively transient in nature, or it may involve a number or a group of illnesses that are characterized by a major disorder of affect. Psychomotor retardation, inability to concentrate, loss of spontaneity, impaired social relations, physical changes and somatic preoccupation are part and parcel of the depressed state. A sensitive in-depth appraisal of depression was made by Bibring (1953).

It is bewildering to the clinician to survey the conglomerate of disorders classified under the rubric of depression: depressive syndrome, neurotic depression, reactive depression, psychotic depression, masked depression, depressive equivalent, postpartum depression, involutional state, transient situational disturbance, cyclothymia, neurotic decompensations, identity crises, etc. Sometimes depression is confused with schizo-affective or schizophrenic disorders. Schizoids are often perceived as depressed.

Everyone is depressed at one time or another, and depression is the most frequent complaint encountered in clinical practice. It has been proposed that "sadness" be used to describe normal phases and that "dysphoria" refer to symptomatic states of depression (Klerman, 1975). Paul Hoch (1972), a sensitive and astute diagnostician, bluntly pointed out that even a differential diagnosis between neurotic and psychotic depression is not always easy to make and that many discussions are reduced to scholastic exercises and mental acrobatics to justify a diagnosis that is tentative at best. The word "depression," when used without qualification, leaves much to be desired both nosologically and psychodynamically. Hoch stressed that, on the basis of his observations and considerable clinical experience, the manic-depressive and the neurotic depressive make suicide gestures just as frequently, but that the likelihood of the completion of suicide is greater in the psychotic.

Guze and Robins (1970) used 17 follow-up studies of individuals who suffered from affective disorders and concluded that the risk of suicide was 15 percent for a lifetime prevalence. However, they considered the risk to be higher during the active phases of the disorder.

The statistics may not appear to be large, but if one-half or more of completed suicides suffer from primary affect disorders, then the suicidal risk is 30 times greater for them than for the general population (Robins et al., 1959b).

Suicidologists are by no means in agreement about the role of depression as the specific cause of suicide. Choron (1972) noted:

> Suicidal thoughts and impulses appear practically in every depression. There is, however, considerable disagreement among students of suicide with regard to the extent to which depression is responsible for suicide, the results of studies vary between roughly 25 and 75 percent. This is quite different from the question of the rate of suicide among the depressed. The figure most often cited is 500 times the national suicide rate of 0.01 percent (11 suicides per 100,000) (p. 76).

Choron estimated that although half of actual suicides may be suffering from some form of depression, only five to 15 percent of the depressed eventually commit suicide. Pitts and Winokur (1964) concluded, on the basis of their own work and of reports from other countries, that the percentage was higher than the most frequently cited five percent and that a more accurate figure was about 16 percent.

While depressive reactions present an extremely large hazard, there are also some optimistic notes. Depressive states can be self-limited, and remissions may take place spontaneously. Some depressives benefit from hospitalization and the psychotropic drugs, as well as from supportive psychotherapy. In cases that cannot be contended with by other means, electroconvulsive therapy may be the treatment of choice. Also, there is increased recognition that lithium carbonate can bring about remarkable changes in selected patients who give evidence of bipolarity or a manic potential (Klerman, 1975).

Mania appears to be diametrically opposed to depression. However, there is no doubt that the euphoria—the false elation, the inability to concentrate, the flight of ideas and the pressure of speech —represents a denial of depression. The patient may escape detection when he is mildly elated and hypomanic. In severe states, however, it is apparent that the individual is behaving in an omnipotent, omniscient or vainglorious and belligerent manner that is markedly inappropriate. In advanced states of mania, there is a progressive lessening of controls and the patient is unable to make realistic decisions. At such times, behavior may become erratic, and both suicidal and homicidal impulses may become overt. Since the maniacal patient is unable to perceive reality objectively, his gratification is illusory. Controls deteriorate, and it becomes essential to offer the patient protection against self-destruction; hospitalization is required. Poor judgment makes such individuals accident-prone, and it becomes equivocal as to whether the self-destructive act is accidental or self-inflicted.

THE SCHIZOPHRENIAS

Definitions of schizophrenia have persistently created large nosological problems. A multiplicity of theories abounded even before Bleuler (1950) used the term "Group of Schizophrenias." The question arises whether it is one disease, a family of diseases or even distinctly unrelated forms of behavior. There are those who refuse to acknowledge that schizophrenia is a disease but hold, rather, that society insists on creating labels and that the prevailing social norms serve as guidelines (Szasz, 1961). American psychiatrists are often accused of overdiagnosing schizophrenia. Laing (1976), an existential psychoanalyst who objects to the term "schizophrenia," hypothecates that the tactics and strategies of the so-called schizophrenias are helpful, and that such people are healthier before therapeutic intervention. He suggests that the role of the therapist should be to help such individuals to use their tactics for growth purposes. Laing is therefore proposing that the defensive measures used by individuals who are allegedly schizophrenic should be respected and that an abrupt termination or withdrawal of their symptomatology could be detrimental. Boisen et al. (1954) discussed schizophrenic ideation as a striving toward solution of conflict.

Geneticists and psychophysiologists have insisted that organic etiologies are often overlooked in favor of psychodynamic explanations. It can be stated that there is no clear-cut, well-defined understanding or diagnosis of schizophrenia. In spite of the vicissitudes inherent in a lack of knowledge, we cannot disregard this disproportionately large group of individuals who are considered to be schizophrenic and who may commit suicide. Farberow et al. (1961c) cite from the "Check List of Suicidal Potential for Hospitalized Schizophrenic Patients" that those individuals diagnosed as schizophrenic constitute about 70 percent of the total number of suicides and also constitute about 68 percent of the general mental hospital population. While we might have our misgivings about classification systems, we cannot deny that individuals who carry a schizophrenic diagnosis present a large lethal potential.

Farberow et al. (1961c) reported on the results of a systematic comparison between 30 hospitalized schizophrenic patients who committed suicide and 30 hospitalized schizophrenics who served as controls and who did not commit suicide. The purpose of this study was to differentiate between these two groups in the hope of finding differences that might help in intervention procedures within a mental hospital milieu and also to apply such information about schizophrenic suicidal behavior to other psychotic categories. Their thorough, comprehensive clinical study of 60 schizophrenic patients is exemplary in its attention to every sphere and detail of the patients' lives. A multidisciplinary approach was utilized in these investigations.

The results were not remarkable. Schzophrenics who were in a mental hospital proved to be under severe stress. It is also manifest that when a schizophrenic is under stress his ability to deal with disequilibria is even further diminished. Over 70 percent of schizophrenic patients who committed suicide had a history of a previous attempt or of marked suicidal ideation. An important aspect of the study was the recognition that in spite of their psychosis these individuals were motivated and were, in effect, trying to do something to alleviate their tension, restlessness and anguish.

A few interesting facets emerged from the same Farberow et al. study: One is that stress cannot be defined on an objective basis, so situations that would be considered to be nonstressful for most people cannot be perceived as having a similar effect on schizophrenic patients. The schizophrenic may leave the hospital milieu for a new situation where conditions are optimal and yet, because of intrapsychic forces or unpredictable, paradoxical stimuli unique to him, may be under tremendous stress, and this stress may be inexplicable unless one can comprehend the distortions. To a naive observer it would appear that there was no apparent stress present in a seemingly innocuous adjustment.

Another fascinating addendum that emerged from the study has to do with the popular conception of the schizophrenic as deluded, hallucinating and confused in his thinking—that in response to a voice he is directed to kill himself or another and he is impelled to carry out the command. This is not in keeping with the findings that emerged from the Farberow et al. study. In most cases where there was a completed suicide, there had been an improvement in psychic organization and control. This, then, would contradict the belief that the schizophrenic patient who terminates his life is on the lowest level, or at least on an extremely low level, of psychic disorganization. One can theorize that as the schizophrenic patient comes closer to the necessity of making a higher adaptation, irrational forces may become too urgent, threatening and formidable. The exact nature of the forces that can precipitate lethality offers a fascinating avenue for investigation. A thesis suggested by Farberow's speculation is that psychosis may be thought of as a barrier against lethality. The implication is that when the psychotic state is in remission or partial remission, the new means of coping are inadequate to contend with the underlying stresses. This thesis may explain the paradoxical effect of tranquilizing and psychotropic agents in the sense that when psychosis is ameliorated or reduced, the patient must then confront intolerable insights that were masked, perhaps protected, by the psychopathology. When one considers the vast conglomerate of variables involved in the schizophrenias, the innumerable difficulties in adjustment become far more comprehensible (Arieti, 1955; Bellak, 1958; Kallmann, 1950; Kety, 1965).

THE ORGANIC PSYCHOSES

The arteriosclerotic, the senile, the alcoholic, the toxic, the infectious and the traumatic psychotic share extensive pathology that may produce psychiatric emergencies. Outbursts of irritability, mania, explosive rage and depression are typical and can be easily provoked by an external event or by cerebral malfunction. Because of their unpredictability, such outbursts may result in violence to oneself or to others. Individuals with chronic organic disease may become isolated, constricted, alienated, depressed and self-destructive. Their problems are no different from those of others suffering from a depletion of resources or an inability to maintain ego controls. Under proper supervision this is less likely to happen, but loss of capacity to reality-test makes it easier to become paranoid, terrified and inundated. Under such circumstances the possibility of self-destruction is intensified.

In discussing acute organic reactions, Hoch (1972) pointed out that completed suicide and suicidal attempts can take place when a patient who is in a confused state jumps or falls out of a window because of inadequate precautions. Misinterpretation and misidentification are frequent, and when an individual is in a delirious state, he may be completely disoriented. Hallucinations and delusions may be so intertwined with accidental factors that the mode of death could only be classified as equivocal.

An acute organic reaction may occur in any number of diseases that have an effect on the nervous system through direct or indirect means. In the area of suicidology, the intoxicants (particularly alcohol), quick-acting barbiturates and large overdoses of psychotropic drugs, predominate. However, bacterial and viral agents can also produce an effect on the brain. Such histological modifications may be subtle, and even individuals with infectious disease involving the cortex may not disclose overt clinical manifestations and reactions. Hoch (1972) points out that an autopsy may be required to give evidence of gross edema of the brain. It is, therefore, logical for the pathologist or neurologist to make an attempt at a diagnosis on the basis of the discernable clinical findings, but this is not always so simple.

In cases of pathological intoxication, a confusional state can coexist with delusions and large surges of affect. Paranoid aspects may coexist with visual and auditory hallucinations. This configuration may result in depression and/or excitement with maniacal fury and can lead to homicide or suicide. It is obvious that when there is an accompanying depressive affect the suicide risk becomes greater. Hoch noted that many of these individuals resemble the patient having an epileptic attack or an epileptic equivalent.

Tolerance to drugs, particularly alcohol, may be due to metabolic factors. Hoch emphasizes that there are individuals who are so extremely vulnerable to alcohol and to other drugs that even a small amount may produce toxicity. In a sensitized patient, minor incidents are misconstrued and misinterpreted so that inconsequential situations can result in a homicide or a suicide. The lethal time factor may be small and last for a few minutes or for several hours. The patient may fall asleep, with a complete amnesia, or become comatose, but irrevocable havoc may have ensued. Since many organic conditions are associated with an overlay of depression, additional confusion, disorganization and disorientation with a clouded sensorium can make for a self-destructive outcome (Hoch, 1972).

PSYCHONEUROSIS AND PERSONALITY DISORDERS

All symptom-syndromes evolve from multiple influences and provide the individual with the armamentaria to adjust and to exist. However, all defenses have their deficiencies and are not foolproof against the unpredictable traumata that can impinge on the organism. The outcome of intrapsychic, primary process conflagrations and extrapsychic events is subject to the ability of the ego to defend itself. Ineffectiveness and deficiencies in the psychic defensive system are crucial when crises arise and the individual is required to function beyond his means. Support from outside influences such as relatives, friends, therapists, etc. is paramount when an individual faces ideation, wishes and the impulses to terminate life. Even with poor and inadequate controls, the supplementary resources, dyadic relationships and succor from ancillary sources can be lifesaving.

Unfortunately, many professionals—psychiatrists, psychologists and social workers—have concluded that only individuals who suffer from major psychiatric disorders—pathological states that are characterized by the psychoses or organic states—are likely to terminate their lives. This misconception has resulted in an often cursory evaluation of many patients who suffer from less severe pathologies, such as the personality disorders and the psychoneuroses.

It is undeniably true that people with less anguish, less despair and more strengths and resources are less likely to destroy themselves, but this represents an overgeneralization.

A diagnosis of psychoneurosis or personality disorder suggests that the patient may have active pathology but is not likely to harm himself. The clinician who makes such a determination may consider the patient to be benign and tends to regard him as unlikely to inflict injury on himself. There is, then, a feeling of relief which is not always justified. Although the patient may be querulous, somatically preoccupied, anxious, obsessive and phobic, the clinician regards such an individual as unlikely to surprise him by committing suicide.

Sifneos et al. (1956) supported this contention that neurotics were less efficient in self-termination and were less likely to ingest large doses of barbiturates than psychotics. However, this study was done in a general hospital. Unfortunately, this optimistic attitude is predicated on the implication that an individual who presents himself with a well-demarcated personality disorder or a neurosis invariably possesses adequate defenses. In addition, there is a presumption that the pathological state will remain stable. However, large decompensation can change the picture. Depressives and schizophrenics do not have a monopoly on suicide.

Although the neuroses and the personality disorders have most recently been discussed in concert (MacKinnon and Michels, 1971) and their symptoms may be closely related, this does not imply that they are the same or that they can be treated similarly. It is, however, important to note that a crucial difference between neurotic symptomatology and characterological disturbances is based on the fact that in the former category an ego-alien discord exists. The neurotic recognizes that his symptoms are foreign, unwarranted, and not a part of himself. On the other hand, the personality disordered or the characterologically disturbed individual perceives his defenses as part of a mosaic. He construes them as valid components of his personality, he accepts them, and they are for all practical purposes regarded as ego-syntonic. He refuses to concede that there is anything wrong; rather, he insists that his pathology is an extension of or an expression of his personality.

There is a large overlapping of symptomatology and life-styles. Most clinicians now agree that the characterologically disturbed—the personality disordered—are in the majority (Grinker, 1975). It is possible to make the assumption that, when one is discussing a hysteric, an obsessive-compulsive, a person in an anxiety state or even a depressive, the patient is quite likely to be characterologically disturbed or have a coexisting personality disorder. It is, however, imperative to note that insight therapy is possible only when the individual perceives that the rationalizations and the intricate configuration that he has constructed are pathological. Antisocial behavior or sexual deviations and drug dependence are predominant, and the defensive capabilities are subject to imponderable variables. It is simply impossible to assign or label a patient and conclude on this basis that the patient will not self-destruct.

Although exhaustive cases can be cited to document decompensation and suicide subsequent to a careful assessment and diagnosis of neurotic states or personality disorders, a few representative illustrations will suffice:

> A seductive 45-year-old female, who was successful in enticing males in spite of her chronic frigidity, became severely depressed. She felt that she had lost the ability to manipulate her synthetic femininity. This was further complicated by her husband's death and her inability to "turn on" new males. When she looked in the mirror, she perceived a middle-aged woman with dry, wrinkled skin. Her estrogen and progesterone level had declined. Her physician's diagnosis was "menopausal state." In such a case, without support, a new conquest, or therapy, the ultimate fate could be suicide.

> A neurotic depressive always received secondary gain from her helplessness, her psychomotor retardation, and her crying spells. Her husband became tired of her and left for a few days.

The outcome was suicide. Instead of her husband it might have been a lover or significant other who became ill and was no longer able to gratify her oral-dependent needs.

The sophisticated man-about-town, oozing with charm and charisma, earned his livelihood with very little effort, but his latest venture turned out to be a terrible fiasco, one that would inevitably result in a long jail sentence. His psychopathy failed, and suicide was the result.

An obsessive-compulsive woman organized her home with marvelous efficiency. Her entire life was centered about her children. Her greatest pride was her ability to regulate and control. A breast malignancy resulted in a radical mastectomy. She lost her shaky feminine identity and overdosed with 100 tablets of pentobarbital that she had patiently accumulated.

A dissociated man, who had suffered hysterical fugues in early life, married, with two children, was arrested after an amnesic episode during which he had been involved in a homosexual relationship. He slashed his wrists with a razor while on bail awaiting trial.

A cyclothymic, 20-year-old woman, who had significant mood fluctuations, felt euphoric at a party, shared a dose of heroin with a mainliner and subsequently died of hepatitis.

It is possible to go on ad infinitum with every symptom-syndrome. At one time or another, any one of them may prove to be inadequate. Perlin and Schmidt (1975) note:

> Suicide may occur during relapse of the mental illness present at the time of original attempt or in association with a new psychiatric disturbance—for example suicide in the course of a schizophrenic relapse or in association with psychotic depression. "Early" or "late" suicide associated with acute presenting illness, a chronic illness in relapse, or a new illness is likely to produce fluctuating patterns in the suicide rate over time in long-term follow-up (pp. 153-154).

In summary, self-destruction is not limited by status, profession, socioeconomic stratification, talent or sagacity. The more anguished are most likely to be vulnerable, while individuals who suffer from personality disorders or the neuroses are statistically less likely to commit suicide. However, such a diagnosis does not make them immune. Psychopathology is no more the sine qua non for self-termination than perturbation or inimicality per se. Lethality kills. The inadequate protection afforded by psychopathology—the symptom-syndromes—or by therapists and significant others can obliterate the capacity of the ego to withstand those rigors that are intolerable or unique for those individuals whose psychic reserves are torn asunder and depleted.

CHAPTER 6

INTERVENTION IN
SUICIDOLOGY

PRIMARY, SECONDARY AND TERTIARY PREVENTION

Prevention, intervention and postvention correspond with primary, secondary and tertiary prevention. Although it is sometimes helpful to segmentalize intervention and discuss the components individually, they represent a continuum that is closely intertwined and tautological. Prophylaxis and postvention are, in effect, intervention procedures, and they overlap. When primary intervention succeeds, the presuicide is recognized, and appropriate measures are taken to avert a suicidal attempt or a lethal outcome. The key is an active educative process that provides basic information and recognition of the clues and the cues of suicide. The cancer prevention program is an excellent model.

An informed and sensitive person, whether he be parent, spouse, friend, teacher, clergyman or even a stranger, senses and picks up the danger signals—the cry for help—during the prodromal period and takes appropriate action. The action need not be dramatic when lethality is relatively low. It may be that only support and understanding are required. For example, the Samaritans offer a sustained friendship that has proved to be effective (Varah, 1966; Fox, 1976, 1978b). Higher degrees of lethality call for the more affirmative action of immediate referral to a physician, psychiatrist, psychologist or an emergency center. It is far wiser that the layman err by being overly cautious and prevene/intervene at once.

The clinician who makes a tentative diagnosis and treats a presuicide now becomes involved in secondary prevention, most frequently thought of as intervention. This requires assessment, counseling, the utilization of various modalities of therapy, psychotropic drugs, electroconvulsive therapy and hospitalization.

In tertiary prevention, which corresponds to postvention, the suicide has been completed. The emphasis now is two-fold. One is to help the survivors—again prevention, perhaps to save them from a similar fate—overcome the psychic metastases that were incurred, and the other is to carefully reconstruct the events and circumstances that resulted in the suicide, in order to learn more about predisposing causes and how to apply this information in saving others. In this sense it is like an autopsy, that is, to determine the variables and dynamics of the fatal outcome in greater depth. This is essentially a research function.

The demarcations of primary, secondary and tertiary intervention are moot. The goal is to learn how to counter life-threatening and self-destructive behavior. The priorities of individual sucidologists may vary, but the goal will always be prophylaxis. It is, therefore, not surprising that the summary of the National Institute of Mental Health Task Force in Suicide Prevention, *Suicide Prevention in the 70's* (Resnik et al., 1973), proposed that the order of emphasis be on research first, followed by education and training. Treatment and service were considered next in order. The thesis is that effective prophylaxis depends on an understanding of the dynamics and the psycho-socio-dyadic-existential crisis of completed suicide that is predicated on methodologic and empirical knowledge. In accord with this rationale, tertiary prevention is nuclear. There is, of course, the inclusion of other kinds and types of life-threatening and self-destructive behavior that must also be researched (Menninger, 1935, 1936, 1937, 1938).

Three major areas were regarded as paramount by Resnik et al. (1973): (1) The training of suicidologists, particularly those who are actively engaged in research; (2) the increased utilization of paraprofessional personnel who have had training and experience in crisis intervention; and (3) preparation and dissemination of information and educational material to individuals who are not suicidologists.

Some suicidologists might object that therapy and service were considered last by Resnik et al. However, therapy and service must be based on a sound structure. One cannot contend with the probability of impending death if this probability is based on metaphysical theory, hunches, improvisations or omnipotence.

Farberow et al. (1973) assessed and outlined the needed research studies for the future—plans that mental health disciplines must implement in order to facilitate the prevention of suicides. Their recommendations were focused on (1) identification, assessment and prediction; (2) effectiveness and effect, developmental correlates as well as physiological and biochemical aspects that may be involved in suicide; (3) the involvement of multidisciplines for recommendations of methodological principles and standardization of criteria for reporting; (4) the development of a national data bank that would bring about a refinement in statistical analysis; (5) the utilization of the projective techniques and other tests (they considered such tests as the Rorschach, the Thematic Apperception Test, the Bender Gestalt, the Sentence Completion and the Minnesota Multiphasic Personality Inventory as potentially helpful means for assessment of suicidal behavior); (6) more openness and the sharing of available information to reduce taboos that still exist and remain as barriers in promulgating more efficient techniques; (7) increasing studies of the environmental factors in differentiating epidemiology and demography as factors that potentiate suicide; (8) a study of the concepts of afterlife and the influence that such thinking has on suicide; and (9) more concerted investigations about the relationship of aggression, violence and hostility.

These extensive research plans are all-encompassing and promising. There were 250 references listed in this comprehensive outline.

INTERVENTION PROCEDURES AND TECHNIQUES

Significant Others

Suicide prevention is carried out by caring people—parents, spouses, relatives, friends, teachers, clergy etc.—who may note excessive perturbation, inimicality or signs of lethality. They might take note of anhedonia, dysphoria, depression or disquieting behavior that causes them concern about an individual's state of being. This may take the form of an interest, or demonstrate, in one way or another, that the cry for help has been heard. Some may have read or heard about the early signs—the clues and cues associated with suicidal behavior. Others may be responding intuitively, but nevertheless provide help during a crisis.

Since the majority of presuicides elect to see a physician or have been persuaded to do so by someone who had not been successful in contending with their state of mind, the physician may also be in the first line of defense. He may be consulted when improvement is not forthcoming or when reinforcement is required. His interest, concern and, perhaps, medication may serve as preventive functions to the presuicide who is now his patient. If he is perceptive, he may note a masked depression or signs that suggest that a self-destructive course is operative or is in the offing. His care alone may suffice and alleviate the crisis. He may, on the other hand, recognize high lethality and refer the patient to a psychiatrist, psychologist or crisis intervention center. Presumably, at this point more specialized and sophisticated care is available. It is, however, important to note that the first line of defense may be non-professionals—people who are related, who care or who are concerned about others.

Telephone Emergency Services

Such services are manned by nonprofessionals, volunteers who are interested in being helpful. Their clients are most likely to be isolated, alienated individuals who have no one to appeal to or who prefer not to make their plight known and wish to be anonymous. Telephone services vary widely in the quality and extent of the aid that they offer and should not be confused with a suicide prevention center which offers telephone service in conjunction with professional backup resources that could be delivered immediately.

In order to investigate the quality of service aspects, McGee et al. (1972) made a series of 76 calls to 19 emergency crisis services in the Southeastern United States. They recorded the time elapsed before the call was answered and how long it took to be in contact with a counselor. Eight different systems were identified. Their conclusions pointed to inadequate and sometimes dangerously low-quality service, particularly if a 24-hour answering service was not in effect. McGee et al. (1973), in discussing crisis intervention activities for the next decade, noted that, at best, a program makes the attempt to intervene when suicide is already a factor. It was their recommendation that crisis intervention services should be administered by community agencies and need not be separate and autonomous or necessarily tied in with health or mental health institutions. However, they stressed that crisis intervention services should be able to render complete intervention when life-threatening behavior is involved. Emphasis was laid on the necessity for thorough training of nonprofessional and paraprofessional personnel and the essentiality of a multidisciplinary approach. Telephone service alone was judged to be inadequate; accessibility of professional help was deemed necessary. There was heavy emphasis on the suicide's need to have contact with professionals made available to him, and telephone service was merely a referral device that should be broadened. In short, the telephone service could not be relied upon to serve effectively without backup and follow-up services.

A Multiservice Approach

An innovative program initiated by the Lincoln Community Mental Health Center in affiliation with the Albert Einstein College of Yeshiva University was described by Rutz, Vasquex and Vasquex (1973). The focal point of this approach is the Mobile Crisis Intervention and Suicide Prevention Unit. The mobile crisis unit consists of multidisciplinary teams who receive an intensive two-month training in psychopathology, direct confrontation therapy, small group behavior and the history and culture of the Puerto Rican and Black societies served by the Center. Provisions were made for backup services so that partial hospitalization, emergency consultation and education were immediately available. More than one-third of the staff were nonprofessionals; that is, they were community mental health workers who lived in the area. A telephone call requesting help mobilized the team. The first priority was to localize and identify the causes of the crisis and to utilize not only their own resources but those of the community. Although this nontraditional approach was set up to meet the needs of urban ghetto groups, there is no reason why it cannot be extended.

The program presented above might be an answer to the misgivings voiced by David Lester (1972) when he discussed the failure of the suicide prevention movement. He considered that the failure was due in large part to the fact that the suicide prevention groups were not properly geared to prevent suicide because they rarely prevene. He pointed out that they postvene and intervene and that the telephone answering referral services are not resorted to by the individual who is most likely to self-destruct. It is, however, pertinent to note that even the projected, highly idealized preventive procedures of the future can at best only reduce the number of suicides —suicide cannot be eliminated as a mode of death. If, as Shneidman (1976) has suggested, the suicidal phenomena are events that involve existential-social-psychological-dyadic events, then to eliminate suicide is, for all practical purposes, to eliminate the unhappiness of human beings. Shneidman states:

> Some students of human nature believe that the urge towards self-destruction is ubiquitous and that a certain amount of it is an inevitable and constant price of civilization, if not of life itself. Primarily, prevention would relate to the principles of good mental hygiene in general (p. 20).

The Samaritans

It would be remiss not to include the role of the Samaritans, who are essentially a suicide prevention agency. Dr. Richard Fox (1976), a psychiatrist, who is the United Kingdom representative to the International Association for Suicide Prevention, is an honorary consultant to the Samaritans. Fox felt that the recent decline in the number of suicides in Britain has been related to the Samaritans' activities. An overall evaluation of Samaritan towns, presumably

those where Samaritans' activities were in effect, showed a decrease of
5.8 percent, whereas there was a rise of 19.8 percent in the incidence
of suicide in towns used as controls.

Although the Samaritans were founded by the Reverend Chad
Varah, it is a nonsectarian society that is predicated on the concept
of befriending lonely people, with no obligations or strings attached.
It was not envisaged as a form of therapy or of counseling, and there
was a taboo against proselytizing, whether religious or political. In
1959, Fox was among the first psychiatrists to consider the issue of
whether the suicidal individual was suffering from psychiatric problems or whether friendlessness, loneliness and alienation were the
preeminent causes. Fox (1976) described in some detail how a
Samaritan branch works:

> Volunteer recruitment may be by personal contacts, the
> branch speakers, or by actual advertising. Ex-clients, those who
> have made suicide attempts, and those who have received psy-
> chiatric treatment are not automatically excluded. An applica-
> tion form is required that includes solemn commitment to ob-
> serve complete secrecy in relation to all matters concerning
> clients. Two references are also required. There is no age limit
> and recent years have seen a swing toward youth among both
> volunteers and leaders from what was in many branches a pre-
> dominately middle-aged movement.
>
> The initial interview is conducted in the Center or the volun-
> teer's home and the successful applicant then goes into manda-
> tory preparation classes that introduce him to the structure and
> the working of the organization; the befriending of people with
> sexual, marital and psychological problems; the recognition of
> those in need of medical care; and legal aspects of the work.
> Role play is increasingly used with mock telephones and there is
> a national cassette library of training tapes. People unsuitable for
> this type of service usually eliminate themselves during the
> training process.
>
> A period of observation of supervised telephone duty and a
> final interview follow. The acceptance rate varies widely from
> branch to branch and from time to time. Of a particular sample
> of 100 consecutive volunteers to the London branch, only seven
> made it to full Samaritan status, but the national average is
> about one-third acceptance.

At any one branch, 100 volunteers are considered the minimum for a full twenty-four hour manned service. A decreasing minority of branches has the phone switched automatically to a volunteer's house at night and branches such as Central London and Birmingham can have as many as 200 or 300 volunteers so that the administrative problems become complex (p. 515).

There is a hierarchical system, with a branch leader. Regular reports are required, and a branch leader can terminate a relationship if he feels it would be advantageous to the client. The volunteer befrienders are known only by their first names and a branch number. In an acute crisis, the Samaritans have a flying squad available which can function as an emergency team. If the emergency is medical, such as an overdose, ambulance service is arranged. Except for a few paid personnel, the majority of the work is done by volunteers, and therefore the budget is low. New clients have risen 30 percent annually since 1964, when there were over 12,000. In 1972, the number had increased 75 percent from 89,000 to 156,000. Fox (1976) considered that the Samaritans were responsible for one-third of the decline in suicide during the decade following 1963, to the lowest rate the British ever had.

In a personal communication, Dr. Fox has called the author's attention to a controversy that has been touched off about the statistics quoted above in an article by Barraclough et al. that appeared in *Lancet* (July 30, 1977) and was expanded in *Psychological Medicine* (August 1978).

Fox (1978) noted:

> There is an academic dispute going on just now about whether a Samaritan branch in any particular locality can be shown to exert a suicide prevention effect. Dr. Christopher Bagley, in 1968, compared 15 towns with Samaritan branches with 15 that did not have them and concluded that there was a significant preventive effect. Dr. Brian Barraclough and his colleagues have just published a study which they say shows that there is no effect. The jury is still out (p. 24).

One cannot ignore the outstanding contributions of the Samaritans and their dedication in building up a systematic befriending of lonely, helpless and isolated human beings and offering them a sustained relationship throughout their periods of distress.

Suicide Prevention Centers

The inception of the first suicide prevention center was less than 20 years ago, and it began its functions under the aegis of a United States Public Health Service project grant for a five-year period. Administered through the University of Southern California, it was established in the Los Angeles community (Shneidman, Farberow and Litman, 1961). It has served as a prototype of the growing network of the centers in the United States and throughout the world. The manifest purpose was to contend with both long-range and immediate prevention of self-destruction. Three main goals were given priority: (1) clinical aspects, involving selection, diagnosis, referral and therapy; (2) community aspects, intended to integrate the suicide prevention centers of public health agencies and to bring about cooperation with the various health departments as well as the police department and coroner's office; and (3) research aspects, not only to obtain psychiatric, psychological and social work data but also to implement and check out hypotheses pertaining to life-threatening and self-destructive behavior. Although expansion and elaboration have taken place, the goals enumerated above are still basic to the function of a suicide prevention center.

Assessment and Prediction

Although clinical assessment is indispensable in an evaluation, it is still undeniably a qualitative process. Data derived from ratings, tests, profiles and other sources add weight to, corroborate and may even change clinical impressions. The chronic problem of validity and reliability comes to the fore. There is, of course, a multiplicity of variables. Any questionnaire, test or diagnostic instrument that could predict the possibility of impending lethality with accuracy would be a boon to suicidology. Some of the most fertile minds in the field have been occupied with this research aspect, and numerous instruments have been developed, ranging from simplistic questionnaires through the most sophisticated approaches. Unfortunately, to this date these instruments have not been successful. This is not to say that they have been useless; many of them have supplied leads that are being used in new research projects.

There are infinite problems that relate to the reliability of the informant in test administration. Also, there is the problem of how to rate the data that are obtained. Data can be circumstantial, and on this basis alone it is not possible to be predictive. Data may also prove to be vague and ambiguous, and the source may not be dependable. Although an individual would have great difficulty in giving phony responses to the Rorschach, it is possible to do so with scales of intent. Finally, data that are introspective are often a reflection of how the individual interprets past and present states of mind and affect. Patrick and Overall (1969) found that asking the patient questions about suicidal concerns and plans was no more or less effective than the administration of a brief psychiatric rating scale in differentiating suicidal from nonsuicidal individuals.

Nevertheless, research suicidologists must attempt to refine the variables in assessing suicide risk. Motto (1974) has pointed out that although clinical and subjective impressions must be improved, even imprecise instruments may supplement a purely subjective evaluation. Diggory (1974) addressed himself to the complexities of predicting suicide with philosophical erudition:

> To be seriously concerned with suicide prevention entails a task that is more challenging than any which most psychologists have undertaken, that is, the task of predicting which persons will exhibit a highly specific, very infrequently occurring behavior. The prediction problem will be solved only when we have systematic, reproducible procedures for assigning to every individual a statement of the probability of his committing suicide together with a carefully calculated error interval for that probability. If that is a realistic goal, then no doubt we will approach it slowly, and before we reach it we will have used many procedures that will be better than those we now use but not as good as the one we seek. If one were to say that the prediction of suicide is no goal but a phantasm, a wraith, we have no present information with which to refute him. The

belief that suicidal behaviors are predictible can be valid only as a belief in principle, not in fact. But as a belief in principle, it is simply a special case of every scientist's article of faith that the universe contains regularities that can be discovered and understood by rational inquiry (p. 59).

Psychological Tests

In general, psychological tests have proved to be disappointing in predicting suicide. The Rorschach, the Thematic Apperception Test, the Bender Gestalt and, for that matter, older psychological tests have proved to be unreliable thus far in differentiating suicidal and nonsuicidal individuals (Lester, 1974). Some studies appear promising but later prove to be either inconclusive or invalid. Specific signs that an individual was in a vulnerable or lethal state that would definitely or probably result in suicide have not been discovered. Future research may be fruitful, but specific signs that are pathognomonic or prove to be differentiating are not now available. The Rorschach has been the test of choice for those investigating suicidal risk. Although the Rorschach can, in the hands of an experienced clinician, provide a wealth of intrapsychic data, as well as illuminate nuances and facets of personality structure, perhaps too much is expected of this instrument. Depression, morbidity, dysphoria, impulsivity, etc., can all be picked up from the Rorschach. However, the variations in the personality structures of those who self-destruct are so numerous that is it unreasonable to expect one or even a few signs and/or content per se to be sufficiently definitive to predict a lethal outcome. Neuringer (1974) noted that the Rorschach can still be a potent instrument for assessing suicidal risk, but he raised some doubts about the interpretation of the results. Neuringer grouped Rorschach studies into four classifications: (1) determinants and ratios, (2) single signs, (3) multiple signs, and (4) content. It was his suggestion that clinicians should attend more carefully to suicidal content when it is manifested on the Rorschach. He considered this significant in the sense that self-destructive behavior was close to the surface and that this represented a communication to the clinician. Lindner (1950) referred to card IV as the "suicide card," and he noted that responses carrying such projections as a "decaying tooth," "a rotten tree trunk," "a pall of black smoke," etc., carry suicidal overtones and morbid thought processes. It must, however, be noted that there are countless individuals who give such responses and are depressed but who do not commit suicide.

Farberow (1972a), in an unpublished paper on *Use of the Rorschach in Predicting and Understanding Suicide,* felt that the Rorschach could be a much more useful instrument if clinicians could conceptualize suicide and its dimensions. He stressed that the act cannot be predicted and that it is the state of mind that must be perceived in combination with personality vulnerabilities and inadequate controls. These factors play a vital role in the probability of suicide. Farberow also questioned whether such an entity as suicidal personality or personalities exists. Those suicidologists who are seeking common denominators in their search for a suicidal personality or personalities on the basis of tests may be engaged in a fruitless endeavor. However, this does not obviate the need to search for predictors.

In reviewing tests that are frequently used, Lester (1974) concluded that neither the Thematic Apperception Test nor the Bender Gestalt gave a reliable differentiation on the basis of signs. In several studies in which the Rosenzweig Picture-Frustration test was used, results were conflicting. The Minnesota Multiphasic Personality Inventory has proven to be of little use, and the data have been nonconclusive. Although item analysis offered some hope of success, data from study to study differed on the specific items that supposedly differentiated the self-destructive from the nonsuicidal patient. In profile analysis there is still the problem of what aspects of the profile are significant enough to be utilized as signs. Lester (1974) summarized his criticism as follows:

> Although the overall impression from these studies is that they have not proven to be of much use, the conclusion may be quite helpful for two reasons. First the studies have been quite poor methodologically and it may be that more adequately designed and executed studies would be more successful in iden-

tifying predictors. Secondly, the majority of the studies using standard psychological tests have tested attempted suicide after a suicidal act. Thus, by design, the studies are not investigating predictors, but rather postdictors (p. 73).

TREATMENT

The treatment of an individual who manifests moderate to high lethality presents a crisis situation for both the patient and the therapist. Every clinician must establish some guidelines in contending with such an emergency since procrastination, miscalculation, inadequate evaluation or incompetence can lead to a fatal outcome. In encountering a potentially suicidal patient, the clinician cannot adhere to his usual schedule of seeing a patient for either a half-hour or 50 minutes. He must be flexible and willing to readjust his schedule and in some instances see a patient for two hours or even longer. Prescribing a drug and making an appointment to see the patient again in a few days or even the next day may invite disastrous consequences. This is particularly true of the patient who is in an acute phase (Moss and Hamilton, 1957).

Therapists must participate actively with the life forces. In searching through the literature, the author has not been able to find a more profound and simple exemplification of what it means to intervene with death in the offing than this passage from Stoller (1973) :

> Those who admire quiet, reflective therapists who listen un-cowed by long silences, capable of an interpretation that hovers at just the right level between what the patient already knows and the part that is hidden, may be dismayed at my grossness with Mrs. G.—my talking, interrupting, joking, anger, sarcasm, argumentativeness, disbelief, inpatience, pushing. I believe I have good reason for employing such techniques. With all psychotics (except those with autism since childhood or with organic brain disease, such as severe toxic delirium or the result of chronic LSD use) , I always talked to the sane remnant of the patient, no matter how small it may be. A bit of sanity is there in the patient at least as a memory of what once was; usually it is somewhat more, a little creature (identity) all wrapped around with psychosis, hidden but peering out of the darkness and listening. As it comes to trust the therapist, it

increasingly reveals itself. I think that trust depends on my having two insights: first that I am at ease with the psychotic part, and all its crazy primary-process glory, and second, that I do not get so swept up in the psychotic part of the patient that I do not also recognize the sane part. Only if I am familiar with the psychotic process and person—only when I truly demonstrate an understanding of its nature—can I fight against it. So long as a patient feels one disagrees, because of ignorance, insensitivity, or a puritanicalness, he will not listen. But if the therapist can be trusted not to be either frightened off or seduced by the madness, the sane part will know that the therapist is safe enough and that ultimately he is its friend, not the psychotic part's (p. 305).

It is essential in the first meeting to estimate and determine the strength of the life forces—as against death wishes—whether Thanatos is overriding Eros. If the balance is precarious, it becomes the clinician's duty to insure protection. This may call for frequent sessions, hospitalization, collaboration of a dyadic figure, cooperation of significant others that may include community agencies such as day care centers, etc. "Frequent sessions' should be interpreted as seeing the patient one or even more times a day. The therapist must be available to the patient on a 24-hour basis. Litman (1957) has pointed out that accepting no more than two to three highly lethal patients is the better part of valor. Even one or two such patients can be emotionally corrosive.

It is imperative to develop a therapeutic alliance in the very first session. This should be differentiated from the transference, which may not be manifest in the early stages. Certainly a positive transference is helpful in therapy but initially it should be differentiated from the therapeutic alliance or working relationship (Greenson, 1967). The working alliance represents a commitment from the patient. This is, in effect, an agreement that a serious life-threatening problem exists, and it is understood that the patient will abide by the rules of the agreement or contract. Both the therapist and the patient then accept basic provisions of mutual trust and agree to live up to their respective commitments. The patient must be in a state of mind where he can give unequivocal evidence that he will call the therapist immediately if anxiety becomes heightened and/or any lethal aspects manifest themselves. The therapist must agree to be available to speak to the patient and to see the patient if an emergency situation arises. This is the prerequisite for ambulatory therapy; if the clinician feels that the patient will not be able to live up to the specific conditions of the unwritten contract, he is placing himself and the patient in a position of risk.

It is obvious that most psychotic patients are not in a position to adhere to such expectations, and they should, therefore, be hospitalized. In cognitive disorders, alcoholism and with patients who demonstrate impulsive psychopathic tendencies, hospitalization is indicated. This also holds true for the presuicidal patient who does not express any affect to the therapist during the first hours (Litman, 1957). Some patients who agree quickly to a working alliance and accept its provisions may do so glibly in order to avoid hospitalization, or there may be a transient flight into health that can only be sustained briefly. Some patients put the therapist through a series of crucial tests, make needless demands and call at inopportune times to ascertain whether he is willing to live up to their exorbitant demands.

Therapists should not hesitate to make use of other available resources to help themselves cope with unreasonable behavior in order to keep abreast of any shifts or fluctuations. The fact that another or others are aware of the patient's (and the therapist's) dilemma can be lifesaving, and there are many cases in the literature where alert significant others saved the patient's life. Litman (1957) cites a case that is illustrative: The patient had been referred by a physician to the pyschiatrist. He was estranged from his wife; after meeting with his wife's lawyer he became suicidal. In the meantime, he had cancelled his appointment with the psychiatrist. His brother and then his father proved to be unavailable. He called the psychiatrist, who was unable to speak with him because he was engaged with another patient. Then he called his wife, but her line was busy. At this point, he became acutely lethal and took an overdose in his office. After some hours, the psychiatrist attempted to return the patient's call, but there was no answer. Since it was rather late for the patient to still be in his office, the psychiatrist called the wife. Apparently she cared enough to respond and found her husband in his office unconscious. Litman stressed the fact that fortuitous factors can be important and that the patient might not have attempted suicide if he had been able to reach his brother or father or wife and that the enlistment of his wife's aid by the psychiatrist saved his life. The other lesson to be reiterated is that the therapist who accepts a suicidal patient must be available even when having a consultation. Answering a call immediately rather than returning it a few hours later can mean the difference between survival and death.

After making an appraisal and deciding that hospitalization is in the patient's best interest, the therapist must not be dissuaded by the patient's or his family's rationalizations that he might lose his job or his government clearance, that economic loss might ensue, that there would be a loss of face or that he, the patient, might be disgraced in the eyes of the family, friends, etc. The clinician who agrees to ambulatory care against his better judgment may be faced with a malpractice suit and vociferous condemnation by the very individuals who tried so hard to persuade him not to hospitalize the patient. Whenever a therapist is in this difficult situation and his recommendations are not accepted, he should suggest consultation, and if that fails, send a certified letter to an appropriate member of the family or enlist help from a community agency.

There are exceptions to every rule. If, after careful evaluation, the clinician feels that the patient's lethality is moderate and of short duration, that the patient is not psychotic, and that he does indeed have a therapeutic alliance with the patient, he may be willing to assume the attendant responsibility but to share it with a responsible person who is sufficiently involved with the patient to serve as an ancillary. If there is a sudden shift or reversal, hospitalization should be considered. Sharing the risk may be complicated if the ancillary figure produces hostility in the patient. In such cases, it might be expedient to split the transference with another therapist. Ingenious planning and subsequent modification may be required until stabilization is effected.

Drugs and hospitalization can be avoided in many instances. This approach should not be followed when high lethality exists, and the therapist should not feel obligated to accept individuals who are completely isolated and alienated and require long and intensive therapy, even if these individuals are not psychotic. Infantile patients with large pregenital problems and little ego strength, who function on a borderline level, are best off under custodial care. Hospitalization may result in regressive attitudes and behavior, but this is far preferable to playing a guessing game with death.

In the first period of therapy, whether lethality is moderate or high, the emphasis must be on a reduction of intrapsychic chaos and rage. It is necessary to lessen dysphoria and establish more cohesion and integration in order to bring about some measure of equilibrium. Therapy in its early stages is, to a large degree, supportive. There are exceptions when the patient does achieve some insight, but the emphasis must be on placating archaic forces and strengthening coping mechanisms. When there are sufficient signs of ego strength and flexibility and the superego ferocity is no longer a threat, then the patient is ready for psychotherapy. The avid clinician who is overly anxious to bring about insight on the basis of his own insight may provoke an exacerbation. Transference must be watched carefully and contended with in such a way that the patient can be dependent during the crisis period but can become autonomous later through therapy. Many therapists tend to give interpretations prematurely to a patient who is emotionally defunct and bankrupt. Interpretations should be postponed until the patient is ready to perceive them constructively (Fromm-Reichman, 1950).

Litman (1957) tends to feel that transference hostility towards the therapist can be exaggerated and that the patient is really crying out for love and protection. The patient may attempt to test and provoke the therapist and thereby court rejection and termination of the relationship in order to rationalize an exacerbation. It is, therefore, important in such cases for the therapist to examine his own countertransference or to make use of a co-therapist or a consultant. Regressive behavior is to be expected, and the patient's dependency may bring about hostile feelings within the therapist, who finds himself expending a great deal of time and energy in contending with the patient. Since the demands of the suicidal patient are often so great and time-consuming, Litman suggests that the therapist should exact a fee that is commensurate with the time and effort necessary and limit the number of highly lethal patients being seen at any one time.

This does not imply that the clinician should restrict the number of low-lethal or moderately lethal patients in his practice. While ambulatory psychotherapy has the advantage of encouraging autonomy, the psychotropic drugs, electroconvulsive therapy and hospitalization may be indicated when office psychotherapy proves to be ineffectual or begins to present hazards. The therapist should monitor his own countertransference reactions since he may inadvertently reveal his own hostility or disinterest in the face of inordinate demands with little or no progress. Under such conditions, it is not atypical for the patient to attempt a rekindling of therapeutic interest by a suicidal attempt or a completed suicide. During an impasse, other opinions and a reexamination of alternatives can be helpful. It is important that the therapist be frank, explain to the patient that he is concerned and that in the patient's best interest he wishes to explore additional options or possibilities. If this is well-timed and tactfully stated, the patient need not feel rejected or abandoned.

PHASES IN THE COURSE OF PSYCHOTHERAPY

Moss and Hamilton (1957) divided the course of therapy into three distinct phases. These phases can be helpful in understanding the dynamics and also give some index of the patient's movement in therapy:

(1) *Acute Phase*: The goal during this phase is primarily to afford the patient adequate security from self-destructive impulses. This requires some restitution—namely, lessening of anxiety through the increase of ego strength with attendant improvement of coping mechanisms, which requires that the patient learn or relearn to interact with others. Suicidal patients are ambivalent about killing themselves, and their ambivalence may persist even

when they are hospitalized. Some welcome the secure milieu, others resent it because their perogrative to take their lives has been abrogated, and still others make a flight into health very quickly in the hope that their surface adjustment will be rewarded by immediate discharge.

The second group remains inert, aloof and uncooperative. It becomes imperative for the staff to intercede and to mobilize their efforts to help the patient communicate and interact. In addition to psychotherapy, physical and occupational therapy, organized activities of a recreational character and even eating arrangements should be focused on decreasing alienation. Nonresponsive patients may benefit from tranquilizing agents or electroconvulsive therapy, and these can have a marked effect on modifying the negative aspects of the acute phase and make it possible for the patient to begin to play a vital role in his own recovery. The therapeutic alliance and the transference are integral in making it possible for the patient to feel less angry and less guilty and to respond to a meaningful figure.

During this phase, the patient is often fearful and humiliated. Concerns about retaliation for his behavior are manifested. He is afraid that he will be stigmatized forever, that he will lose his employment or his status, that he will not be reaccepted by his family or his spouse, that he is mentally ill and that there is no remedy for his plight. The therapist should not ignore these feelings and should not hesitate to reassure the patient. It may be expedient to contend with such apprehension by having others corroborate his reassurance. A letter from an employer attesting to the fact that the patient's job is secure can have powerful impact.

(2) *The Convalescent Phase*: During this period the patient is calmer, demonstrates more appropriate affect and has made a reasonable adjustment to the hospital. He feels less out of place and is much more receptive to clarification of· the dynamics of what has transpired to cause him to behave in such a self-destructive way. His amenability and rapport with the therapist make it possible for him to reveal himself and to examine new routes or avenues that might

circumvent or alleviate the precipitating forces that brought him to the crisis.

The convalescent phase terminates when the patient must return to his former milieu and all of the problems and issues that were associated with it. It must be recognized that even while he was getting along well in therapy he was able to do so largely because of the safe surroundings. During this period when it appears that much progress has been made, the patient seems pleased, his relatives are pleased and complimentary to the therapist, and sometimes the therapist is a bit too pleased because he does not recognize that this may still represent a flight into health or, another term that is often used, a flight into reality.

The patient is very much like an adolescent who is anxious to get into uniform and attack the enemy. However, the first sounds of battle are overwhelming, anxiety is heightened, and unrealistic fantasies become inoperative. During the convalescent period, the suicidal patient has not been able to fully implement insights, and his understandings may be highly intellectualized. Much of his seeming confidence may be fragile and based on wishful thinking. If his therapist has indeed inspired him with confidence and the positive transference is firmly established and if the people about him are seen to be less threatening, he is ready to leave and begin to resume his routine functions. However, if the therapist perceives the wish to be discharged from the hospital to be premature and a resistance against going into deeper issues, he must act decisively against discharge, even if it incurs the disappointment and grumblings of relatives and a temporary negative transference reaction from his patient.

(3) *The Recovery Phase*: The patient is now once again attempting to contend with situations and conditions that had precipitated his suicidal attempt or a lethal state. Moss and Hamilton (1957) found evidence of reactivation in 90 percent of all cases. They found that 80 percent of reactivations took place when the patient was given a pass to go home for a day or a weekend. Some patients worsened when they insisted on leaving the hospital without the approval of their therapist or, in some instances, with the therapist's

consent. In their study Moss and Hamilton found that completed suicide and/or another attempt at suicide occurred in 55 percent of the patients. Others had recurrence, without any conscious fantasies, of suicidal ideation or symptoms that were similar to those that they had experienced previously. It was noted that those who had a meaningful therapeutic relationship and who had experienced genuine insight during the convalescent period were less likely to reenact the past. In most instances this appeared to be related to the transference with the therapist and the fact that what had transpired between them was too meaningful to destroy. In short, the patient was not alone—a significant person was now actively involved in his life.

If so many patients reactivate during the recovery phase, one might well ask why patients are permitted to leave the hospital on weekend passes or are discharged prematurely. Perhaps it would make more sense if hospitalization was prolonged, but economics and reality often preclude this course. There are some therapists who feel that, in spite of the possibility of reactivation, the patient must learn to contend and to face reality as quickly as possible. Many of them consider some reactivation phenomena as part and parcel of discharge and pride themselves on being able to deal with it even though the patient may suffer minor exacerbation or fluctuations. Their attitude is predicated on the fact that they have rapport, alliance and a reasonably good transference, so that the patient need no longer be regarded as actively suicidal.

The Moss and Hamilton study (1957) is by no means conclusive, and many suicidologists might question the large number of reported reactivations. However, it should be noted that reactivations can take subtle forms. They may result in gestures that are played down because the patient has had therapy before, or in ideation which may not be manifest.

Since patients are vulnerable at least three to four months after a suicidal attempt, continuing therapy for them should be arranged. Farberow et al. (1961c) emphasized the need for social service investigation of the home environment and orientation of the family prior to discharge of the patient. Relatives should be warned of the possibility of reactivation. Group therapy or a day care center may be the answer for some individuals who find it impossible to continue individual psychotherapy and for some who might benefit from a combined individual and group experience.

GROUP THERAPY

At the Fifth Annual Meeting of the American Association of Suicidology, Farberow (1972b) discussed the supportive effect of group psychotherapy in the prevention of suicide. He reported on two groups that were functioning within the Los Angeles Suicide Prevention Center. One group was conducted on a long-term basis that was insight oriented; the other group, which was innovative, was, in effect, a nongroup—that is, for all practical purposes it was a drop-in center that did not require any commitment. The first group was comprised of individuals who acknowledged their vulnerability to self-destruction. The nongroup proved to be unique in the sense that chronic, borderline and even the severely disturbed and self-destructive patients were offered the opportunity to face the reality of their predicament and to develop an affiliation and perhaps a commitment to the center. As a result of attending sessions, such patients could develop a suicide identity—but this might be the necessary prerequisite to accepting their vulnerability. The philosophy is similar to that of Alcoholics Anonymous where it is essential that the alcoholic accept the fact that he is indeed an alcoholic before he can go further in contending with his problems.

Billings, who is an advocate of open-ended groups, considers them extremely useful (Billings et al., 1974). He has discussed the long-term group that involved the participation of some 200 individuals over a 46-month period. There were 10 suicidal attempts and one completed suicide during the course of his study, but he considered that the patients involved in the study were in the high-risk category.

Litman (1974) combined group therapy with some of the concepts that have been utilized by the Samaritans. His goal was to reduce alienation and improve interaction in individuals in the high-risk category. He divided 400 high-risk patients into two groups. The experimental group received a continuing relationship maintenance (CRM) service. This provided them with an ongoing relationship with supervised volunteers, either through telephone calls or other means, at least once a week. In effect, the strategy was to befriend them, which is the primary tactic of the Samaritan approach. Ongoing relationships were extended for a period averaging about a year and a half. Litman found that individuals in this group had chronic, long-standing, rather than acute, problems. He concluded that the continuing relationship with such people through CRM was extremely helpful. However, individuals habituated to alcohol were not good candidates for this program.

It cannot be categorically stated that all suicidal patients are good candidates for group therapy. However, group therapy can be a valuable adjunct in prevention, and many unique approaches are being improvised. In some instances, a combination of individual and group therapy can be beneficial. Clinicians should be aware of the diverse and innovative resources that group therapy programs offer. Very often a therapist closeted with his patient may become myopic and fail to recognize that an extension of one-to-one therapy can be provided through this means. On the other hand, before referring a patient to a group, the clinician should familiarize himself with the orientation and goals of the programs and the staff's qualifications and then decide whether this approach will meet the particular needs of his patient.

THE MATTER OF CONFIDENTIALITY

It can be unequivocally stated that every therapist, every clinician, regardless of whether he be a psychiatrist, psychologist, social worker, physician or counselor, is dedicated and motivated to work in the interests of the survival of a patient. The clergy, teachers and others who encounter an individual who is likely to self-destruct would also do what they could to prevent it. However, sometimes it is impossible for them to do so; that is, it is impossible for them to do so alone. It therefore becomes necessary to call in others; the professional who is aware of the suicidal intent needs to communicate the dangers to others who can collaborate and who are willing to intercede and even actively intervene in a lifesaving effort. It may not be possible for even the experienced therapist to develop sufficient data in the first or early sessions, particularly if the patient is psychotic, suffering from organic brain disease, has been misusing drugs, or is markedly ambivalent and intertwined in a dyadic relationship that has yet to be uncovered. The question is, when should confidence be breached?

Shneidman (1975) was emphatic about refusing to serve as a partner in a collusive pact of secrecy when suicide or homicide was involved. This view is shared by most clinicians and particularly by suicidologists. However, there are exceptions, and some clinicians, including Max Siegel (1976),* strongly feel that confidentiality

should not be breached under *any* conditions. His emphatic paper was prompted by the fact that the APA "Ethical Standards of Psychologists" is in the process of revision and a controversy about confidentiality has arisen. Principle 5 of APA "Ethical Standards of Psychology" now reads:

> f. Confidential information may be disclosed without authorization from the client only when and to the extent that the psychologist reasonably determines that such disclosure is necessary to protect against the clear and substantial risk of imminent serious injury or disease or death being inflicted by the client on him/herself or another.

Siegel's proposed substitute wording of this section declares that confidentiality must be maintained without *any* reservations. He states his position as follows:

> In some 35 years of professional practice, I have learned over and over and over again that without complete trust between the patient and therapist, there can only be severe limitations upon the openness of communications in the privacy of the treatment setting. I have learned that I cannot play God,

---

* Max Siegel is President of the Division of Clinical Psychology of The American Psychological Association, formerly President of Divisions 13 and 29 of the American Psychological Association

that I cannot make judgments about when it is proper or appropriate to violate an individual's revelations, confessions or whatever. . . . Therapeutic aims are dependent upon the unqualified acceptance of the privacy of patient communications, and with no strings attached. . . . There was a time that I shared the naive notion that a person could be protected from suicide by hospitalization, or by otherwise having family "take charge." I subsequently learned that people commit suicide in hospitals, strangely enough, and that I could best help by being the one person he or she could trust, completely and unequivocally. . . . As I reflect upon over 35 years in clinical psychology, I am all the more convinced that my failures were most often associated with an absence of mutual respect and trust . . . (p. 1) .

Siegel's proposal and rationale deserve some comment. He would rely completely on his therapeutic relationship, which is based on trust. One is tempted to inquire about the failures that he alludes to. Is it not conceivable that a patient who was unable to develop a relationship of complete trust with Siegel might have been able to do so with another therapist? Is it not conceivable that although a patient's initial interaction with Siegel might have been negative, it might have been altered by another therapist, a consultant, a dyadic figure, a member of the family, a community agency or a suicide prevention center? One is also tempted to inquire how Siegel would contend with the highly lethal individual who gives no evidence of therapeutic collaboration, transference or rapport. He mentions that we cannot play God, but is it not assuming an omnipotent role when one makes the statement, "I am all the more convinced that my failures were most often associated with an absence of mutual respect and trust, and my successes with complete unequivocal acceptance and trust" (p. 1). It is, indeed, an ideal situation when the interaction between patient and therapist exists and such mutual trust has been established. However, it may take hours or weeks for it to develop, and before it occurs, the patient may have already taken his life.

Siegel's argument that people can commit suicide even when they are hospitalized, if they are determined to do so, is correct. It is also correct to state that a patient with a Type A personality who develops a coronary thrombosis might also die in the hospital. Or he may die from another heart attack after he has left the hospital. However, an individual who is suffering from a heart attack belongs in a hospital. Whether it be a heart attack or a high-lethal crisis, the patient belongs in the hospital and is less likely to die a hospital.

Siegel also considers it a naive notion that the family can serve an ancillary role. This attitude runs counter to the utilization of significant others and the fact that dyadic relationships exist and must be contended with during a suicidal crisis.

Shneidman (1975) described a patient he had seen at a suicide center who took out a pistol from her purse and told him she was going to kill her husband and then destroy herself. He told her she could not leave his office with the weapon. She pointed out that he was abrogating the rule of confidentiality—that she could tell him anything. He made it clear that homicide and suicide were not included under confidentiality and that he had no intention of serving as an ally and confidant in bringing about death. Although she responded with hostility, she complied and continued therapy with Shneidman. Perhaps she would not have carried out her threat. But what could have happened if she had her gun and her trust was suddenly dispelled?

Siegel's concept of absolute confidentiality could be a serious blow to suicidology. The one-to-one relationship is undeniably important, but the therapist must recognize his own limitations and cannot always rely on idealized concepts at such a crucial time. He may require help.

There is another aspect that is to be considered. What would the legal consequences be for the therapist who adopted strict confidentiality and was later sued for malpractice because he did not make full use of community resources and available options in order to prevent death?

POSTVENTION

Postvention, a term coined by Shneidman, refers to a series of procedures that may be instituted after suicide. Shneidman (1971a, 1973, 1976) has elaborated on the procedures that can help ameliorate the terrible consequences of self-destruction. Postvention represents a large public health problem because the survivors—the families, loved ones, friends—far outnumber the individuals who have committed suicide. If about 50,000 individuals commit suicide, how many survivors are left to mourn and suffer guilt and anguish? Their number increases regularly each year. Many of these survivors are, in effect, victims who have their lives damned and devastated forever. There are millions of this increasing population who are tortured by self-blame, confusion, ambivalence, shame, loss and hatred. Many brood and spend years searching for targets—motivations that might have been directly or indirectly related to the suicide—in fruitless conscious and unconscious attempts to absolve themselves. Their depression and emotional states make them candidates for a suicidal course. In contending with survivors, the reality of the suicidal event that transpired cannot be repressed, suppressed or denied, and once again preventive measures should be instituted. Concomitant with such procedures, a careful examination of the deceased is required.

Medico-Legal Investigation

The postmortem is the province of the coroner or the medical examiner. Under ideal conditions, he is a physician who is trained as a pathologist, with a good knowledge of forensic medicine. It is his task to determine the exact cause of death as well as the mode of death—whether it was natural, an accident, suicide or homicide. Even after autopsy, an exact determination of death is not always possible, and such terms as "accident-suicide, undetermined" indicate that the mode of death was not clearly established (Curphey, 1961). Such equivocal findings are not infrequent, and even when the pathologist has made a decision about the mode, there may be doubts that persist endlessly. Members of the family may refute or refuse to accept the pathologist's findings and insist that death resulted from an accident, natural causes or even from murder. All possibilities must be carefully considered and investigated.

The psychological autopsy has proven to be a valuable means for a more precise determination (Curphey, 1969). The pathologist, as part of a suicide team, receives input from a variety of community resources—the police, hospitals, medical colleagues, psychiatrists, psychologists, and others. In addition to ascertaining the mode of death for medico-legal purposes, valuable and more accurate statistical information can be gathered for computerization and storage in data banks.

The Psychological Autopsy

This procedure is an attempt to focus on those components and forces that reflected self-destructive motivation. Shneidman (1976) considered its main function was to provide data that would help pathologists when the mode of death was uncertain or undetermined. There are any number of deaths that call for such probing—e.g., did the person jump out of the window volitionally? Was he pushed or thrown? Was he cleaning the window and bent over too far? Did he have a heart attack while he was leaning over to get some air? All four modes of death could be involved in this one situation. An overdose or the ingestion of a toxic substance may be due to poor visual discrimination between two bottles, miscalculation, murder or suicide. An individual may be forgetful about following his doctor's orders, or confused because of alcohol/drug ingestion or an organic disorder. It is even conceivable that the doctor made a mistake and prescribed the wrong dosage or that the pharmacist made a mistake and dispensed the wrong dosage or drug. The person tinkering with a running car in a closed garage might be doing so because of ignorance, cold weather or suicide. One can go on ad infinitum and cite specific cases, all of which indicate the complexities.

The psychological autopsy, through an extensive multidisciplinary in-depth study, attempts to be more precise and seeks to abstain from using the word "undetermined" if at all possible. Shneidman (1976) attributes the initiation of the psychological autopsy to a combined effort of Dr. Theodore J. Curphey, who was chief medical examiner for Los Angeles County, and the staff of the Los Angeles Suicide Prevention Center, in an attempt to help resolve the matter of equivocal deaths. This supplementation of the medical autopsy requires detailed and careful reconstruction. Seemingly irrelevant aspects may be of great significance; occupation, religious practices, medical history, utilization of alcohol, ages of death of siblings and other members of the family, hobbies and life-style can be helpful. Interviewing various members of the family, colleagues and friends can yield material that is crucial to establishing the mode of death. Shneidman (1976) gives an outline for a psychological autopsy in which details and nuances of the deceased's life can be taken into consideration. Curphey (1969) attests to the effectiveness of the psychological autopsy. In 1953, before this procedure was used, he found that, of 188 drug deaths, 74 percent were classified as suicides, 11 percent as accidents and 15 percent as undetermined. With the utilization of the psychological autopsy some nine years later, of 440 drug deaths, 90 percent were classified as suicides, 1 percent as accidents and 9 percent were considered to be undetermined. It would therefore appear that a refinement of techniques led to a more precise determination of the mode of death.

The psychological autopsy in its reconstruction of the suicides' life-style is attuned to the prodromatic factors or signature items, such as depression, drug habituation, risk-taking, perturbation, inability to cope, helplessness, etc. Although a few of these items were not conclusive in themselves, a number of signature items that were synergistic with a destructive life pattern contributed to the configuration that often resulted in lethal consequences.

In reviewing psychological autopsies, Shneidman (1976) found two outstanding, pervasive common denominators. He referred to them as "governing concepts," and they have echoed and re-echoed in the field of suicidology. One was the role of the significant other —the dyadic relationship. His clinical impression was that the interaction with a spouse could often be crucial. The optimistic note of such a deduction is that if a pathological relationship is perceived and ameliorated—if there is a modification or resolution of hostility towards the target whose defenses are poor, limited or depleted —it could make the difference between life and death. Even if therapy failed, Shneidman suggested that a separation could be lifesaving.

The other pervasive concept that has been expounded in suicidology is partial death. Menninger (1938) has espoused this thesis for over 30 years. Partially dead individuals are technically alive but psychically dead. Their lives are meaningless and without purpose; their affect is crippled and they are resigned to eternal nothingness. Their existence represents an exercise in futility. Many perpetuate their ennui with drugs or invalidism of one type or another. Since their partial death offers some modicum of death by way of a cessation of affect, they may maintain it for an indefinite period. However, they represent the hazard of completing their psychic suicide. In assigning lethal ratings to this category, Shneidman, as a clinician, stated that in rating 30 cases he would not include partial death among the first five in lethality but among the first 12.

Treatment of the Survivor-Victim

Every society has devised techniques for contending with loss and bereavement (Mandelbaum, 1959). The mode and period of grief are determined and demarcated. A basic tenet has been that the bereaved requires immediate support—particularly from loved ones and from meaningful and prestigious figures. Sympathy, consolation, encouragement, distraction, abreaction and efforts at restitution are offered to the bereaved. Regression under such conditions is accepted, so crying, helplessness and psychotic reactions are condoned. The initial trauma may cause a flattening of affect, psychomotor retardation, numbness, mutism, panic, loss of identity, depersonalization and denial.

Every religion has its own postvention procedures, and the ceremonial functions that relate to death permit the expression of grief —but in a structured, proscribed manner. There is some latitude, but there are explicit and implicit controls that are operative. Various rites are carried out, and they offer the bereaved helpful outlets for grief but limit periods of regression so that the loss will not permanently impair the living.

An adjustment to any mode of death of a loved one can be a long, painful and tortuous process, but this is especially true in the case of sudden death, as in suicide. Weisman (1975) discussed the degrees of bereavement:

> Bereavement is like dying itself, except that it refers to the process by which a person suffers, sustains, and then recovers from the wound inflicted by loss of someone essential to his reality. Like any wound, it may be short and trivial or very serious, life-threatening and prolonged. During the bereavement process, healing can be impaired, delayed, and exaggerated, with many secondary complications, including that of chronic invalidism (p. 1754).

In situations where there is some foreknowledge, such as an impending operation, a diagnosis of malignancy, chronic illness or the degeneration of old age, it is possible to undergo some anticipatory grief and prepare for the demise. In the case of a sudden death, anticipatory grief is not possible. Even when an individual recognizes the possibility of suicide, it may be virtually impossible to accept such a reality. Lipton (1967) described the trauma of sudden death. The survivor may occlude it, deny it, or appear not to recognize its impact. Reactions may be paradoxical in the sense that instead of profuse crying and loss of control there may be a seeming lack of interest, a matter-of-factness—seeming acceptance. Parkes (1972) suggests that both of these seemingly divergent attitudes are attempts on the part of the individual to bring about a restitution of the love object. The mixed feelings of depression, yearning, search and denial can shift from one end of the continuum to the other.

Subsequent to the Coconut Grove Fire, Lindemann (1944) became extremely interested in the grief reactions manifested by the survivors, and also in the grief reactions of those who had suffered losses in World War II. His conclusions were that unless an individual was able to demonstrate grief after the loss of a loved one, large disequilibria could take place. Such an individual might develop severe emotional problems, somatization, psychophysiological disturbances and problems in social interaction, and even a psychosis could ensue. It was his conclusion that bereaved individuals should be encouraged to express affect and to work it through.

The question arises as to whether intervention is necessary or indicated for every survivor-victim of a suicide. If, as Lindemann suggests, a "normal" grief reaction has taken place and the individual's ego is strong and resilient enough to bear the attendant grief, should preventive and interventive procedures be instituted? Bereavement is a normal consequence of life, and after the death of a loved one, ambivalent though the love may have been, a reactive depression characterized by mourning is to be expected. Should every survivor-victim of a suicide be regarded as presuicidal? How can we determine the criteria to judge whether a "normal" mourning state is a reactive depression or whether it is, in effect, a preliminary to self-destruction? It would appear that there are two options: One is to assess and to evaluate every individual who has played a significant role or has been a dyadic figure in the relationship which resulted in self-destruction. Contact with such an individual should be maintained for a year, or even longer, to determine whether another suicide is in the making. This would represent an attempt to prevene. The other option would be to wait through the period of depression following the acute state of mourning and the prolonged loneliness and at that time determine whether the reaction to bereavement carries a suicidal threat. Weisman (1975) considered a bereavement abnormal only under the following conditions:

> (1) Arrest of the process, in which afflicted patients showed typical symptoms for long periods without evidence of relief, recovery or restitution; (2) exaggeration of symptoms during the course. An example is a mourner who denies absolutely that a death occurred or one who believes in a full hallucination about the dead or, more extreme, communication with the dead; (3) deviant behavior that violates conventional expectations or jeopardizes physical health and safety (p. 1755).

It would seem far more appropriate to utilize the first option and begin to work with the survivor-victims of suicide as quickly as possible and not wait to ascertain if the bereavement is abnormal or atypical. Shneidman (1975) discussed his conclusions based on his long clinical experience as a suicidologist. It was his opinion that the treatment of the survivor-victim.of a tragic death should begin as quickly as possible—within two to three days after the trauma. He also considered that postvention could not be limited to therapies and clinicians alone and that within the next decade it would be practiced by such diversified individuals as lawyers, nurses, friends and even good neighbors. Aside from the significant individual or individuals who were involved in a dyadic relationship and are the primary survivor-victims, there may be a multiplicity of other survivor-victims, and it would not be feasible for everyone who had had a relationship with a suicide to be seen by a therapist. However, once again, in order to prevene, these individuals should be watched carefully. Once again it becomes necessary to listen for the cry for help and to watch for the prodromata of suicide. Mourning is related to death and carries with it large perturbation and inimicality. However, it is the degree of lethality which again becomes the most significant barometer.

Although Shneidman found that survivor-victims were generally amenable to intervention, in this writer's experience this was not always the case. Some refused to interact, found it too painful to bring up matters that pertained to their own feelings of guilt and shame and considered intervention an intrusion that opened up old wounds.

Many of these individuals wished to maintain their suffering as an act of expiation. They felt they deserved the punishment and wished to continue it as long as they lived. Individuals who maintain this attitude fall into the category of the partially dead. In short, they have also committed suicide psychically but remain alive. Early intervention with such individuals may require the help of ancillary figures to bring the individuals into treatment and to prevent the possibility of a completed suicide.

The initial therapy must be supportive and a relationship initiated in which it becomes possible for the gamut of affect towards the suicide to be explored. It is imperative that the therapist not play a judgmental role in this process since great guilt as well as fury towards the deceased may be involved. This eliciting of repressed and suppressed affect may unleash the ferocity of the superego, make life even more unbearable and drive the individual towards self-destruction. The therapist must therefore offer insight only at periods when it is appropriate either to expiate guilt or to help resolve it. Since somatic problems can arise frequently during such a period, in addition to a psychic overlay of insomnia, anorexia and weight loss, guilt, ill-defined pain and malaise, the patient should be encouraged to have periodic evaluation by a physician who is aware of the tragic circumstances. Grief and depression may be masked by symptomatology that involves physical dysfunction (Gero, 1953).

In our technological, scientifically oriented society, nothing seems impossible. Men explore outer space, and interplanetary travel is no longer a fantasy. Immunological research is yielding positive results in transplants; cancer is no longer synonymous with inevitable demise; bypass heart surgery can reverse arterial occlusion and bring a fresh flow of oxygenated blood to the starving myocardium. Gerontologists talk with confidence of prolonging life and soberly make the prediction that survival to 100 or 150 years will soon be common.

Perhaps it behooves us to remind ourselves that man is still mortal. Regardless of advances and progress, Thanatos—death—is built in for all. While the wish or the dream to live on forever may predominate, despite our best efforts and techniques at intervention there will always be some—admittedly a minority—who for reasons that we can not fathom or fully understand decide to terminate their own lives. We must learn to reduce their number.

CHAPTER 7

IMPLEMENTATION

PROBLEMS AND ISSUES

Having read thus far, the reader has, we hope, acquired some in-depth understanding and perspective of the panorama of suicide. This assumed expertise may be accompanied by a confidence that should not be dispelled. However, confidence can be illusory and, when faced with an impending death, may ebb and evaporate under the harsh heat of actuality.

The acquisition of basic principles is rarely sufficient; it must be supplemented by the mastery of implementation skills and the procedures that elaborate such skills in order to attain proficiency. This holds particularly true when life and death are in the balance.

A major criticism of the plethora of articles and books about suicide is their repetitive emphasis on the cry for help and the need to reduce self-destruction, with only infrequent consideration of how this reduction is to be achieved. Guidelines on how to develop an alliance, transference, the dyadic relationship, etc. are set forth in abundance, but there is a paucity of literature and information dealing with what transpires and what specific countermeasures can be employed effectively when one is faced with the imminence of suicide. Reading a map, even if one can, is a far cry from contending with the interminable obstacles that may be encountered in reaching the goal. Two Canadian psychiatrists, Hirsch and Dunsworth (1973), had some pungent comments to make about this matter:

> Until very recently the massive literature had little data on how to actually deal with a person who is contemplating imminent suicide (p. 108).

128

They noted that in the book, *Suicidal Behaviors, Diagnosis and Management* (Resnik, 1968), little more than one page in 500 deals directly with this topic and this appears in the section on "Psychotherapy of the Suicidal Patient," written by Mintz. Hirsch and Dunsworth went on to comment:

> There are almost no data regarding techniques of dealing with patients in dangerous situations who are threatening suicide but not asking for help or who are actively engaged in rejecting it (p. 108).

In answer to this criticism it is, perhaps, easier to try to inspire than to be specific. Perhaps the implementation techniques and processes are not well defined. Perhaps the professionals are attending and responding to the basic principles of suicidology but are acting under terrible stress and urgency in a highly individualistic manner and are loath to reveal unorthodox or exceptional techniques that are not fully in accord with their psychotherapeutic training. Perhaps suicide is not the exclusive province of psychotherapists and it is unrealistic to expect them to provide divine guidance and absolutes. Perhaps nobody really knows *exactly* what to do when dealing with an imminent suicide. The variables are innumerable, and the therapist dealing with an imminent suicide tries to survey the situation, keep his cool, utilize the principles of prevention, and improvise on all available options that are consonant with both his life-style and his therapeutic style. Stoller (1973) exemplifies this kind of therapist. The same criticism that has been leveled against suicidology—the vagueness about the specific utilization of procedures—was made about psychoanalysis for years. Glover (1955) and Greenson (1967), along with a few others, have attempted to provide a modicum of clarification.

Resnik, Davison, Schuyler, and Christopher (1973) addressed themselves to this problem in suicidology and pointed out that in addition to the urgency of the situation the therapist is often confronted by a situation that is alien to his own intrapsychic state and to his training as well. The involvement of the spouse, dyadic figures, the extended family, significant others, community resources, etc.

can be taboo since it represents an invasion of the sacrosanct therapeutic relationship. Although most therapists recognize the necessity for abjuring their customary modes of interaction, they are not always capable of functioning on their optimal level under such conditions. It is not unlike the predicament of the surgeon carrying out a life or death procedure on a kitchen table or in a tent with some floundering, poorly prepared laymen serving as his assistants.

Resnik et al. (1973) raised another cogent question:

> When the clinician does have a motivated patient, other problems still remain. How can he approach the suicidal patient in a way that will maximize the chance for a positive outcome? Psychodynamic individual psychotherapy requires time, intellect, philosophical commitment, and an evolving relationship for success (p. 460).

The American Association of Suicidology is aware of and sensitive to this problem, and at the 1978 meeting in New Orleans considerable time and attention were devoted to an innovative training program for the development of a dynamic intervention approach that is primarily designed for lay personnel but can also be helpful to professionals and paraprofessionals.

It is a basic assumption that while aptitude, ability, interest and motivation are important, implementation is predicated on a learning process. The intensive, prolonged training in medicine illustrates the highly structured protocol for teaching the art and science of implementation. The student is not admitted to medical school until he has given evidence of his capabilities, especially in the physical sciences. Subsequent to acceptance, he is subjected to the arduous task of learning the basic principles of medicine in two years. The process of implementation extends over the next two years in the forms of rotations and clerkships in teaching hospitals and clinics, during which he is introduced to techniques and procedures. After the completion of this program and the attainment of the degree, the recipient is further confronted by more concerted implementation as he embarks on his internship. It is not uncommon for uncertainty and misgivings, with a mobilization of anxiety, to occur at this time.

It is obvious that perfect implementation programs do not exist. Physicians jest cynically amongst themselves about the July transition, when medical graduates assume the functions of interns, interns take on the responsibilities of residents, junior residents become seniors, and new chief residents are chosen. It is common knowledge that many physicians are reluctant to admit their patients to the hospital during this period when the house staff is learning to implement. Implementation is lifelong in medicine, with staff meetings, seminars, postgraduate and continuing education courses, professional meetings, etc.; all are required to meet new criteria, exigencies and the recertification that is becoming mandatory.

The subject matter, the purpose, and the length of time that is optimal in gaining skills that are to be effectively applied vary in every discipline. It is imperative to stress the translation of awareness, perspective, orientation and knowledge into implementation.

We all know how to do many things. The small boy who has watched his father carefully thinks he knows how to drive a car. He may become so imbued with his know-how that he implements prematurely. It can also be embarrassing for a father whose lack of know-how in assembling a mechanical toy results in many hours or days of frustration. Our lives are marked by countless episodes of ineptitude, clumsiness and misconstructions that are manifestly attributable to inadequate implementation but are quickly suppressed or repressed. A curse of our times is the how-to-do-it books, particularly in health areas, that influence and encourage the suggestible to blindly embark upon dangerous courses. This should not be confused with positive and constructive programs where excellent provisions are made for implementation.

A didactic approach is rarely effective on any level. For example, cardiopulmonary resuscitation instructions can be printed on one page, with another page for diagrams, and can be memorized with relative ease. Following through on this basis alone could be tragic and/or fatal. The American Red Cross, hospitals, chapters of the American Heart Association, the YMCA and others realize that they must offer highly structured programs to prepare the individual to act immediately and appropriately. The American Heart Association carefully evaluates its implementation process of manikin practice, questions the quality of instruction and recommends retests of proficiency at least once a year. The American Cancer Society has been equally involved in developing and disseminating pragmatic approaches to detection. It is the general consensus of suicidologists and the American Association of Suicidology that a focus on education and training is the sine qua non of implementation and that many useful paradigms are available. Frequent references have been made to primary, secondary and tertiary prevention, but a detailed and comprehensive discussion of the attendant complexities is required in order to pursue the goal of prevention.

AWARENESS, TRANSLATION AND IMPLEMENTATION

In the context of suicidology, awareness represents a recognition based on the communication of facts, feelings and observations that alert and cause the sensitive and empathic individual to take notice. It is characterized by a responsive concern that may rise to the proportion of alarm. If it goes beyond that point, it can lead to panic—catastrophic behavior which precludes intervention.

Translation is perceived as a precursive, prefigurative process that involves decoding the presuicidal signals and tuning in on the multiple manifestations of the psycho-socio-dyadic-existential condition. Translation is essential but preliminary to and discrete from implementation.

Implementation refers to an active process wherein appropriate measures are taken to prevene, intervene and postvene. The three phases—awareness, translation and implementation—are part of a continuum that must be symbiotic to be effective. In medicine the physician becomes aware of the patient's discomfort/disequilibria under the rubric of diagnosis. He then translates this symptomatology, utilizing anatomy, physiology, pathology, etc., and with his clinical acumen and experience pieces together a syndrome. This makes it possible for him to proceed with attempts at cure or amelioration. Awareness and diagnosis are indispensable, but without implementation they offer nothing beyond reassurance when the condition is functional or benign. There is small satisfaction in making any diagnosis unless there are prospects of some positive steps at intervention. Identifying a presuicide and labeling him as being highly lethal or manifesting high suicidality is merely a qualitative estimate or determination of a poor prognosis unless appropriate, specific countermeasures are instituted. The aim of all science is description, prediction and control. The exploration of countermeasures for presuicides should be and will be never ending.

It is interesting to note that systems of implementation may undergo evolution. In his pristine period, Freud naively assumed that bringing unconscious material to the surface and then translating and interpreting it were sufficient. Freud soon realized that he was overly optimistic and that his technique was not only ineffective when deeper layers of intrapsychic defenses remained intact but failed to modify character and life-style. Greenson (1967), in discussing the implementation processes of psychoanalysis, differentiated four distinct procedures; confrontation, clarification and interpretation were preliminary steps, the fourth was working through. All too often, in cases of repeated suicidal attempts, with various periods of remission and reactivation, the patient was in psychotherapy but had been subjected to, or insisted on subjecting himself to, only an intellectualized or supportive experience in which the crucial working through had not been accomplished.

RESEARCH AND IMPLEMENTATION

The emphasis on implementation does not contradict the priorities proposed by Resnik and Hawthorne (1973)—that research in suicidology should precede education and training, and that treatment and services should follow in that order. It is clear that without research, education and training would suffer and a void would exist in primary, secondary and tertiary care delivery. Although the research function is absolutely necessary, the priority of research over implementation in suicidology is debatable. This does not imply that available resources for research should be withheld or denied but, rather, that research should proceed concurrently with and not to the exclusion of care and services to facilitate and improve implementation. Research and implementation are reciprocal; research stimulates, overlaps and is often derived from implementation techniques and procedures. The discipline of psychoanalysis involves research, explorative-diagnostic and therapeutic functions.

A study of 22 patients that exemplifies the application of research to care delivery was instituted by John H. Greist of the Department of Psychiatry and David Gustafson of the Department of Preventive Medicine at the University of Wisconsin School of Medicine. The study used a computer to try to identify presuicides and to determine whether the computer could predict which patients were planning self-destruction. Greist, Gustafson et al. (1973) developed a computer-based information system which utilizes the cumulative knowledge, judgment and clinical expertise of eight experienced psychiatrists. The system was not intended as a substitute for or replacement of the individual clinician but, rather, was used to integrate and synthesize pertinent knowledge and periodically reassess future models so that the patient might be in a better position to define his subjective state. Unlike the individual therapist who, for one reason or another, neglects to ask or omits a question that might be crucial, the computer never forgets. It is not a substitute for clinical evaluation but an adjunct that may prove to be a complementary and helpful predictive instrument.

The interface consists of a screen upon which questions appear and a typewriter keyboard on which the patient types out his answers. The computer was so programmed that questions that directly reflect suicidal intent were strategically interspered with other queries. Open-ended as well as multiple-choice questions were incorporated, and there was opportunity for the patient to provide his own answers when he thought the given multiple choices were unsatisfactory or inadequate. The patient could see his answers on the screen and by pressing a key could change his answers. A sequence was established that enabled the computer to branch according to the patient's responses and to ask successive questions to follow up an earlier answer in greater depth. Computers are readily available; the charges for non-prime time are minimal.

On the basis of his experience, Greist suggested that it is easier for patients to answer direct, emotionally-laden questions to an impersonal computer than to a clinician who may be uncomfortable or who may have reservations about probing sensitive areas.

Outcome categories were combined so that they differentiated only between those who would make a suicide attempt and those who would not make an attempt. The computer accurately predicted 70 percent of the suicide attempts as against the therapist's 40 percent. For the cases in which no suicide attempts were made, the computer was 90 percent correct and the clinicians 94 percent. The sample was admittedly small.

Greist, Gustafson et al. (1973) stated:

> Although the computer interview is no panacea in the difficult clinical area of suicide-risk prediction, the approach has the obvious merits of low cost, short development time, widespread and instant availability, standardized collection and evaluation of data, and easy modification to incorporate new knowledge or to test new hypotheses (p. 1331).

In a follow-up article, Greist, Gustafson et al. (1974) bring up a cogent point:

> The computer interview cannot be compared with, and is not intended to replace a person-to-person interaction. It presently has no way of picking up nonverbal aspects of communication. and it probably does not engender strong transference feelings. A computer interview can, however, be compared with reading a good book—it provides information and offers an opportunity to reflect (p. 221).

Gustafson and Greist et al. (1977) describe an ongoing study in which patients are interviewed on the first meeting by the computer and are subsequently seen by therapists, who are asked to give their estimate of the probability of suicide. Gustafson et al. concede that because the sample size is small it will be a number of years before the system can identify those who will attempt suicide. The preliminary results were based on 30 patients who had been followed after a three-month interval. Four individuals in this group made suicidal attempts, and even though conclusions cannot be drawn at this early stage, the results so far agree with the conclusions reached in the 1973 pilot study.

This material is included to illustrate how research can be applied quickly and effectively even while authentication is still in progress. The primary care physician, the internist, who does not have the time or the expertise to evaluate the patient thoroughly could find it expedient to use such a screening instrument even though the results are tentative. Psychotherapists, who have doubts or misgivings and wish corroboration, as well as clinics and hospitals, could also find it valuable since the computer printouts that record the responses would be available for analysis.

REPRESSION, DENIAL AND IMPLEMENTATION

A thorny problem that stands in the way of implementation in suicidology is the phantasmagoria of interrelated variables. This conglomerate has been portrayed in the literature as being a denial of death, a repugnance and repudiation of death, diverse rationales of immortality; an impossibility because it has never been experienced; a magical act; a malignant or undesirable introject that will be extirpated or exorcised; a return to an idyllic period of the past with a reunion with beloved objects; a metamorphosis by which all of the tragedies of the past and present will be eradicated and a new purified being will emerge; a redemption of all sins, real or fantasied; the existence of life beyond the grave and the possibility of influencing and controlling the living; the supplantation of a battleground by Elysium; and, paradoxically, exaction of vengeance for all of the inequities and injustices of life. These are just some of the attitudes and beliefs for which there is absolutely no substantiation but still permeate our society.

In the Victorian era, the misconception and the attendant dishonesty about sex were particularly prevalent. Erotic behavior was countenanced only under formalized auspices, although everyone was well aware of the fact that illicit relationships existed. Children were regarded as immune from erotic impulses. Although everyone was cognizant of clandestine and surreptitious urges, they were regarded as sacrilegious. Acceptance of death, particularly by suicide, is still in the process of emerging from this static morass of hypocritical sanctimoniousness.

Freud's genius and fortitude made it obvious that sex and its manifestations have their onset with life itself and are not phenomena that occur suddenly at puberty. Society has now granted itself permission to explore the biological, the physiological, the psychological, the social and the existential impact of sexual urges. However, in the matter of death by suicide, the denial, self-deception and the hypocrisy linger on.

Freud himself, that heroic advocate of enlightenment and exploration of the psyche, was not immune from the repression of a patient's suicide. Freud found himself discomfitted and thwarted by his inability to remember the name of Signorelli, an artist whose frescoes he admired and wished to discuss. When the name of Signorelli was mentioned, he was able to overcome his block, and his associations led to a patient who had committed suicide. Although Freud wrote about this episode of repression, it was not until later, in 1911, in the *Psychopathology of Everyday Life,* that he gave an extended version of his repression and related it to a patient's self-destruction. Holden (1978) commented on Freud's initial reluctance to fully disclose his associations with the suicide and questioned why he did not elaborate further with an analysis of this patient. Perhaps Freud (1954) answered this question when he somberly stated that in spite of denial, death evokes a reverberation of one's entire existence. It might be added that this is not only a traumatic but a stigmatic experience.

Needless to say, repression and reticence do not serve the cause of implementation of primary, secondary and tertiary intervention. Denial is even more serious. It can be anticipated in patients, but it cannot be accepted in professionals, who are required to face up to a rigorous honesty in order to maintain their competence. No one in the literature has been more incisive relative to competence than Lesse (1975) :

> .. . A suicidal attempt by the patient while in active therapy, may often be the psychiatrist's or psychotherapist's fault since suicidal attempts can be prevented, and suicidal drives can be blunted and eliminated in most acute suicidal situations (p. 311).

Although Lesse uses a few diplomatic, qualifying words, this a clear indictment of professionals who are unequal to the task of blunting/eliminating suicidal drives in the course of psychotherapy. There are those who would consider Lesse's remarks too severe. There are, admittedly, some patients who are so determined to achieve their goal of self-cessation that neither the tightest security measures of the psychiatric hospital nor the skillful intervention of an experienced clinician will prevail. However, when active therapy is in progress, a suicide cannot and should not be attributed so quickly to the patient's preordained fate or his resolution to die. Such an attitude may represent a denial by the therapist. Implementation failure may be, and has been, directly linked and related to a multitude of manifest and subtle factors (Holden, 1978). The therapist may have underestimated the prevalent or fluctuating lethal intensity. The therapeutic alliance may have been short-lived or may have been abruptly aborted. The strength of the transference may have been poorly gauged; it may have shifted—too loving, too hostile. The therapist may have inadvertently become a dyadic figure in the drama, all the while being oblivious to the nuances of his own verbal or behavioral interaction with the patient. He may have rejected the patient, unaware of his own negative counter-transference, or demonstrated overt indifference or hostility. His own morbid feelings of futility and disposition to self-destruction may have reverberated. The interactions between the doctor and a suicidal patient are complex, to say the least. Stone (1971) has discussed the therapeutic interventions that can be designated as malignant in that they can precipitate suicide.

Lesse is a highly regarded, astute clinician not given to making drastic or dramatic statements, and some therapists will, no doubt, be offended by his bluntness. Litman (1956b, 1968) examined the reactions of 200 therapists who had lost patients by suicide and concluded that they responded very much as any individual would to a fellow human being's death and that, additionally, they defended themselves and attempted to justify their treatment through a process of intellectualization. The above quotation from Lesse is unlikely to serve as balm for a therapist's troubled superego.

Even if one does not accept Lesse's statement completely, it is indisputable that many psychiatrists and psychotherapists are insensitive, poorly prepared, poorly trained or not trained to treat highly lethal patients. They suffer from an educational deficit, a myopia or a hiatus in implementation skills.

It should be stressed that such therapists are not necessarily incompetent. They may be proficient in their modalities, provide sophisticated psychotherapy to a wide variety of patients and possess an excellent comprehension of the psychodynamics of depression (Lesse, 1975), but these competencies are not necessarily adequate for contending with the psychopathological conflagration inherent in a lethal crisis. Since every clinician treats dysphorias and depressions of various types and degrees with attendant-suicidal fantasies, ideation, gestures, etc., and since most patients either respond to therapy or medication, have a remission, continue to be chronically depressed or see another doctor and do not commit suicide, false feelings of competency and security may result. On a number of occasions, the author has heard from colleagues the identical, anguished litany that is loaded with disbelief, shattered omnipotence and denial: "How could this happen to me? No one ever did this to me before."

A model for ameliorating this state of affairs exists in the discipline of medicine. Technically, every licensed physician has the unlimited privilege to practice any or all phases of medicine even if he is not board certified in a specialty. The primary-care physician or general practitioner may consider himself capable of treating a wide spectrum of problems. For example, he is quite likely to accept cardiac patients and offer them good care; but when a patient with intractable angina, a coronary thrombosis or congestive failure does not respond to his treatment, he would immediately ask for a consultation with a cardiologist, hospitalization, or both. Because continuing education is increasingly mandatory, he is likely to elect courses in cardiology on pragmatic grounds, and as a result of his increasing competence reduce the necessity for frequent referrals to cardiologists. Psychiatrists and psychologists must make the same decision to limit their ministrations to those who fall within their area of expertise. Since suicide is so prevalent and insidious in our culture, the psychotherapist must opt to either learn more about primary, secondary and tertiary care implementation or refer such patients to others immediately.

Paraprofessionals are in a similar position, with a major difference being that they are not doing "active therapy." Although the nurse, the crisis prevention worker, the Samaritan, etc., are unlikely to delve into depth therapy, they, too, are beset by issues related to effective implementation, and they, too, must recognize their limitations and the need for continuing education and reinforcement. Uhleman, Hearn and Evans (1977) reported on the use of microcounseling versus programmed learning for hotline workers in London, Ontario, at the Tenth Annual Meeting of The American Association of Suicidology, in Boston. Most suicide prevention centers have developed training programs as well as supervision for their paraprofessionals.

It is an ironic commentary on the formalized deception fostered in our society that the saving of a life is associated with a title of prestige. When an individual collapses, the melodramatic call rings out, "Is there a doctor in the house?" Some doctors cringe and fail to identify themselves because if they are highly specialized their general training has long since become obsolete and they have vivid premonitions of a red-hot malpractice suit. A boy scout who has learned to do cardiopulmonary resuscitation or Heimlich's maneuver may be far more proficient than a physician who is not intimately involved in primary care. Certainly a general practitioner, a cardiologist, an anesthesiologist or a pulmonary specialist would be extremely welcome, but the assumption that these indidivduals are close at hand or that the patient will still be alive when a physician is available is presumptuous.

Americans in general have demonstrated a contempt for the barefoot doctor model or the medic; the saving of a life is associated only with physicians and intensive care units. But who is so stupid as to refuse mouth-to-mouth resuscitation from a bowlegged tailor who is at the head of his CPR class, or a tourniquet from a bald barber who still lives up to the ancient tradition of his trade? Unknown multitudes have been saved by policemen, firemen, ambulance personnel or bystanders who have been motivated to learn first aid. The term "first aid" is very appropriate because without it the patient would in many instances never reach the physician and the supportive, sophisticated technology that awaits in the emergency units.

The old attitude toward medical emergencies is slowly changing, but in the area of suicide, the public does not yet recognize the possibility that a compassionate layman can render first aid and that a paraprofessional can be compared to a medic. There will never be a sufficient number of professionals who are readily available or easily accessible. It therefore becomes essential to enlist and to motivate as many people from related professions and the public in general to become familiar with the basic first aid procedures of intervention in suicide. The task of reducing this all too frequent mode of death requires structured, concerted effort.

THE ETHOS, THE MEDIA AND IMPLEMENTATION

Although a proliferation of articles and books on suicidology has saturated the psychiatric and medical journals and has had considerable influence, the primary impact has been on the professional. The leaders of the professional groups whose works have been cited in this book have sought with tireless tenacity to communicate their growing concern. Other groups of humanistic, sensitive and aware people have emerged but with little structure and only the vaguest concepts of crisis intervention. Hampered by lack of funds and relying on inexperienced volunteer personnel, their cohesiveness has centered about their common purpose. These pioneer groups have been the embryonic suicide crisis intervention centers, offering direct and immediate links to those contemplating self-destruction. Many of these centers are now meeting the accreditation standards established by the American Association of Suicidology under the skillful guidance of Dr. Richard K. McGee, Chairman of the Certification Committee.

It would be remiss not to include the expanding influence of the Samaritans and their continuing, positive worldwide effect in "befriending."

Winkelstein (1977) has stated assertively that prevention and curative functions are not synonymous and that it might be expedient to demarcate them into two distinct systems. This is applicable to the approach of suicidology, wherein treatment is the function of the professionals but prevention falls within the domain of paraprofessionals, volunteers and all concerned people. Obviously, some overlapping is to be expected.

Undeniably, constructive forces are in evidence. However, aside from minor gleams of hope, the general climate remains bleak and the statistics for self-destructive behavior continue to escalate.

Gray (1977), writing in *Lancet,* expressed it well:

> The main reason why people choose to act in a way that puts them at risk is because their concept of the future is different from that of those who give them advice (p. 1339).

It is extremely difficult to prevent something that so many people refuse to concede exists; if, indeed, they admit it is a reality, they claim that it does not apply to them and that they can dissociate themselves from it, as if it were like a mirage. How is it possible to take constructive action against a threat that is either not perceived, misperceived or, to make it worse, regarded as unimportant, an unsuitable subject for discussion or even for consideration? If this amblyopia were applied to germs—diseases—and there were a denial of pathogenic micro-organisms, there would be no health precautions, and there would, as in the past, be epidemics and plagues.

Saward and Sorensen (1978) note: "The most effective preventive measures seem to be those that require the least individual effort such as the public health management of water, sewage and food" (p. 891).

Attempts to decrease the incidence of suicide will be exercises in futility unless the channels of information and education are greatly expanded. We enjoy a technically adequate communications system. However, the potential of these resources to improve the quality of life has not been realized. Obviously, the fault lies not with the communications systems but, rather, with the programming that the media, rightly or wrongly, thinks will attract and hold the greatest number. Given a choice on prime time TV between an educational suicide prevention program and a banal family comedy, we can be sure of what the Nielson ratings would reveal. Saward and Sorenson (1978) suggest that the media has a more powerful effect on life-styles than do the professionals.

Suicide education will never win a popularity contest, but we are living in a iconoclastic Zeitgeist, and the archaic, repressive forces meet less opposition from more resilient superegos and more tolerant ego mediation. Other areas once considered to be forbidden, anathema to us, and out of bounds have been covered by the media. Suicide will probably never be free of its ghastly, ghostly taint, but suicidologists are optimistic that increasing numbers can be persuaded to cast aside primitive misconceptions and learn to implement those fundamental principles that can prevent needless deaths.

Caustic criticism of the media for our failure to gain their cooperation in recruiting the legions vital to our cause is neither diplomatic nor psychologically sound. The media is only too happy to oblige when the demand is clearly apparent. The public is extremely interested in and fascinated by suicide if the circumstances are grotesque, bizarre, involve prominent figures such as movie stars, writers, millionaires or the infamous, and if the self-destruction can be related to a sexual, scandalous or titillating motif.

Occasionally, material on suicide can be presented thoughtfully and sensitively. Some years ago there was national coverage when a young reporter killed herself on TV after reading the news and announcing her own impending death. Sally Quinn of *The Washington Post* is to be commended for her in-depth coverage of this poignant event in August, 1974. Her comprehensive, detailed account was, for all practical purposes, the equivalent of a psychological autopsy.

The increased collaboration of the media has resulted in a constant stream of information that would have been considered unfit for reader consumption a short time ago. Such topics as drug and alcohol addiction, homosexuality, venereal disease prevention, birth control, and especially the association between cigarette smoking and lung cancer, where there is a conflict of interest between the media and the sponsor-advertiser, would have been taboo.

Most newspapers have one or more regular columnists who answer questions and write brief articles about medical matters and human relations, but self-destruction is given short shrift or is conspicuously absent.

Publicity is freely given for the Heart Fund, American Cancer Society, Multiple Sclerosis, Muscular Dystrophy, Cerebral Palsy and a host of other causes which solicit funds. Suicide prevention centers fail to attract sponsorship and function on meager donated funds. In obituary notices, the suggestion is frequently made by the family of the deceased that in lieu of flowers donations in memoriam be made to any number of causes. The author has yet to read one appeal made by a bereaved family to donate money to the American Association of Suicidology (AAS) for research, or to a suicide prevention center. This would indeed be a dead giveaway.

Suicidologists are not deterred by the general complacency, and numerous measures have been and are being instituted to dissipate apathy. Such measures are an integral aspect of and cannot be dissociated from the practice of suicidology. The leading and most vigorous organization in the field of prevention has been the American Association of Suicidology (AAS). The AAS is a multidisciplinary organization and invites the participation of all those who wish to become involved (see appendix for further information).

There are still the inevitable questions as to whether we are doing enough and whether our efforts are directed on target or are too peripheral and tangential. Perhaps we should attend more to the caretakers such as physicians, psychologists, social workers, clergy, etc., many of whom have had only superficial experience with suicide prevention.

Medical students are often woefully unconcerned about this problem, and more suicide curricula would be helpful. These students are usually required to complete only one course in psychiatry, and additional training is through a clerkship. At St. Elizabeth's Hospital in Boston, all Tufts University medical students on rotation receive orientation in suicidology, and this author has found that for the large majority this represents their introduction to this subject. First-year psychiatric residents are often in the same position, and their background in suicide intervention is sketchy.

Seminars or programs for journalists and columnists could be offered periodically in an easily accessible metropolitan hospital. Dr. Bruce L. Danto, Director of the Detroit Suicide Prevention and Drug Information Center and President of AAS, has worked with the police department, and he noted (1978):

> ... such an approach by a suicidologist can be most timely, as police agencies are looking for meaningful contact and dialog with mental health professionals. Police officials are urging police agencies to acquire professional training in human behavior. Conjoint programming with crisis intervention and suicide intervention workers could prove to be a very helpful contact (p. 1).

Clergymen, lawyers, barbers, hairdressers and bartenders are often in the position of being confidants, and many of them would welcome programs of intervention training. One recently completed program, under the auspices of the University of Rochester, was well received.

Miller (1978) brought up other interesting possibilities. He suggested that one goal might be the establishment of a permanent "Center for the Study of Suicide" on a major campus. He offered another suggestion that about every five years we zero in on a high-risk group as a target population:

We could then concentrate much of our "national effort" on reducing the suicide rate of that group. A similar goal would involve the selection of a particular geographical area (such as a state, county, or a reservation) where the suicide rate is unusually high. By focusing our "national attention" on reducing the area's suicide rate, we could demonstrate that "suicide reduction" is more than merely a fantasy (p. 3).

Miller (1978) also proposed that the federal government might be prevailed upon to instruct the National Institute of Mental Health to increase its effort in the area of suicide. Miller suggested that large-scale fund-raising efforts such as those conducted by other organizations were desirable. He also felt that someone in a high executive position must have suffered a bereavement as the result of suicide and that such an individual would not only be amenable but very much interested in playing a helpful role in an effort to reduce self-destruction.

A permanent foundation established to study the aspects of all forms of self-destruction would be a boon to humanity. A good model is the Sloan-Kettering Institute.

Ingenious means are infinite, and we can be sure that their cumulative effect would reduce the incidence of suicide, but this goal will require training programs that are dynamic, relevant and applicable.

CHAPTER 8

SUICIDE PREVENTION

THE TRAINING MANUAL

The *Suicide Prevention Training Manual,* officially introduced at a program session at the annual meeting of the American Association of Suicidology in New Orleans in April, 1978, is innovative in a number of respects: (1) Input was derived from the combined experience and judgment of highly respected figures in the field. (2) It is comprehensive. (3) It provides for a program that meets varying needs. Although it is primarily intended for the layman, it can be a significant and valuable tool for the instructors and professionals as well. (4) The information is succinct but highly detailed. (5) The emphasis and the focalization are realistically directed at prevention. (6) It lends itself to a flexible approach so that branching out, unlimited modifications, additions and improvisations of the workshop problems are possible. (7) It requires intimate involvement and offers maximal opportunity for group participation. In short, it is an excellent vehicle for learning implementation technique.

Guides, manuals, didactic instruction, programmed learning, sensitivity training, tapes, etc., have been used by many crisis intervention centers in the past. Role playing and acting began with the history of civilization, and psychodrama has been used as a therapeutic technique for at least a half a century. The manual is unique not because it establishes a precedent but because its inclusivity and versatility provide for broad, multifaceted utilization.

The 14 workshop problems will be quoted verbatim as they appear in the *Suicide Prevention Training Manual,* and they will be

147

followed by the author's comments, which are elaborative and in no way a substitute for the valuable and pertinent course material contained in the training manual.* It must be reiterated that the manual represents a carefully structured and constructive compendium—a program that offers the opportunity to acquire implementation skills. The mere listing of the workshop problems and the discussion that follows are a far cry from a shared, methodical supervised group experience.

The workshop problems serve as a springboard for the author's comments, which are intended to illuminate and explore possibilities and complexities that are raised by the problems, to compare and contrast the professional and the lay approach when it is possible to do so, and to draw from his personal experience in coping with similar issues. The training manual is readily available at nominal cost, and further information can be found in the appendix of this book.

WORKSHOP NO. 1

Problem: Describe a person who is likely to commit suicide, listing as many specific characteristics as you can think of below.

In attempting to answer, the professional is likely to think in terms of categories where vulnerability is present, particularly depression. He would include the psychoses, other symptom-syndromes and also reactive factors that were intolerable to the ego.

The less sophisticated might attempt to compile an endless list of traumata: bereavement and other objects of loss such as health, job, home, money; intractable pain or disgrace; sadness, helplessness, loneliness, rejection, guilt, futility, inability to cope; abuse of drugs, excessive use of alcohol; and incarceration. The list could go on and on. A person whom the professional would describe as most likely to commit suicide would probably present an amalgam of some of these characteristics.

---

* Used with permission from the American Association of Suicidology and from the Health Information Services, Merck Sharp & Dohme Division of Merck & Co., Inc.

Even if the list included no apparent reason for suicide, all of the specific characteristics would still be correct. Unfortunately, they are also incorrect. There may be evidence of depression, anxiety, perturbation, dysphoria and inimicality, but none are pathognomonic, nor are they predictors of suicidality per se. Since a large majority of people who suffer from the categories and characteristics enumerated above do not commit suicide, it is not possible to define a specific type of person who will do so. It is, however, conceivable that anyone may momentarily feel the urge to self-destruct. Although some people, when anguished, bang their fist against the table or through a window, some others, during even a brief eruption of lethality, terminate their lives.

It behooves us not to ignore, dismiss or take any person for granted when the signals, whether they be veiled, coded or overt, are perceived. Since overlearning is essential to full comprehension, a review of Chapter 4 and the two that follow will prove helpful.

WORKSHOP No. 2

Problem: A friend you have known well for several years confides that he is very disturbed by thoughts of suicide. He is frightened and would like help, but is worried that if people find out about this problem it will damage his career and his home life. What do you do? What could you avoid doing?

In this case, the cry for help and the ambivalence are evident. A suicidal attempt has not yet been made, and there is still time to intervene. How much time? How serious is the threat? This cannot be determined until A has told B (his confidant) more about his intent and B has elicited more information about A's ideation, motivation and plans for self-destruction. Subsequent to this essential process, B must decide on the best course of action, and he must also decide on what role he should play in implementing it.

It is extremely distressing for anyone to hear such news from a friend. If B does not have warmth and compassion for his fellow man and does not have some frame of reference, then he is ill prepared to absorb the impact of his friend's predicament. If B's reaction is negative—shock, disbelief, indifference, coldness, sarcasm or condescension—it could well precipitate further exacerbation. Callous remarks such as, "You must be kidding," "Is this for real?" "Come on, now, you're not going to commit suicide," "Cheer up!" "You have a good job, a good wife, a beautiful house," "What the heck is wrong with you?" "I know a hundred guys who would love to be in your shoes," "Take your wife out to dinner and a show," "Maybe we'll get together some night," represent a brush-off, a clear-cut rejection. After having mobilized his resources and pocketed his pride to confide in and appeal to his friend, A now feels humiliated as well as totally rejected.

Let us now assume that friend B is a humane and sensitive person, and although he was initially caught off guard by his friend's confidence, he adapted quickly and responded immediately and sympathetically. "Tell me more about these feelings of committing suicide." He listened attentively and without interruption while A discussed his depressive state of two years' duration and revealed that he had experienced some physical symptoms at the time as well. A had seen his physician and had touched vaguely on his feelings. His physician gave him the impression that he had little faith in psychotherapy and told him that he could find nothing physically wrong with him. B was able to get A to confide that he had lethal instruments in his home and insisted that they be gotten rid of. A sighed with relief at his friend's authoritarian but thoughtful and quiet approach.

B explained that thousands of people on every socioeconomic strata were in therapy and that a therapist would not willfully violate confidences or harm a patient. A agreed that it was illogical to consider a therapist as a hostile agent and that perhaps he would arrange for an appointment but that he would like to get his bearings first. B picked this up at once and suggested that he would attain his equilibrium not by postponing a visit but by seeing someone at once. A admitted being uncomfortable about "asking around" and giving himself away. B also did not know of any professionals, but after a minute or two of thought, he dialed his own internist and in A's presence explained that he had a friend who was troubled by suicidal thoughts and that he, B, felt a consultation was in order. He was given two names and was told that both were highly competent. At this point, B handed the phone to A and stated simply, "I'm your friend and I know you need help. These people are experts; call one of them and make an appointment."

A became more anxious again and turned his head away from the telephone. "What shall I say? Let me think about it. I'll call tomorrow . . ."

"Now is the time. Simply ask for an appointment and tell him that it's urgent. If his secretary answers, do exactly the same thing. It's not likely that you'll be asked to tell anything that is personal. The purpose of the appointment is to do just that."

"What if he asks who referred me?"

"Tell him that Dr. Y referred you. When you see him, you can explain the circumstances."

A dialed very slowly. The first doctor was unable to see him for a week. He would have settled for this, but B encouraged him to call the other therapist. The second doctor agreed to see him at 7 a.m. the next morning when he mentioned that it was urgent and that he had been referred by Dr. Y. He was asked to give his name and his telephone number, which he did with trepidation.

B smiled for the first time. "Good. It wasn't any harder to arrange that than to call any doctor." A was silent for a short time and then appeared to be relieved—less tense—and spoke more spontaneously. He seemed less frightened. They talked for a while longer, and B made it clear that he would continue to be available. He offered to drive A to the doctor's office the next morning. A extended his hand and said, "It's not necessary, I wouldn't let you down." At this point, B felt that he had accomplished his purpose. Sometimes, as in this instance, the intervention process proceeds smoothly.

However, there are any number of cases in which the well-intentioned friend may find himself nonplussed or at his wits' end. A, the friend who has confided his suicidal ideation, may refuse to cooperate and become irritable and cantankerous. Although frightened, he may suddenly develop rage and perceive intervention as a coercive intrusion. He may demand to be left alone. Although admitting that he has a loaded gun at home or enough drugs to constitute a lethal dose, he may refuse to give them up. Sometimes an individual may grudgingly surrender such items but be able to replace them quickly. For example, if a magazine or bullets are removed from a gun, or even if the gun is also taken from him, an individual with a license can buy replacements immediately. In states where a license is required to carry firearms, it is wisest also to ask him to surrender, at least temporarily, the license as well. Even this has shortcomings because there are so many other ways an individual can destroy himself. The person who smiles as he gives up lethal instruments should be suspect. Any jocular or sarcastic comments such as, "You're taking all my defenses away," or "Now you're making it impossible for me to kill myself," are equally suspect.

A may become abrupt and angry when the subject of seeing a therapist is broached. His answer may be, "If I wanted a therapist, I would have seen one. I came to talk to you and now you're putting me off. I can see I'm not going to get any help from you; you think I'm crazy."

B must be patient, steadfast and tenacious in order to prevail. He must attempt to continue the dialogue at all costs and revive the initial trust that led A to confide in him. The conversation may go on for a long period of time, perhaps hours. The outcome may convince B that he did get through and that he had aborted an attempt at self-destruction. There are, however, instances when after even hours of effort A does not yield and rejects any plans that would reduce risk. B is now in the same position as a therapist and must immediately call upon other resources. Again, the matter of breaching confidentiality arises and must be quickly resolved. It may be possible for B to call A's physician if he knows who he is. Another alternative is to call a relative whom A respects. If there is no family and no physician, then the next course of action would be to ask for guidance from a suicide prevention center or the emergency unit of a hospital that has psychiatric backup. In some cities, the police department works in conjunction with therapists who are on call. A

person in a highly lethal state must not be left alone, and persistent
efforts should be made to save his life.

When an individual confides in a friend, who often is a peer
figure, about his poor controls and impaired coping abilities, a shift
transpires in the relationship that may impose a burden on the
friend that he is ill-equipped to bear. In seeking out such a friend,
A may not have chosen wisely. A vulnerable but well-intentioned
friend, B, may so compound A's difficulties that he may produce a
malignant effect. This could also occur even when B is familiar
with intervention principles, and even with a therapist, but it is
less likely to take place with individuals who are experienced in
implementation techniques. There are many well-intentioned friends
who cannot assume the positive role that is required to guide an
individual through a jeopardous presuicidal or lethal state. A friend
in such a quandary would be well advised not to attempt a heroic
stance but to seek immediate consultation rather than involve himself in a struggle that may intensify and become even more complicated. If physicians can seek help and advice without loss of
integrity, there need be no sacrifice of self-esteem in emulating them.
This is not to suggest that a cry for help should not be answered but,
rather, that an individual who can barely keep himself afloat is a
poor substitute for a lifeguard or even for someone who can swim.
However, the friend may be the only one available at that time to
keep his friend afloat—alive—until his cry for help is answered.

Still another issue that may arise when a friend has brought up
suicidal inclinations is a conflict of priorities. It is one thing
when A calls B or comes to see B at a mutually convenient time.
He may spend an hour or more, and while it may conflict with other
commitments, B can cancel or postpone them with the simple and
honest explanation that he is involved in a matter of grave importance. However, let us now assume that A, intent on self-destruction, comes to see his friend B on a Sunday afternoon and after two
to three hours of discussion remains unconvinced that he requires
treatment. He does feel somewhat better, buttressed by B, and
shows no inclination to leave. B has read about such matters and
has also taken a crisis intervention course. He knows that A should

not be alone. How long can he stay with A? B, an attorney, has a family and many other commitments. It is clear to B that A should be evaluated by a therapist in order to determine whether he should be treated on an outpatient basis or hospitalized, but A refuses to budge. B has made him feel safer, and A insists that there is absolutely no need to see anyone else and says that he's beginning to feel much better. After another fruitless 30 minutes of attempting to get A to see a therapist, B invites him to dinner and suggests that he stay on. A now declares that he is much better, less "uptight," and says that he will return home and think things over. B is ambivalent about the next alternative. Perhaps his misgivings are unwarranted; maybe he has exaggerated the situation and is overreacting. A appears improved; he is bright and after thinking it over will probably call a doctor the next morning.

While B is having dinner with his family, A calls on the phone. He feels better, is appreciative, but has a question. B is tempted to tell him that he is having dinner and will call him back. But this could be interpreted as disinterest and rejection, so in spite of his wife's annoyance, he listens. A repeats that he is better but now he has some cramping in his stomach and is worried about falling asleep. He had a nightmare the previous night. Would it be all right if he took two 5–mg. tablets of Valium that his wife's doctor had prescribed for her? The directions on the bottle said to take one tablet three times a day, but her doctor told her she could take two at bedtime. Again B tells A that he should see his own doctor or a psychotherapist and that his wife's medication was prescribed for her and not for him. A thanks B profusely and assures him that he will be in touch.

At 11:30 p.m., when B is attempting to interest his wife in a romantic interlude, the phone rings. A is still feeling "pretty good," but he has taken the Valium anyway but is not sleepy and wants to discuss his nightmare of the previous night. His voice is strident, and he is obviously anxious. B curses to himself and again advises A to discuss his nightmare with the professional. As the conversation continues, B's wife takes off to the guest room. B decides that it is too late to do anything about A and spends the next two hours attempting to placate his wife.

B arises early, drives to his office to review his notes for a case he is to present in court that morning. It is too early to call A. He would appear to be oversolicitous and it might alarm his friend to receive such an early call. He has breakfast with the opposing attorney to see if a settlement can be reached. Unsuccessful, he is in court until 12:30. When he returns to his office, his secretary informs him that A has called twice. When he calls back, there is no answer. While he is talking long distance with a client, his secretary interrupts and tells him that there is an emergency call from A. He tells her to put A on "hold" and inform him that he will speak with him in a few minutes. A hangs up. B calls him at home, but there is no answer. Growing increasingly concerned, B is only half-listening to a new client when his secretary buzzes to inform him that A is in the waiting room. B breathes a sigh of relief.

After his client leaves, B thinks for a minute and then dials A's home. It is 4:15, and A's wife, who is a schoolteacher, is likely to be home. She answers immediately, and B gives her a quick and frank resume. She does not appear to be surprised and informs B that A had been seen by his internist two weeks before and had been referred to a psychiatrist because of his depression. Also, their marriage is on the rocks, and she is contemplating divorce. A had made no mention of this in his discussion with B. A's wife agrees to call the psychiatrist and promises to come to B's office as soon as she makes the call.

A is agitated when he walks into B's office and sits first in one chair, fidgets, and moves to another chair. He apologizes sheepishly for taking up B's time and mentions that he has been wandering around most of the day, had not kept the 7 a.m. appointment with the psychiatrist, had not gone to work and now wants some advice about taking a leave of absence from his job. At this point, B tells him that he has contacted his wife in order to enlist her help and that she is on her way. A's agitation increases, and he begins walking about the room. B, who is somewhat concerned that A may walk out, asks him to sit down and explains that he thought it was necessary for him to get in touch with A's wife and that A obviously needs help. A sits down as his wife enters the room. She says, without any preliminaries, that she has called the psychiatrist and that he would see A at 6:30. It is now almost 5 p.m. A is abashed when she brings up the internist's recommendation of two weeks ago, but says nothing. B breaks the silence, "The doctor is obviously willing to go out of his way to see you so quickly. It's about time that you agree."

A's wife says, "This hasn't been a happy period for me, but I'm going with you; maybe this will change the situation."

An analysis of B's behavior and management is in order. On the positive side, his orientation and crisis intervention were helpful. He was concerned, nonjudgmental, addressed himself directly to the primary issues, gave of himself freely, was encouraging and supportive, and attempted to prevail on his friend to accept professional care. Most important, in spite of his friend's negative attitude and denial, he was able to maintain the trusting relationship and a dialogue at the expense of considerable frustration to himself. Ultimately, by enlisting a significant other he accomplished his goal and may have been instrumental in saving his friend's life.

From another perspective, his implementation was poor. He was too ambivalent about taking action after the first meeting. He had no affirmation that his friend would not make a suicidal attempt beyond a vague response that he was feeling better. He was in no position to make a full evaluation himself, and he had not been able to elicit the marital discord and the internist's recommendation. He permitted himself to be seduced and blackmailed into playing an archaic but ostensibly supportive role in which his friend was the controlling figure. His friend was baiting and testing him with calls and questions which he could not refuse to answer because of the underlying threat of suicide. Because of his own anxiety and guilt that he might precipitate or activate suicide, he waited and endured too long before taking affirmative action. When he failed in his attempt to persuade his friend to consult with a professional and when he received no positive assurance regarding his friend's suicidal intent, he could have accomplished the same purpose with facility and with much less inconvenience and upset to himself by doing what he ultimately did, calling his friend's wife or a significant other—a relative, a doctor, a clergyman or a suicide intervention center.

How could a professional deal with this same problem? Although A is a fictitious figure whose problems, symptoms and dynamics are idiopathic and at best obscure, the professional would initially attempt to develop a rapport, using a quiet, thoughtful approach. He would encourage the patient to bring up his presenting symptomatology—namely, the suicidal ideation—and then try to allay the concern that treatment would be deleterious to his career or his home life. In the course of establishing a working relationship, a therapeutic collaboration, he would investigate the dyadic configurations and make some decisions about whether it could provide therapeutic leverage. If the dyadic figure or partner was suicidogenic, the therapist would take measures to intercede, even if this necessitated the separation or divorce from the malignant other in order to protect the patient from a suicidal course.

The ongoing comprehensive evaluation would include attending to mental status, orientation and the sensorium. The patient's stability and ego state in terms of control would be determined, with emphasis on the reactive forces. The therapist might use an anamnestic approach in taking the medical, developmental, social and emotional history. He should determine onset of suicidal thoughts, previous suicide attempts, ideation, plans and gestures. He would explore the content of dreams and fantasies. In the course of his evaluation, he would take into account the dysphoric state, depression, decompensation and episodes of psychosis. He might perceive dynamics that would lead him to masked or obscure channels or a clearly defined syndrome, or he might be in a position to make only a tentative or differential diagnosis. Above all else, he would concentrate on an assessment of suicidality and lethality. If the patient proved unresponsive or additional material was required or desirable, he would request psychological tests.

In the event of an acute psychotic state with high lethality, the therapist would insist on hospitalization. In making a decision about treating a highly lethal patient on an ambulatory basis, there is once again the necessity of establishing priorities. The therapist, whose time is taken up in treating patients, teaching, perhaps writing, having a family life, some hobbies and recreation, cannot forego everything in order to be at the beck and call of more than one or two highly lethal patients. The experiences of B in helping his friend A demonstrate some inconveniences; if these were multiplied by three or four others they would create havoc in the life of the clinician. When the risk of lethality is high and the possibility of transference is good and if the therapist has the time and is willing to make the commitment to see the patient frequently and to be available to the patient day and night, the decision for outpatient treatment may be viable. If, however, the therapist already has one or two such patients, wishes to maintain a close relationship with his family and friends, and hopes to retain his own health and sanity, he has only two options. One is to refer the next highly lethal patient to a colleague who he knows is equal to the task; the other is to hospitalize the patient, treat him, and when lethality has been reduced, see him on an ambulatory basis. This, of course, does not apply to people who present low or low-to-moderate lethality, who are part of the patient load that every therapist carries in a busy practice.

In the case of low or moderate lethality, it would be expected that the patient has enough ego strength to cope with anxiety from one session to the next. Sometimes brief telephone conversations are required initially, but with support and insight, the calls for succor would not be so insistent that the therapist would be subjected to interminable telephone calls or unscheduled walk-ins.

Mr. A may, after evaluation, be diagnosed as an obsessive-compulsive who decompensated and became depressed when his wife threatened to divorce him. Would it be possible to hypothesize that his wife was a surrogate of his mother whom he needed desperately, and that therefore his wife's rejection of him brought forth smouldering rage and fantasies of killing her which were turned about and became directed at himself? In order to contend with these fantasies, did A seek out a substitute whom he could manipulate and who would provide him with warmth and affection and thus mollify his anger and fury? In this situation, A's wife would be the dyadic figure. For A, treatment might symbolize his weakness and his need for dependence and might have reactivated the excessive anxiety that he experienced during childhood. Now, this same concern was expressed and focalized about being humiliated by his peers at work and being regarded as cowardly at home. If this was indeed the case, Mr. A's prognosis in the hands of an experienced therapist would be good, and hospitalization would not be required. After a short period of dependence on the therapist while there was reinforcement to his ego and perhaps a positive change in his marital relationship, A would experience a fading of hostility, less need for a substitute dependent relationship, and a lessening of suicidal ideation. Providing A with unlimited attention and love and permitting him to manipulate would only serve to bring about a wider rift with his wife, and the friend who encourages his passivity could end up inheriting him. The treatment plan might be to work through passive-aggressive components into more mature channels.

WORKSHOP No. 3

Problem: The woman who lives next door, whom you've known for years but have not socialized with very much, has changed since her husband's death. She stays to herself, has dropped out of activities, lost weight, looks unkempt when she comes out to go grocery shopping, and her bedroom light is often on late at night. At first you thought her behavior was typical of mourning, but it has now been well over a year since the death of her husband and she seems to be getting worse instead of better. What do you think these signs suggest and what would you do about them?

Depression and grief go hand in hand. After a reasonable period of time, the painful process is usually worked through or blunted so that the individual can adjust. Transient episodes of dysphoria and depression are not atypical, but a depression related to mourning that is also chronic and intensifying is highly suggestive of self-destructive intent. Symbolically, such an individual is living a psychic death. The withdrawal signifies a refusal to accept the death of a loved one and to resume one's life. Guilt, recrimination and rumination about the past revive and maintain the image of the deceased. All activities from which pleasure might be derived are forsaken, and this masochistic behavior may represent an incubatory period for suicide. Although still existing, such individuals play out the role of someone who is already dead. In short, their behavior is the equivalent of death. They can be committing suicide passively, and within a given period of time they may die sub-intentionally or intentionally. Older people may refuse to see a physician and die of medical neglect. The mode of death is all too often labeled as natural or accidental.

Chronically bereaved persons tend to be reluctant to accept the overtures of well-intentioned interventionists. Very often, members of the family and friends have failed to prevail and have been discouraged by the rigidity and the refusal to respond. However, this does not preclude intervention by others who remain constant and through tactful, nonintrusive means seek to develop a meaningful relationship with such an individual which can lead to therapy. The term "tactful and nonintrusive" describes crucial approaches in helping such people. One must imagine the plight of human beings whose depression and grief have cut them off from all human relations.

Sometimes a considerate, sincere and consistent approach can be effective. The next-door neighbor drops by casually on shopping days and offers a ride to the depressed recluse, Mrs. DG. The offer may be refused at first, but it is made again and is finally accepted. They stop for coffee or lunch; there is small talk. The offer is not to shop *for* Mrs. DG, but to shop *with* her. An attempt is made to develop a sharing experience. The neighbor introduces her to a friend, asks for small favors, borrows a dish or some onions she forgot to buy, asks for a cookie recipe. She treats Mrs. DG as a peer—not a sorry lost soul; she helps her to regain self-esteem. When Mrs. DG expresses her feelings of melancholia, she listens sympathetically but introduces the subject of medical and psychotherapeutic help whenever possible in a matter-of-fact manner, with the offer to facilitate it.

However, Mrs. DG may be too guilt-ridden and does not wish to be tempted by the outside world after she has resigned herself to a psychic death. In attempting to draw her back into the world, well-meaning others are in fact separating her from the beloved object with whom she is still united. They may become agents of the devil and deepen her plight with what she perceives as harassment. The telephone rings for the third time, and each call is from a neighbor who wants to know how Mrs. DG is feeling; is she feeling better; is there something they can do for her, perhaps some shopping. Each time she answers, "No, thank you." The phone rings again. She decides not to answer. It must be someone else calling to distract and thereby disturb her tomb-like existence.

Ten minutes later someone rings her bell. She asks who it is from behind the door, and the neighbor identifies herself. "I tried you on the phone and there was no answer. Are you all right? Is there anything I can get for you?" Mrs. DG abjectly answers, "No, thank you." She now decides to take the phone off the hook and just leave it that way. She has thoughts of dispensing with the telephone.

The doorbell rings again. Someone has brought her a little gift— a pie, a basket of fruit, a book. Momentarily she is polite and opens the door slightly. The good neighbor practically pushes her way in. Mrs. DG is wearing an old bathrobe, looks dishevelled with hair uncombed. She explains that she is tired and was lying down. The good neighbor tries to be cheery and to enter into a dialogue. Mrs. DG wearily repeats, "I must lie down now." She opens the door with the entreaty, "Please, I can't talk with you now."

The woman next door has tried everything to be helpful to her neighbor and had alerted and enlisted the help of others. She has been kind and thoughtful and has tried to be tactful and not to be intrusive, but her best efforts failed. She is now somewhat concerned that if she continues to intervene the pressure might have an adverse effect on Mrs. DG and might cause her to do something desperate.

How would a professional deal with this situation? Suppose one of the neighbors has a relative or friend who is a psychiatrist, and invites him to dinner. After dinner she discusses the situation with him in some detail. While he is giving it some thought, she invites a few interested neighbors to drop over, in the hope that a professional may be able to provide some cues.

The psychiatrist starts off defensively. "If this were a patient who came to my office, I would evaluate her. I would insist on a physical examination and perhaps have her hospitalized. I could put her on antidepressants in conjunction with psychotherapy and, if necessary, ECT." His hostess interrupts to point out, "The problem is how to get her to a therapist. She won't talk to us, won't let us in, and just doesn't respond to anyone. She looks worse and worse."

Someone points out that she has no relatives. Someone else suggests a minister, but it is known that Mrs. DG did not have any church affiliation and that the young minister who had conducted the services following her husband's death has left the ministry and returned to the university for graduate study. A neighbor turns to the psychiatrist, "Why don't you call her; you're a professional. Maybe she'll answer her phone. Or, you could just ring her bell and tell her who you are. Tell her you are our friend. Maybe she'll let you in."

The psychiatrist's hostess interrupts with the comment that it would not work. She had already told Mrs. DG that she had a friend who was interested and concerned about her and would like to see her, and that Mrs. DG has made it clear that she did not want to see a doctor. She had also become extremely upset and said that she was sick and tired of people trying to run her life.

The psychiatrist thinks for a minute. "Does anyone know the name of her physician?" Nobody does, but a woman recalls that a youngish doctor in the neighborhood had attended Mrs. DG's husband before his death. Maybe he was her doctor, too. His name is Dr. White. The psychiatrist nods, mentions that he knows the physician slightly, goes to the phone and calls him. Dr. White is courteous and understanding. He remembers Mrs. DG because he had treated her husband for coronary disease prior to his death. He had seen Mrs. DG once about that time and found her to be mildly hypertensive. She did not keep her appointment for the next visit and he had sent her several reminders to come in. On one occasion when the secretary called her and she refused to make another appointment, he had spoken to her personally, and her answer was that when she was ready to come in she would call. Dr. White admits the gravity of the situation but points out that she had poor rapport with him and that in his opinion it would be unwise and probably cause even more upset if he called.

Dr. White mentions that Mrs. DG and her deceased husband were formerly patients of Dr. Smythe, whose practice he took over when Smythe retired six or seven years ago. The psychiatrist picks this up at once. "Where is Smythe now?" Dr. White recalls that his colleague had moved with his wife to a rural area about 30 miles away.

It's worth giving it a try, the psychiatrist comments as he dials information. There is a Dr. Smythe, and he comes to the phone and listens to the story. He remembers Mr. and Mrs. DG and had been unaware of the husband's death. He wishes he could be of help but he is old, infirm, with "a bad case of arthritis" that makes it impossible for him to drive. However, he is certain that Mrs. DG would speak with him. He had been her primary care physician for 35 years, and even after his retirement she had sent him Christmas cards for some years. Yes, he will call her and express his belated condolences. He cannot come to see her because he doesn't have a car. The psychiatrist's hostess immediately offers to pick up Dr. Smythe and drive him over. Dr. Smythe agrees. He will inform Mrs. DG that he is going to be in the neighborhood and that he would like to drop in on her. He seems certain that she would see him and that he could help her. He is right.

The moral of this fictitious tale is that in some instances, even a professional may be able to prevene or intervene only by improvisation, and a retired old doctor, or a postman, or a streetcar conductor can play the lifesaving role.

When the workshop was introduced to the membership of the American Association of Suicidology in 1978, the professionals were divided into small groups, and role-playing was utilized to make them familiar with the problems in the manual. This select, sensitive group used their collective expertise to explore the infinite actions and counteractions that are demanded by a commitment to life preservation. The experience was instructive, frustrating and even pathetic when brilliant strategic maneuvers were foiled by equally effective countermeasures. For some, the involvement was so real that they were veritably exhausted. The workshop proved to be an excellent exercise for deflating omnipotence.

WORKSHOP NO. 4

Problem: A friend tells you about a college student who is away from home for the first time and becomes anxious over his failure to get straight A's, even though he is doing much better than average. He breaks up with his girlfriend and begins drinking and using drugs. He talks about being a burden to his friends and a disappointment to his family. You know that he recently tried to buy a pistol, saying it was a gift for his father. What do these signs suggest and what would you do about them?

It is difficult enough to intervene and to arrange for treatment for someone who is close by. It is even more difficult to deal with an impending suicide from afar. The exact condition and the resources for intervention are unknown.

The sequence of events described above carries deathly connotation. Loss of one's ego ideal and self-esteem, loss of a significant relationship, resorting to alcohol and drugs to ameliorate these losses and, finally, buying a pistol portend lethality. The urgency of such a situation cannot be stressed enough. If the young man is a student at a university, it would be imperative to call the counseling service and speak to someone in authority at once. Invariably, counseling services in universities have backup from mental health professionals. A small college is unlikely to have a counseling service but may have an infirmary with a consultant available for crisis intervention. The dean might be called, and in a small college he is likely to know what professionals are available. Police departments may have trained personnel or professionals who are on call and available for such an emergency. Above all, some friend should be instructed to stay with the potential suicide and not leave him alone. There are mixed blessings here if the friend is immature, but if he is instructed not to leave the potential suicide until help arrives he can serve the purpose. It is, of course, implied that the student's family has already been notified and that some responsible member is on the way to make the necessary arrangements for evaluation and for therapy.

In the case of an individual who is not a student but is in similar circumstances in another city, a wise maneuver is to call a local suicide intervention center, briefly explain the situation and ask for the telephone number of the nearest suicide prevention center in that city. An updated listing of all the suicide prevention centers in the United States is available, and most centers are likely to have a copy.

When some parents hear that their children are in jeopardous straits, they call immediately in order to offer help and encouragement, but sometimes they can be directive, overbearing, angry and humiliating. If the parent who calls is a malignant dyadic figure, he is serving as a catalyst for the potential suicide. The parent or parents should respond and offer help, but it might be far wiser for professionals to see the presuicide first and define the situation. Needless to say, this young man's problem is not failing to get straight A's.

WORKSHOP NO. 5

Problem: As a volunteer for Meals on Wheels, you go regularly to the home of an elderly man who lives alone. You know that he has been under treatment for mental depression and he usually is very quiet and uncommunicative. Today, however, he seems happy and energetic. He tells you that his troubles are about over, that he is thinking of getting involved in some activities, and that you won't have to put up with him much longer. What does his behavior suggest and what would you do about it?

The lonely and the elderly are prone to depression. Euphoria represents a denial of the existing depression and many individuals profess a happy state to defend themselves against helplessness and hopelessness. Sometimes euphoric states can be maintained for considerable periods of time. However, it must be remembered that if the coin of depression is turned over, euphoria may be on the reverse, but the coin is the same. The danger here may be far more serious. The statement, "You won't have to put up with me much longer," carries great significance because it suggests that the elderly person is mobilizing to take some action to change his predicament. When an individual makes such a comment, it should be picked up immediately, and he should be asked to explain it. If he indicates a plan to commit suicide, the volunteer should remain with him. A refusal to explain the remark has the same connotation as a plan.

In this case, any rationalization for his statement, "You won't have to be put up with me anymore," should be considered suspect in the light of his depression and withdrawn behavior. Whenever an individual is under treatment and acts in this manner, his doctor should be notified immediately. However, such an individual may refuse to identify his doctor; he may have a poor rapport, alliance or transference with his doctor. Nevertheless, it is the therapist's responsibility to decide the wisest way of contending. Until some disposition is made, the volunteer should remain, and if unable to do so, someone should be enlisted to stay until professional care can be provided. All too frequently, the depressed patient may have the wish to die but his psychomotor retardation, with the attendant anergia and depletion of psychic energy, serves as a deterrent. However, the fraudulent, false elation energizes the patient, and while the layman may be pleased by the sudden shift, the well-trained clinician is all too aware of the possible morbid consequences.

WORKSHOP NO. 6

Leader: I will take the part of a young woman standing on the edge of a bridge, ready to jump. (Note to Leader: If this description doesn't fit you, make a joke about it to put other participants at ease, like "If you feel awkward about this, think how ridiculous I feel.") You are coming along in

*your car and you see me, stop some distance away, and get
out of your car. What do you do now and what do you say?
Just talk to me like you would to that woman.*

This portion of Workshop No. 6 calls for role-playing and provides some experience in contending with a crisis situation in vivo
and in vitro. There is a great difference between dealing with the
above situation and playing the role of a friend or a confidant who
is trying to develop sufficient rapport to persuade the potential
suicide to accept treatment .Here, one is contending with an individual who is about to kill himself or herself now. No one, not even
the most seasoned professional, would feel at ease or know exactly
the right words to say. Sometimes, when a number of professionals
are involved, they use a round-robin approach wherein one starts
talking and after a period of time another steps in, and then perhaps
even a third may take over.

In this case, there is only one nonprofessional present to intervene.
The establishment of a dialogue increases the likelihood for the
maintenance of ambivalence. If an individual is completely and
fully intent on jumping, noticing a car stop will not serve as a deterrent. However, if the potential victim is still uncertain, ambivalence can be increased by offering hope, by opening up lines of
communication that can delay the fatal move. It is then possible that
intervention measures may succeed. Commands, threats, and interro-
gation are not indicated. Tenuous and embryonic though it may be,
some kind of interaction that is in concert with reality should be
established and continued as long as possible. Reasonable questions
can be asked, and questions should be encouraged and answered in
an optimistic but truthful and sincere manner. Every effort should
be made to obtain some leverage. The tenor of the conversation
should have a calming effect so that it will reduce the volcanic intrapsychic urge to destruct.

In spite of the awkward situation, an introduction can pave the
way. "I'm Tom Smith. I'm an insurance agent, and I was driving
by and I saw you. Can I help? Is there anything I can do for you?"
If the individual remains silent, he may continue, "It can't do any
harm to talk about it." If the individual signifies that he or she

does not wish to talk, one can repeat, "What harm can it do? Why not get it off your chest?" If the individual begins talking at all, there may be some opportunity for a dialogue. "Is there someone whom you would like to talk with? I may be able to arrange it." If the individual hesitates, "There's a gas station with a phone about a half a mile away, and if you want to speak with anyone, I can get hold of him for you." If the individual appears to be interested, one might then suggest, "Why don't you come down, and we can both drive over." If there is still refusal or hesitation, one can pursue this line and inquire, "Who's the person you have in mind?" In a time of crisis such a person must be significant. Another suggestion might be, "Why don't you come down and tell me more about this person?" Any and every postponement increases the possibility for survival. If the conversation becomes animated, or if the ambivalence shifts in a positive direction, or if the reality aspects and hopes for some solution take hold, the potential suicide may decide to come down.

Although it is conceivable, it is highly unlikely that either a lay person or a professional would encounter this type of crisis. However, it can happen, and establishing a dialogue is crucial to the outcome. A checklist of questions is contained in the manual for the group to evaluate and criticize the intervention process.

Workshop No. 6 (continued)

Problem: The 12-year-old daughter of a friend of yours has reacted badly to her parents' divorce some months ago. Always a quiet, withdrawn child, she has become even more so. She no longer sees her friends, she dropped out of the school orchestra, and she spends most of her time alone in her room. Her father was always very close to her and protective of her, and you suspect that she feels deserted by him and that she believes he would not have left if he really loved her. Her mother, with whom she lives and who feels guilty about the effect of the divorce on her daughter, tends to let her alone, to do what she wants. What is your analysis of the problem and what would you do about it?

This 12-year-old is obviously depressed and the possibility of suicide cannot be dismissed lightly. Since a child of this age and this type of character structure is not in a position to refer herself, parental cooperation becomes necessary. In such cases, divorced parents often put aside their acrimony and bitterness in order to help the child. Even if only one parent agrees, some steps can be taken to initiate therapy. If both parents disregard the ominous signs and will not assent to consultation with a therapist, the child's pediatrician would be the best source for a referral. Most pediatricians are keenly aware of the emotional problems of children and have ready access to resources for evaluation and treatment. Because the pediatrician is likely to know the child and her problems and has played a significant role in the past as the child's physician, his judgment would be respected. If it were necessary to call the school to enlist their help, his input and recommendations would be more seriously considered than a call from an interested lay person. The pediatrician would also be in an excellent position to prepare the youngster prior to his referral to a therapist or a child guidance center or a children's hospital that has a psychiatric unit, all with access to facilities with well-trained professionals who could do a thorough evaluation and follow through with therapy. Treatment might even be indicated for the parents, not to reconcile their marriage, but rather to develop a better understanding of their daughter's problems and fruitful ways of providing her with some support and reassurance.

WORKSHOP No. 7

Problem: A woman in her mid-thirties whom you've known well for several years recently found out that she had rheumatoid arthritis. Since then, she has become very negative and morbid. She is convinced that she is becoming hopelessly crippled. She talks of being a burden to the family. Now, when you call her on the phone to ask how she is getting along, she starts to cry and says she has nothing to live for. "I might as well be dead," she concludes. What do you do?

No one can accept a diagnosis of a progressive, chronic disease for which there is no cure and for which the treatment is merely palliative without experiencing depressive repercussions. This applies not only to arthritis but also to diabetes, cardiovascular disease, obstructive pulmonary disease, hypertension and a host of other ailments. Even if the physician has been tactful in explaining the situation and outlining his proposed treatment, a period of depression follows. The individual's entire life-style may require modification. Many individuals adapt with the help of their physician; those who do not respond should be referred for psychotherapy.

A process of reality testing can be helpful to such a patient. "There are many others who have the same illness and have been able to live on and go about their tasks for many years. If I follow my doctor's advice with regard to diet, exercise and medication and I make other essential modifications, I can still look forward to living and I can still derive some happiness from life."

Even in cases of malignancy where surgery and radiation are required, multiple sclerosis, cerebrovascular accidents, or spinal injuries with paralysis, people can still find means of self-actualization, realization and attainment. Every major professional association makes provisions and provides facilities to enable members who suffer from physical disabilities to participate at meetings. Some years ago, a professor of neurology at Harvard Medical School who suffered from arthritis deformans was able to continue his teaching in spite of serious progression of the disease. He grasped chalk between the knuckles of his fingers and was able to illustrate complex brain function with his precise diagrams on the blackboard.

Great danger exists when an individual equates his illness with death. Such people may remain in a state of psychic death for the remainder of their lives. Others hasten the process by self-destruction.

In the case of the woman discussed above, her last statement—that she might as well be dead—carries a menacing ring. This statement demands careful investigation. She may be suicidal, depressed, or both, and her physician should be notified of her emotional state. Rheumatologists are conversant with the psychosomatic implications

of arthritis, and the doctor would be in a good position to refer her
to a colleague who has an interest in physiopsychological interrelationships.

Preliminary to referring her, her friend might well attempt a
reality testing approach to help her recognize that her dread of the
future is predicated on her morbidity and that it is not inevitable
that rheumatoid arthritics are doomed to hopeless invalidism. This
woman's dire vision of the future is strongly suggestive of a psychopathology that may have long antedated the diagnosis of arthritis.
There is here the implication that she has been struggling with and
perhaps masking a grave psychic threat and that finally the sword
of Damocles has fallen. Psychotherapy would appear to be indicated
for her regardless of suicidality.

WORKSHOP No. 7 (continued)

*Now we'll try a slightly different situation. You (designate
someone in the class) will portray a worker in a suicide prevention center. You answer the phone and I'll be the caller.
(Note to Leader: When the person answers the phone, say
"I'm sitting here with a gun in my hand and I'm going to
blow my brains out." During the conversation, if appropriate questions are asked, reveal that you are a middle-
aged businessman, that you lost your job after giving 15
years of your life to the company, that you had to dig into
your savings, and that now you might not be able to send
your children to college. Say that you discovered some time
ago that you would never fulfill your dream of becoming
a top executive, and now you can't even support your own
family.*

Such a call is grim indeed, but the worker should bear in mind
that if an individual with a loaded gun were truly determined to
blow his brains out, he would not call a suicide prevention center,
which he knows full well is committed to deterring people from
killing themselves. One can therefore assume that the caller is
ambivalent and still hesitant about carrying out his threat.

This could be a prank call, but the worker must treat it seriously, and the attempt must be made to disarm the man via the telephone. One logical approach would be to point out that it is much easier to talk without holding a gun in one's hand. After the worker has given his own name and identified himself, he might well ask, "Have you put the gun down? Good. Now tell me more." In eliciting the rationale for the wish to take his life, the manifest problem is economic loss, but the problem that is far deeper is another kind of loss—the loss of virility. He should be encouraged to go into greater detail about his age. He might still be comparatively young, and 15 years is not an inordinate period of time. He might be reassured with the trite comment that many people don't have money to send their children to college, that children often find ways and means of going. There are always other jobs. Many dreams are unfulfilled. This type of man requires restitution, and after having established some rapport with him, the worker should stress that if he came to the center, resources would be available and could be explored to help him. The 15 years he had spent on his job might make him attractive and valuable to another company. Stress could be placed on his value, significance and importance to others; it should be emphasized that staying on a job for 15 years was indicative of stability. This approach would emphasize the initial attempt at restitution.

It must not be forgotten that the caller has a loaded gun. If his response has been positive and he has divulged his name and address, arrangements should be made at once to secure and remove the weapon. This should not be postponed. If he refuses to accept such an arrangement and insists on "thinking it over," the police should be called, and the worker should accompany the plain-clothes-man to the caller's house.

WORKSHOP NO. 8

Problem: We'll take one more example for practice. Suppose you (indicate a person from the class) are a police officer called to the scene where a woman is standing on a ledge ready to jump. Explain how you would approach the scene and then act out what you would say. For variety, I'll ask you (indicate person from the class) to portray the woman on the ledge and to act according to the principles of suicidal behavior that we've covered so far.

There is a variation here from the problem in Workshop No. 6 in that a police officer has been called to the scene, and one can assume that a crowd has gathered. If the police have received some training in crisis intervention, they would dispense with shrieking sirens when responding to such a call. A crowd is not likely to disperse even if the policeman suggests it. At such times, people are fascinated by suicide. There may even be a few cruel bystanders who will taunt and tease the unfortunate person, urging him or her to jump. The officer's first task is to make use of his authoritarian position and take charge by calling to the woman on the ledge and giving his name. At this point, if there is a crowd, they're likely to quiet down in order to better witness the drama. Since shouting in order to communicate with someone high up on a ledge is unsatisfactory, the officer might suggest that they could converse more easily if he came upstairs. If there is no opposition from the victim on the ledge, he might proceed to do so and also urge the boisterous onlookers to quiet down. Other police may arrive at the scene, and they may be helpful in keeping order. The officer may have radioed for help while he was on route. His next task would be to position himself as closely as he could to the potential suicide but not encroach in such a way as to threaten or cause the victim to jump. His general approach would be similar to that already described in Workshop No. 6.

Hirsch and Dunsworth (1973), who researched this type of problem, concluded that in such cases a determined person will jump but those who demonstrate hesitancy, misgivings or ambivalence on a high building or a bridge where they are attracting public attention are responsive, and even nonprofessionals can be successful in deterring them. The implication is that two discrete categories of suicidal people select the high building, bridge or public place where they will attract attention.

Although most suicidologists would agree with the procedures discussed in Workshops No. 6 and 8, Hirsch and Dunsworth (1973) stated:

> There are almost no data regarding techniques of dealing with patients in dangerous situations who are threatening suicide but not asking for help or who are actively rejecting it (p. 108).

They reported that the police have had greater experience in dealing with such problems. In 1970, efforts of the Emergency Service District Units in New York City were futile in 123 cases in which people fell or jumped from high structures, with subsequent injury or death. However, there were 163 cases in which the efforts of the service units were successful and death and serious injury were averted. Hirsch and Dunsworth quoted Deputy Commissioner Wilfred N. Horne as stating that all of the rescues in this group were accomplished ". . . either through voluntary submission or subterfuge or cajolery on the part of the officer." Horne trains his personnel to use the practical, strategic approach of trying to establish confidence and trust while providing the potential victim with hope about his current problems or dilemmas. The potential suicide is then offered either food, drink or cigarettes in order to obtain "an opportunity to grab him . . ."

Some suicidologists might object to the use of the words subterfuge, cajolery and grab. This may be an issue in semantics—terms such as placating, calming and convincing would be less likely to carry the connotation of deceit. Others might object to "grabbing" and using the temptations of food, drink or a smoke as means of taking the individual into custody. Although the goal is the same—to save a life—the suicidologist might be concerned about the violation of trust—tempting the patient and then grabbing him. An interesting question could be posed here: After prevailing on a suicidal individual to leave his or her perch and come down for some food or a cigarette, how many suicidologists would permit the victim to return to the ledge or the edge of a bridge?

Workshop No. 9

Problem: A member of your women's club, whom you know well and see socially from time to time, has taken an overdose of sleeping pills. She was treated in the hospital emergency room and released. You have heard that the act was precipitated by her husband's unfaithfulness, but you don't know if that is true. You want to help, but you don't want to embarrass her. How would you evaluate the seriousness of the situation and what would you do about it?

This is a delicate situation. Many people are sensitive and loath to discuss intimate problems even with close friends. It might be unwise for a friend to revive and reactivate the situation that had already resulted in a suicidal attempt.

The friend should concentrate on her concern and on her willingness to be helpful. Her main effort should be on motivating the patient to seek consultation with a therapist. Emphasis should be placed on the fact that professionals see such problems frequently and can help to resolve such issues.

If in the course of conversation this woman does confide in her friend and appears more anxious and perturbed afterwards, she may reactivate if she is left alone. A member of the family or a responsible friend should stay with her, and, in the meanwhile, arrangements should be made for her to be seen by a professional. A situation such as this cannot be modified quickly by a simple cathartic approach, and even if she professes to feel better after having abreacted, the possibility of another suicidal attempt or gesture is present.

Although society has become more permissive, unfaithfulness in a spouse can provoke emotional turmoil and upheaval. However, this does not justify taking one's life. It should, therefore, be tactfully suggested that even if this woman feels better, her problems remain unresolved. All too frequently a friend may accept the rationale for a suicidal attempt at face value—in this case, that the husband's unfaithfulness precipitated the act. The story of infidelity could be a distortion or hearsay, and it may even be conceivable that the woman is defending herself against her own erotic feelings by projection. The friend should be extremely careful not to support or reinforce suspicions and hearsay but should, rather, insist that further clarification under objective auspices be sought. It would, therefore, be wiser for the friend to address herself to the problem of whether this woman was self-destructive rather than to the unfaithfulness aspects.

Since the woman was treated in a hospital emergency room and released, some discreet inquiries might be made as to the policy and conduct of emergency room personnel in that hospital with regards to suicide and crisis prevention. Again, it is easy to be presumptuous. Although it is conceivable that she was not fully evaluated in terms of suicidality, it may also be that she was indeed seen by a professional and arrangements were made for therapy but that she had refused treatment suggestions, signed herself out, or could not be hospitalized on legal grounds.

Workshop No. 10

Problem: After a weekend at home, your college roommate slashes his wrists one night in the dormitory. The cut is not serious and he stopped the bleeding himself and applied a bandage. He laughs it off as a prank and asks you not to say anything about it. You know he has had serious fights with his father, who feels that his son is not "manly" and athletic enough. What would you do?

It is probably easier for a roommate who has also been a confidant to guide an individual into treatment in such a situation than it would be for a casual friend who stops by. The roommate should quietly confront his friend, "No one slashes his wrists as a joke. You're selling me short and you're selling yourself short by telling me a story like that. I know you've been having trouble at home and that you've just come back from a weekend there. I know you trust me because you've discussed problems you have at home with me before. I know how unhappy you are. Now tell me what has been going on."

The friend may refuse to discuss the situation, or he may bring up some of the precipitating events. However, none of the manifest material that he could bring up would justify his ending his life. The roommate must therefore persist. "You've given me some idea of what went on, but what you did cannot be explained so easily. I think you ought to see someone who is trained to help you. I'm your friend, but right now you need a professional."

Hopefully, the roommate would bring up his despair or depression rather than react with bravado or silence. If the roommate continues to deny the desperate feelings which caused him to behave in this way or becomes angry, perhaps even furious, because his friend is persistent, then the counseling service should be contacted. Any clinician who heard this brief version would know that the events outlined would not provoke the young man to slash his wrist and would hypothesize the simple dynamics that the overpowering rage and wish to kill his father retroflexed.

WORKSHOP NO. 11

Problem: You are a professional counselor. A man is referred to you by police after a nearly lethal suicide attempt. He comes to you because he is afraid that the police will give him trouble if he doesn't. He apologizes for the incident, thanks you for your time, and says that he is all right now and that it won't happen again. How do you evaluate the danger and what do you do about it?

Individuals who come for evaluation and therapy under coercion are frequently uncooperative. They are likely to be uncommunicative, give as little information as possible, manifest hostility or even threatening behavior in order to cow the therapist, or be excessively polite in the hope that this will be interpreted as contrition. The patient may also be persuasive and attempt to con the therapist into going along with him and giving him a clean bill of health.

The first step is a complete and thorough evaluation. It is in no way different from that done for any patient who has made a serious suicide attempt. If the working alliance—the therapeutic alliance—has been established, the plan and goals for treatment should be established. If a patient continues to be uncooperative and insists that he is "all right now," then an attempt must be made to confront him with his underlying, unresolved problems. It should be stressed that uncovering these same problems can result in a reactivation of suicidal impulses. Confrontation should take the form of a logical explanation in which the therapist indicates that he will not be beguiled and will be firm, yet kind and considerate.

An attempt should be made to reduce the external pressure and the loss of autonomy suffered by the patient by being referred under police auspices. The therapist should make it clear that he is working not for the police but for the patient. If the patient is not highly lethal and does not require hospitalization, the counselor should persuade the patient to return for the three to six sessions of further evaluation that might establish an alliance and reinforce the relationship. During this time the patient might be offered the option of consulting with another professional. However, if all efforts fail, the seriousness of the situation should be brought to the attention of his family, his physician, or a suicide intervention center.

Workshop No. 12

Problem: You are a lawyer called upon by the widow of a client who committed suicide. She obviously is upset and talks about how shocked and lost the children are. She acts confused and doesn't seem to know what to do. What would you do?

The lawyer is faced with two problems—legal issues and a grief reaction. If he is emotionally constricted or interested only in performing legal functions, then he will not respond to this client's grief and depression. It would be very easy for him to rationalize this attitude, particularly if he is unable to perceive the magnitude of the impact that the suicide has had on the family of the deceased. He might be embarrassed and abashed because of his own guilt feelings about such matters. However, if he is a sensitive and thoughtful human being, he probably would not confine himself to legal matters but would encourage the widow to discuss her anguish. He could tell her that her feelings might be useful in shaping plans for the future and that by being made aware of what she has been experiencing he would be of greater help to her as an attorney.

He can encourage her to make use of the available community resources. On the other hand, if he perceives her as being helpless, he can, as her attorney, obtain her permission to contact individuals and agencies that might be responsive to her and to her family. Although he might not be aware of all the various resources, his professional contacts could easily identify them. He could also be a supportive and reassuring figure by calling his client periodically in conjunction with his legal services.

Workshop No. 13

Problem: A man who used to be in your car pool has withdrawn from other people ever since his wife committed suicide. He formerly was friendly and active, but now goes to work alone, eats alone, and has quit the company's bowling league. He has lost weight, looks tired and closes himself in his office for long periods of time. What can you do?

This man is in a similar situation to the woman described in Workshop No. 3. His grief and guilt have resulted in an existence on a psychic-death level. Such individuals may discourage intervention, and one must adopt a strategic approach in attempting to develop an interaction with them. The subject's superior at work could play an instrumental role through a kindly, low-key interaction—perhaps a short chat with him initially and then other conversations in which he could voice both his respect for him and his concern about his health. It is conceivable that this approach might produce some kind of interaction. The supervisor might persuade him to have a physical examination to check on his weight loss, and then inform the physician of the man's changed behavior. Relatives and significant others should be alerted. Despite his withdrawal, the people in his car pool should keep in touch with him either by calling him on the phone or dropping in on him periodically. They may receive a cool reception, but their persistence and their show of interest may help assuage his guilt. He requires some restitution. Befriending by the Samaritans could be helpful to such an individual.

People who have condemned themselves to a living death can be extremely difficult to approach, and it must be recognized that even the best efforts may not succeed. They have doomed themselves, sentenced themselves, and they refuse to consider any alternative to their self-imposed punishment. Patience and commitment are required to gain accessibility. Sometimes intervention is not effective until a suicidal attempt or a serious gesture has been made. Such self-punishment may partially alleviate guilt and increase receptivity to intervention measures.

Workshop No. 14

Problem: You are a school guidance counselor. A teenage student seems embarrassed and despondent after his father's suicide. His friends avoid him, his grades have dropped, and he may be jeopardizing his chance to go to college. What do you do?

Although much younger, the teenager is not unlike the man discussed in Workshop No. 13. He may or may not respond to the school counselor, but a poor initial reaction should not deter the counselor, who should make use of his authoritarian position to insist on evaluatory, preliminary sessions at frequent intervals. He may in this way gradually develop a relationship and provide some restitution by serving as a surrogate for the deceased parent. He might encourage the teenager to talk about his father in order to determine the quality of the relationship and the significance of the loss. If the counselor feels unequal to the task, he should use his influence to persuade the young man to go to a therapist, a suicide prevention center, or a clinic that offers extensive and intensive care. Members of the family should be enlisted. Often, they, too, are responding similarly, and family therapy might prove to be an extremely valuable expedient.

A Global Training Proposal for the Inculcation of Humanism

Views about education are widely divergent. There are those who adhere to the traditional curricula of the past. Ultraconservatives still hold to a rigid, strictly disciplined program that is well standardized and in some respects is a simulation of the ratio studiorum: Those who succeed scholastically would matriculate in universities, where they would prepare for careers in law, science, medicine, education, etc., or if they excel in mathematics they would go on to an institute of technology. This attitude conflicts with the views of more flexible educators who consider hobbies such as photography, ceramics, or almost any project that the student chooses to select as viable means of self-actualization and as a form of enrichment to the core curriculum. In recent years, some schools, not without the opposition of some parents, have added piecemeal courses in sex education, drug, and alcoholic dependence.

Those who are not prepared and in some instances are barely literate may be admitted to flexible universities or colleges which have adapted to the influx. These institutions use a variety of rationalizations for their open programs and have created a multitude of subdivisions with such euphemistic names as University X, School of Basic Studies, or College of Practical Arts and Letters which is, in fact, a secretarial school. Many of these schools, facaded by a university, teach high school subjects, without requirements for an area of concentration, and then award the graduate a degree which is just as meaningful as the previously earned high school diploma. Community colleges are even less expensive and more cooperative. In some states, every resident who has a high school diploma is entitled to admission to an institution of higher learning.

In spite of the educational pandemonium, every year thousands on all echelons and in every discipline manage to satisfy the established criteria and take their place in society, presumably ready to begin their careers.

Aside from formal technical training, the question also arises as to how well these graduates are prepared to interact maturely and humanistically. How many of them have learned what it means to value and to preserve their own lives and the lives of others? How many have developed an appreciation of the crucial import of those early years in character formation? How many have learned to tolerate their own limitations and the limitations of others? Above all else, how many appreciate the inexorable function of destiny and the ultimate termination of life itself? For that matter, how many physicians and health service providers have a stage-by-stage understanding of the vagaries of the life cycle from birth to death? The greatest deficiency in our educational system is the failure to provide courses in human relations that concentrate on the preservation of life and are taught from kindergarten on through college and beyond.

The training that is offered, if offered at all, is conspicuously vague, inconsistent, segmental and improvised. For example, the dangers of drug dependency may not be introduced until high school, when a considerable number of students may already be users. Sex education may be introduced when some members of the class are already pregnant or have venereal infections. Even in schools where psychology or human relations are taught, references to vital areas are fragmented, glossed over or omitted as inappropriate. "If you're interested in such matters, you can make it your major in college." In college, the answer is graduate school. But how many colleges or graduate schools offer comprehensive courses or seminars in suicidology, thanatology—death and dying—crisis intervention, etc.? The point is that an individual may obtain a doctorate in medicine, psychology, theology or education and, at best, barely have touched upon a panorama of universal issues that affect all mankind.

For all practical purposes, life begins with birth, and since it would be inappropriate to intrude on the fetus, teaching human relations and the value of life should be initiated as soon as minimal comprehension is evidenced. Parents inaugurate the process. "No, don't hit your little sister! You will hurt her and make her cry. Do you remember how it hurt when you fell and you cried? Why don't you tell me why you're so angry? You say you don't like her? But she's a tiny baby, and she was asleep. Why don't you like her? You were angry when I picked her up? Oh, then you're angry with me. Now sit down here beside me and tell me about it. You don't want me to pick her up. It makes you angry. Now I understand. But when you were very little, I picked you up too. I love you very much. Now let's play with your blocks."

This represents an early symbolic lesson in suicide prevention. The lines of communication are open, the child is encouraged to express affect and learns to interact with a loving, caring figure. Expressed in simple dynamic terms, the parent has interpreted primary process id feelings, is attempting to expand ego functions, and all the while is structuring a superego that will later spontaneously curb such behavior without great attendant conscious or unconscious guilt. Not once did the parent say, "You're a naughty boy. If I catch you near the crib, I'll spank you, and I'm going to tell your daddy about this. Now get out of my sight! Play in the next room."

If this process is continued and fostered by surrogates, teachers, from kindergarten on, the forces that are inherent for the preservation of life would be reinforced.

The teacher asks her class, "How many of you have a dog or a puppy? Raise your hands. What is your's puppy's name? What do you do with your puppy? Do you play with it? Do you feed it? Do you get angry with it?"

"Yes, when he runs away."

"Why did he run away?"

"I pulled his tail."

"Why?"

"Because I felt like it. He won't do what I tell him."

"Do you sometimes disobey and run away?"

"Yes, and my mummy punishes me."

"How do you feel?"

"It hurts."

"Did it hurt your puppy when you pulled his tail?"

"I kicked him, too. I think he was crying."

Others are asked to respond about their personal experiences in disobeying and in feeling hurt. Someone brings up the fact that being scared is more painful than being punished. There is no complete agreement. One child boasts that he is not scared, but others concede that being scared plays a large role when one is punished. Discussion centers about whether animals can be frightened and whether it hurts them as much as it hurts children. Also, the teacher asks for some suggestions for how to train animals to be obedient. Next, someone brings up taking a sick cat to a veterinarian. A little girl mentions that her kitten cut a paw and her mother stopped the bleeding with a Band-Aid. One child insists that it is good only for bleeding. Another mentions that it is also good when you bruise yourself. The teacher asks if everyone knows how to apply a Band-Aid. A child chimes in that hands must be washed first. Why? The subject of germs comes up, and that you can't see them. Someone mentions that even if a finger is bleeding, it should be washed first.

The next day the teacher brings in Band-Aids and shows how to use them and how to go about washing. There is further discussion of germs, that they can be seen but only under a microscope. Also, if the bleeding cannot be stopped, the Band-Aid won't help. The teacher says that the next step is to seek help from a mother or a teacher or any other person. A child mentions that it may be necessary to go to a doctor's office. Another shares his experience of having his toe sutured in an emergency room, deeply impressing the others. He confided that he was scared at first but that after a few minutes it didn't hurt.

On another level, the school nurse demonstrates the use of the instruments that a doctor may use in the course of an examination. Older children can be taught about the techniques used and the precautions taken in dealing with simple emergencies. The emphasis from the beginning is on humanism—sharing, learning to be helpful and effective in difficult periods of someone else's life and, above all else, experiencing the gratification that can be derived from playing such a role.

A child in a class is seriously ill. What can be done to make him feel better? One of his best friends mentions that he's very interested in baseball, and someone suggests they could send him cards with pictures of baseball players. A few would like to call and speak with him. Others suggest writing him a letter telling him that they are sorry that he is ill. One child is not participating and brings up the fact that he doesn't care about his sick schoolmate. He is asked to tell why. "He punched me for nothing." The ill will is resolved when there is an admission that the punch was provoked—he offers to send a funny card.

On another level, a videotape depicts an angry scene between a boy and his father. The boy is forbidden to use his bicycle. In a rage, he sneaks out and rides off at top speed. He is hit by a car, and in the last scene is being placed in an ambulance. The discussion centers about what factors were contributory and whether rage and guilt might not have played a part in his self-destructive behavior. The class is asked to give some examples of similar behavior. Guilt and reflex anger as possible causes of accidents are explained in simple terms. The conditions under which people are prompted to hurt themselves or others are discussed.

In the primary grades, one teacher can incorporate this humanistic protocol in her regular classwork routine. Later, it should be carefully programmed. A number of teachers, a team, could participate, and if sufficient interest is demonstrated about a specific aspect, provisions should be made to invite experts to speak.

If traumata, injury to a fellow student, hospitalization, death of a student or bereavement in a student's family occur, priority should be given to discussion of such an event. There should be a sharing of feelings, an opportunity to express grief and exploration of those resources from within and from without that can provide sustenance and restitution for loss.

Some graduates of a program that incorporates humanism might still be semi-literate and poorly trained for their chosen careers, but they would all have acquired some basic guidelines for preserving and treasuring their own lives and the lives of others. Such a comprehensive program would serve to inform and sensitize countless young people and to develop in them an awareness and an openness that could be disseminated to their elders and to others.

Saward and Sorensen (1978) stated:

> The responsibility for the prevention of disease and disability through health education, improved life-style and environmental control permeates all aspects of society: the individual, the family, the school, the work place and every voluntary agency

and level of government. We believe that we can evaluate our collective sensibility to that responsibility without further medicalization of our society (p. 894).

In summary, the preservation of life theme would include a meaningful and dynamic overview of the life cycle and all of its stages from birth to death, carefully programmed to have meaningful impact on various age groups. Bodily illness, emotional stress and disorder, psychosomatic relationships and mental illness, as well as drug and alcohol dependence, sexual adjustment, delinquency—asocial and antisocial behavior—crisis prevention and suicide prevention, would constitute major foci on the art of living.

The presentation would be nontechnical but intertwined in a humanistic mosaic. Shneidman (1970, 1975) referred to the psycho-socio-dyadic existential state, and suggested that an understanding of this configuration is a prerequisite for effective intervention. This gestalt can be utilized in the interests of prevention through educative means.

The graduates of the program outlined above would not be expected to emerge as doctors, but as humanoids. Those who did emerge as doctors, mental health professionals or whatever discipline, would be in a better position to combine caring with empathic care.

CHAPTER 9

MANAGEMENT

Suicidologists and therapists are unlikely to see a patient immediately after a serious suicide attempt. They may see such people before the attempt or after medical measures have been instituted in the hospital emergency room. Ambulance personnel, policemen, firemen, lay people who have some knowledge of first aid, and physicians have the responsibility of keeping the victim alive immediately after a suicide attempt. This ordeal is seldom discussed in the suicidology literature, where the emphasis is on prevention and intervention—that is, recognizing the prodromal signs of the presuicide and arranging for assessment and treatment in the hope of averting a suicidal attempt.

When an obstetrician is asked for the best prophylaxis against pregnancy, his wry response is "abstinence." Suicidologists would affirm that the best way to preserve life is not to destroy it. However, Ross et al. (1971) estimated that 350,000 Americans make suicidal attempts every year and that this number is increasing steadily. Other, far higher estimates put the total in the millions (see Chapter 3). In the 15 to 30 age group, suicide is outnumbered only by accidents and homicides as the mode of death. Ross (1971) stated that in one representative month 144 suicidal patients were admitted to the emergency service at UCLA Hospital. Many had multiple admissions, and some repeaters had been admitted for the sixth or seventh time. This problem is not an isolated one and is shared by other large urban hospitals. At St. Elizabeth's Hospital, which has the

187

largest psychiatric unit in a general hospital in Boston, the demand for beds for attempted suicides is ever increasing. One can only surmise how many attempted suicides do not receive medical care. There may be no one available to call for an ambulance, or a family may shrug off a coma and unwittingly let the victim "sleep it off" to an eternal sleep.

A patient who is in therapy may call his therapist, or a friend or a relative may call the therapist to ask for advice subsequent to a suicide attempt or "accident." Offering such advice constitutes an acceptance of responsibility. The accuracy of information given by an anxious and frightened caller is questionable. A "few" pills may be two or 22. Two drinks may be 3 ounces or an undetermined amount, if the quantity was not measured. "Just some bleeding" may call for a pressure bandage. Drowsiness with confusion after ingestion of an unknown toxic substance may be a prodrome of coma. Some patients may have swallowed every drug in the medicine cabinet, and the relative who reports only the missing half-dozen Valium capsules is providing the therapist with misleading information. It is far better that a medical resident be sarcastic and exasperated after he has needlessly examined a patient than for the advice-giving therapist to receive a letter from an attorney announcing a law suit for negligence.

Recently, a man called and introduced himself, with an apologetic laugh, as the brother of a former patient. This man's adolescent son had returned earlier that evening and had gone upstairs immediately. Approximately a half-hour later, he was found fully dressed and sound asleep in his parents' bedroom. The father tried to awaken him and smelled beer on his breath. The parents decided to let him sleep for an hour, but then the mother became distressed when she could not awaken him. She called her husband, and together they failed to arouse him. Their best efforts resulted in a flicker of the son's eyelids. They called their physician, but he was unavailable. Next, they called the husband's brother, the former patient, and he suggested that some professional advice might be helpful. The father could not resist imparting the information that his somnolent son was an excellent student, did not smoke pot, and that this was probably the first time in his life that the boy was drunk. He was planning to let his son sleep on. Again he laughed nervously, "Kids do these things." But he was disturbed and apologized again for bothering a stranger. Then he paused. He was obviously worried and needed direction.

The advice was brief. "Call the police for an ambulance."

This man had the courtesy to call back the following evening. His son was still in the intensive-care respiratory unit after gastric lavage and endotrachial intubation. The gastric return had been analyzed and proved to contain Doriden, a sedative and sleeping medication that had been prescribed for the mother. The boy had ingested almost a full bottle. The empty bottle was found by the parents upon their return from the hospital. The young man had made a suicide attempt for reasons unknown; fortunately, his life was saved after some days of intensive care. (Doriden, the trade name for the generic drug glutethimide, carries even greater hazard and potential for lethality than the barbiturates. Davis and Cole (1975), highly regarded psychopharmacologists, see no reason for prescribing this medication since less expensive and safer drugs are equally effective. An overdose of Doriden can result in erratic fluctuations of consciousness, convulsions and coma.)

The reader might well inquire whether it is necessary to advise calling an ambulance for an adolescent who has had a few beers and returns safely home to sleep it off. The answer is simple. If you, a professional, are called by someone who is obviously distressed and appeals for help and advice, and if you do not have enough information or history about an individual who cannot be aroused after three attempts, and if you do not know the amount of ethanol that was consumed or whether some other drug may have been taken in conjunction with alcohol, then you are not in a position to offer any other advice.

Not unrelated to the preceding is the question that is frequently asked by students and others: How does one differentiate between a suicide gesture and an attempt? The answer is "guess." Although this answer may not be well received, it is important to stress that all too often gestures terminate lives and that the outcome can be the same for both. The gesture that is often regarded as a device or a bid for attention should be heeded and treated seriously.

First aid before the patient can be delivered to the emergency room is vital. However, clues to what has transpired must be discovered before effective action can be taken. If the individual had shot or stabbed himself, there would be bleeding and a knife or a gun nearby, and an attempt could be made to control the bleeding. If an unconscious person is found in a garage with the doors closed and the car motor running, carbon monoxide poisoning would be indicated and resuscitation measures could begin.

Most people survive a suicide attempt—others die. In any case, when one can identify the means and the locus of the self-inflicted injury, lifesaving measures can be initiated. There is some evidence that the availability of lethal means plays a role in how the suicide is attempted. Since we live in a drug culture and there is apparently an unlimited supply of drugs, most emergency rooms are plagued and deluged by people who have overdosed. These individuals may arrive at the hospital fully conscious or with varying degrees of consciousness. Some may be semi-stuporous, others may be comatose and still others dead. In many instances, perhaps in most instances, there is little or no information about the drug or drugs—the amount taken, or, in the case of a comatose patient, how much time has elapsed since ingestion. A comatose individual arriving unaccompanied, or accompanied by an obviously unreliable informant, provides little or no help to the physician. A relative who has brought along the empty bottle can be of immense help in providing a rational medical approach. If some medical history is available—i.e., previous cerebrovascular accident, severe hypertension, etc.—then treatment can be focalized. Otherwise it becomes necessary to rule out the numerous possibilities that may result in a loss of consciousness. If a careful physical examination does not yield any clues and a diagnosis cannot be established, the physician is quite likely to think in terms of an overdose and to take appropriate measures.

It is not unusual for a patient who is in treatment and makes a suicide attempt by taking an overdose to call the therapist after a change of heart. Sometimes a relative will call the therapist to ask what to do. The therapist should first instruct the caller to summon an ambulance, and then briefly attempt to determine what, how much, and when the drug was taken. The patient's status should be elicited, i.e., conscious/unconscious, cyanotic. If the therapist was the prescriber of the drug, he would be in a position to gauge how many tablets or capsules were in the patient's possession. If the patient is conscious, the therapist might suggest to the relative or friend that while waiting for the ambulance he attempt to give the patient an emetic and save the vomitus. Okun (1971) suggests that a lay person administer syrup of ipecac, found in many medicine cabinets, which induces vomiting through its effects on the medullary center. If this is not available, an attempt may be made to force emesis by stimulating the back of the throat and the soft palate. Emesis should never be attempted if the patient is in a coma or appears to be unconscious.

MEDICAL EMERGENCY CARE FOR DRUG OVERDOSE

The therapist should call the emergency room of the hospital to which the patient has been referred and give them whatever history and information are available about the patient. Identification of the drug or drugs the patient may have ingested is particularly valuable. This is the greatest help in the problem of treatment in the emergency room.

If the patient has ingested the barbiturates, glutethimide or other depressant drugs that act on the central nervous system, it is imperative to act quickly because of their rapid absorption. The first step is to rid the body of the toxic substances, regardless of what they may be. The next step is to treat the patient symptomatically in order to keep him alive. If the toxic substance has been identified, an antidote may be available. Okun (1971) noted that there are excellent antidotes for the narcotics but not for other drugs. A patient who has ingested other drugs may require extensive and ingenious improvisation in his medical treatment. If the patient has survived the preliminary intervention measures, intensive care is then required to contend with any drop in blood pressure and to maintain an open airway.

Many psychotherapists are unaware of the nightmarish events that occur when the patient is brought into the emergency room, and it might be instructive to provide a summary. The following account represents an abbreviated extrapolation from the guidelines set down by Dr. Ronald Okun (1971), who has established a protocol that has been successful in dealing with many patients who were overdosed and comatose.

Emetics are used only if the patient is fully awake, and apomorphine, which is more effective than ipecac, usually induces vomiting in five to 15 minutes. However, it should not be used if the patient has previously ingested a depressant to the central nervous system such as a barbiturate. Apomorphine may produce cardiac arrhythmia, and in that event appropriate steps must be taken. Activated charcoal acts an an absorbent, but there is a difference of opinion as to whether it can be bypassed in favor of gastric lavage. Although some physicians have felt that hypnotic sedatives and tranquilizers that had been ingested more than four hours previously were absorbed, Okun (1971) and others have found that even 24 hours after ingestion it is still possible to recover comparatively large quantities of the drugs.

If the drug has been identified, and classified with regards to its short- or long-term action, as, for example, in the case of a barbiturate, then diuresis or hemodialysis may be instituted. Alkalinization of the urine in conjunction with forced diuresis increases the clearance of the barbiturate. Adding Mannitol to the diuretic may further improve elimination. However, Okun warns that the large urinary output involved in massive diuresis can affect fluid and electrolyte balance. Insufficient fluid replacement may bring about dehydration and must be carefully attended to.

The treatment should be geared to the patient's condition, and any number of changes can ensue. Nonresponsive patients require modified or additional procedures. Treatment also depends a great deal on the depth of the coma. In deeply comatose drug-overdosed patients, the following regimen is utilized: After the initial evaluation and a thorough examination with special attention to vital signs, the patient is checked every 15 minutes to note changes that may have occurred. Oxygen is administered. A patent airway is maintained and, when indicated, endotracheal intubation is performed, a procedure best carried out by an anesthesiologist. When necessary, a tracheotomy is performed. Gastric lavage is instituted, and if productive, is repeated. A nasogastric tube is inserted following lavage, clamped for two hours, then unclamped and connected to low suction for another two hours. At this point, an enema is indicated. An electrocardiogram is followed by monitoring on the cardioscope. A complete blood count is done, and special tests are performed. Blood levels are checked for barbiturates, glutethimides, salicylates, etc., if the drug has not yet been identified. In the case of the barbiturates, it is important to determine the type—long- or short-lasting. Repeat tests may be necessary. A catheter may be inserted, and the urine measured for flow, pH, and specific gravity every hour.

The above is an abbreviated outline; any number of complications may occur that require modification and additional treatment. For example, the patient may remain hypotensive, or if the cardioscope indicates abnormalities, measures must be taken to stabilize the heart. Arrhythmias can result. Pulmonary problems may occur and recur. Shapiro (1971) has delineated conditions that require the services of a respiratory care specialist. The patient is turned every 60 minutes to minimize the danger of atelectasis and pneumonitis. If pulmonary edema occurs with oliguria, dialysis may be utilized.

Emergency room protocol and procedures may vary from hospital to hospital, region to region, and standards of management and care in a large metropolitan teaching hospital that is well-staffed may differ from those of a small rural hospital where emergency services must be improvised. Issues that are often debated relate to indications for emesis and lavage.

Freidin (1977), who is Director of the Primary Care Center in Boston City Hospital, noted that most toxic substances provoke spontaneous vomiting, but went on to state, "However, when there is a doubtful history, emesis should be induced if there are no contraindications (p. 8)." He listed the absolute contraindications as coma or stupor and evidence that caustic alkalis or corrosive acids, petroleum distillates and strychnine had been ingested. Freidin has found syrup of ipecac to be effective in about 60 percent of patients in 15 minutes. He mentioned that the length of time after ingestion beyond which emesis will be of little benefit is undetermined but suggested that "small but probably insignificant quantities of barbiturates can be recovered from gastric contents four hours after ingestion." However, Okun (1971) and others have recovered comparatively large quantities of the drug 24 hours after ingestion.

Freidin (1977) does not even mention apomorphine and reserves gastric lavage to those cases where vomiting cannot be induced or is contraindicated. Lavage is uncomfortable to the patient and may cause serious trauma and even apnea during the procedure. It does not completely empty the stomach, and the volume of fluid may force the drug beyond the pylorus. The major advantage of its use is that results are immediate.

There are, obviously, arguments for and against the use of emesis and/or lavage. Concern about charges of inadequate treatment and the possibility of litigation may motivate the physician or emergency room director to strictly adhere to those procedures that are most likely to conform to the accepted treatment in the hospital or region.

If the patient survives and regains consciousness, the psychotherapist is now in a position to make an assessment and decide what measures to take. In older, and even in some younger, patients medical sequelae may develop. Pulmonary, cardiac and neurological sequelae to suicidal attempts are not uncommon. Although younger patients who had been in good health may respond quickly and favorably, older people are often "washed out" after the ordeal.

When a patient is wheeled into the emergency room and the resident mutters, "Another OD," and his colleagues nod in agreement, their bewilderment and frustration are understandable. The suicide attempter is considered to be the cause of his own woes, and many doctors, consciously or unconsciously, feel that they are being imposed upon. There are so many people who are suffering through no fault of their own, and here the physician must make heroic efforts to save the life of an individual who does not value it. This is not to suggest that physicians do not give their full attention to and utilize all their skills in trying to save the lives of suicide attempters. They do. However, all too frequently they resent it.

Shneidman (1971c) refers to the physician's antipathy to such individuals as "The God damned syndrome," and he describes it as an attitude that is characterized by disdain, contempt and hostility. He illustrated this attitude when he quoted a frustrated young physician in the emergency room remarking, "I will show you where to cut the artery next time." Physicians who have had training in suicidology are much more likely to feel compassion for the patient and have some understanding of the torment and self-torture that are antecedents to the attempt to end one's life.

HOSPITALIZATION AS A DETERRENT TO SUICIDE

Management by hospitalization of presuicides and suicide attempters carries both positive and negative implications. Hospitalization is not a panacea. Clinicians who suggest or insist on hospitalization should have a clear rationale for such a decision. Although significant others may be influential in making the judgment, there are usually two parties involved—the therapist and the patient.

However, the determination whether or not to hospitalize is essentially the responsibility of the clinician, sometimes in conjunction with a consultant. If all or most patients who present only suicidal ideation or suicidal fantasies were to be hospitalized routinely, every neighborhood would require one or more hospitals. Although there are large variations and differences of opinion in interpreting guidelines for hospitalization, most clinicians have established criteria for this action. The author is in accord with Slawson (1971), who stated:

> As a general rule, I think that the patient should be hospitalized, unless there is certainty that other dispositions are safe; by safe I mean that they meet the patient's immediate need and show him that his message has gotten through and has been understood. Hospitalization need not necessarily be in a psychiatric hospital; most patients can be treated in a general hospital. The community standards for such care are increasing however, and hos-

pitals have been sued when patients commit suicide on their premises. For this reason, such things as a private duty nurse around the clock and some judicious care in handling the material aspects of the room, such as physical appliances, windows and drapery cords are essential (p. 451).

There are clinicians who may ignore or make exceptions to the guidelines by waiting, introducing another drug, increasing dosages, or relying on an illusory or nonexistent positive transference. The therapists who are awed by prominent patients or their families tend to procrastinate on hospitalization for fear of offending the family or because they are concerned that their competence may be doubted. A request for a consultation should be welcomed if the patient or the family questions the necessity for hospital intervention.

Some therapists are overly cautious because of inadequate training and experience, or a countertransference with an admixture of hostility that may be tinctured with considerable anxiety. Hospitalization offers them an honorable expedient, and they use it with minimum inducement. They may even disengage themselves from any further interaction with the patient at this point.

Presuicidal doctors are notoriously difficult to hospitalize. Aside from the fact that they can no longer deny their pathology, there is a serious threat that they will be recognized by colleagues and patients. When in this position, many request a referral to a hospital in a distant city where their chances of being recognized are slight. In the hospital, they may be aloof, critical, solitary, and uncooperative. They may refuse to interact with other patients or members of the staff whom they defensively perceive as inferior. The milieu for them is stifling, and every therapeutic maneuver is regarded with suspicion, questioned, and subverted. A superficially polite relationship with the therapist is maintained to secure a quick discharge. Such reluctant patients invariably promise to continue therapy when they are released from what is tantamount to an involuntary imprisonment.

Opinions about the indications for hospitalization, weekend or holiday passes, and discharge from the hospital are widely divergent. They range from no hospitalization to extensive, indefinite hospitalization. The statistics for reactivations and exacerbations that lead to a fatal outcome have been extremely high (Moss and Hamilton, 1957). Patients who are discharged remain vulnerable for three to four months. The questions arise as to whether such patients were prematurely discharged, or whether another suicide attempt is unrelated to the length of the period of hospitalization, or whether both early discharge and a latent persistent suicidality are synergistic.

The dynamically oriented therapist would be inclined to regard the length of hospitalization as secondary to making an assessment and setting the goal for reducing and diffusing lethality—in short, crisis intervention. If some restitution can be provided quickly, if the patient responds and collaborates, and if the controls improve, he may be ready for discharge after a relatively brief stay. This obviously cannot apply to all patients. Slawson (1971) suggested that 72 hours might be long enough to make a careful and effective evaluation.

One group of therapists is convinced that there are no indications for hospitalization and would advise against it at any cost. They argue that it does more harm than good and that an individual intent on killing himself will do so anyway, whether it be in or out of a hospital. This view is supported by others on medico-legal grounds, namely, that if the goal of therapy is to encourage freedom for making decisions, then the risk of suicide is justified (Terry, 1975; Cooper, 1975). Comstock (1977), who is a former president of the American Association of Suicidology and a proponent of the development of more sophisticated criteria for hospitalization, made the following observation:

> The possibility exists, although it has been relatively little explored, that hospitalization may increase the risk for later death rather than diminishing it (p. 25).

Comstock (1977) takes note of the wide variations in hospitalizations subsequent to a suicide attempt. In nonteaching hospitals in the United States and Great Britain, they range from 22 percent to 100 percent, with a majority of reports being 60 percent or higher.

She contrasts this with admissions to teaching hospitals, where the hospitalization rate is far lower and varies between 12 percent and 20 percent. She suggests that this large discrepancy may be accounted for on the basis of different standards of practice, although the availability of beds in a psychiatric unit may also be a factor.

Numerous studies are in accord that all suicide attempters should be hospitalized. Kessel (1965) mentions that it is customary in some parts of England to hospitalize all suicide attempters. Motto (1965), Bogard (1970), Paykel et al. (1974) are all in agreement with this precaution. In their studies, Bogard (1970) and Paykel et al. (1974) presented evidence that most of the suicide attempters who are not hospitalized and have been referred for ambulatory treatment never follow through. Motto's (1965) study indicated that the rate of suicide was greater for untreated suicide attempters than for those who had psychotherapy. Kirstein, Prusoff, Weissman and Dressler (1975) tend to agree that outpatient treatment may not be an adequate substitute for hospitalization, but they go on to bring up the following problems:

> . . . Of practical concern is the number of beds necessary to hospitalize all suicide attempters. Furthermore, a number of suicide attempters would be encouraged to identify with a sick, dependent role and look to hospitalization as an escape rather than try to cope with their conflicts. A third area of objection arises from the ethical and legal aspects of imposing hospitalization on a person who does not want it (p. 26) .

There are a number of practical considerations for developing criteria for hospitalization: (1) The criteria could be translated into operationalized rating assessments; (2) the quality of the evaluation process would be improved by focalization on significant variables; (3) patient care would be improved; (4) the assessment procedures would be more uniform; (5) there would be less reliance on "clinical judgment" that can sometimes be a mixture of intuition, ill-founded conjecture or surmise, and may be compounded with excessive apprehension or underestimation of the seriousness of lethality; and (6) it would satisfy the psychiatric utilization of a view with some answers predicated on operationalization of the rating assessment.

A study, with some of these objectives in mind, was conducted with a multidisciplinary team at Yale University by Kirstein, Prusoff, Weissman and Dressler (1975). Nine criteria for hospitalizing suicide attempters were formulated. These included (1) a well-defined plan for self-destruction; (2) a recent history of serious medical attempts; (3) suicidal ideation gestures or attempts related to a psychosis with a delusionary process; (4) the evolvement of suicide ideation into gestures; (5) a firm and rigid anticipation of hospitalization; (6) social isolation; (7) current evidence of a well-defined suicide attempt; (8) voicing persistent suicidal ideation without perceiving any other alternatives; and (9) disappointment with the inability to effect secondary gain as a result of their suicidal behavior accompanied by an inability to modify their behavior.

The four items judged to have the most relevance for hospitalization on the basis of multiple regression analysis were "suicidal risk, thought disorder, serious intent, and major medical effects . . ." (p. 24).

Comstock (1977) cited four criteria for hospitalization. In the first category were patients who failed to respond to crisis intervention and who could not be deterred from their intention to self-destruct. The next group were psychotic patients whose death wishes reflected delusional and hallucinatory states. The third category included "Patients with moderate to severe depression, especially where the dynamics of introjected rage, self-blame and intrapunitive thinking occur with or without vegetative signs of depression" (pp. 26-27). Comstock's fourth criterion covered patients who were unable to interact because of their pathology and therefore could not enter into a therapeutic alliance.

Kiev (1976) approached the problem by using cluster analysis based on a 56-item inventory of responses to life crises. He developed profiles of seven types of suicide attempters: Type 1, characterized by suicidal gesture; type 2, acute depression; type 3, passive-aggressive; type 4, anxiety reaction with interpersonal conflict; type 5, socially isolated; type 6, suicidal preoccupation; and type 7, chronic dysfunctional. Kiev considered that the type 2 patient, who fell into the acute depressive profile, represented high risk and hospitalization was warranted. He expressed reservations about the hospitalization of the other profiles. He felt that type 1, the suicidal gesture patient, need not be hospitalized and that type 3, the passive-aggressive, was not likely to continue with treatment but that a very brief hospitalization might be utilized in an attempt to initiate and establish a working therapeutic relationship. He considered the type 4, anxiety reaction with interpersonal conflict, and the type 5, socially isolated, to be patients unlikely to benefit appreciably from hospitalization. He recommended long-term ambulatory treatment as best suited to the type 5 category. For type 6, the suicidal preoccupation group, he was again inclined to feel that hospitalization was not indicated. For type 7, chronic dysfunctional, management by hospitalization was not well defined.

Cserr (1978), a medical director of a psychiatric hospital, suggests a pragmatic clinical approach. He considers that those who insist on hospitalization exclusively and those who insist on community care in all cases are involved in an unhealthy rivalry. He offers the following indications for hospitalization:

> I am not saying that every time a patient mentions suicide that a decision to hospitalize should be made immediately. Rather, hospitalization is indicated under the following circumstances: (1) If the origin of the impulse is not understood within the context of the patient's illness; (2) if suicidal behavior is likely, either as a regression or manipulation; (3) if other disorganizations are involved which could lead to self-destructive acting out (p. 1).

The emphasis on the deemphasis of hospitalization is reminiscent of a parable. A man of fabled wisdom was asked to adjudicate wide differences that had created a feud between two partners. The first man gave a lengthy, impassioned account of the grave injustices that had been perpetrated upon him. The wise man listened patiently and after a brief pause, nodded his head and told him that he was right. The partner, equally fluent, then proceeded with a series of refutations that demolished his adversary's story. The wise man paused again, nodded his head, and told him that he was right. A curious bystander, who had listened in fascination, had the temerity to enquire, "Please forgive my intrusion, oh learned sage, but how can they both be right?" Again, the wise man paused, looked thoughtfully at the bystander and nodded his head—"You're right, too."

On the one hand, the literature is replete with injunctions for hospitalization when high risk is manifest, and many studies indicate that even individuals who appear to be responding well and are no longer considered lethal can reactivate while away from the hospital on a pass, that people continue to be highly vulnerable for 90 days and longer after discharge from the hospital, and that suicide attempters who are not hospitalized are unlikely to seek treatment on an outpatient basis and are far more vulnerable than those attempters who are treated. On the other hand, there are those who regard lethality as a transient state and that once the volcanic proportions of lethality have been deactivated or reduced, the patient may still require treatment but not necessarily hospitalization. Shneidman (1975, and throughout his vast literary output) has reiterated that lethality, unlike perturbation, is comparatively short in its duration. If the purpose and goal of crisis intervention and even hospitalization are to effect a reduction of the immediate crisis—that is, a lessening or a remission of high suicidality—then the purpose has been accomplished. This transformation has taken and can take place and be effective in a therapist's office, an emergency room, or during a brief, 72-hour stay in a hospital.

The matter can be examined and explored in terms of our expectations of a hospital's functions. There are myths about hospitalization just as there are myths about suicide. The length of time spent in a hospital is not commensurable with the resolution of nuclear issues that provoked the individual to suicide. In addition to providing security, the hospital offers intensive psychotherapy, drugs, and electroconvulsive treatment, in conjunction with habilitative and rehabilitative resources. These may be of great benefit to some patients. Unfortunately, this is not true for all patients; there are those who benefit minimally and others who do not benefit at all.

There are also patients who perceive the hospital as a haven for regression and make every effort to remain indefinitely. The husband of one patient ruefully suggested that hospitals should erect condominiums and provide perpetual care for people like his wife. Whether hospitalization is for 72 hours or longer, it is at best a transitory state. The most extensive hospitalization does not provide assurance for future adjustment, and the vast majority of suicide attempters require continued psychotherapy after their discharge. The overuse and abuse of hospitalization have been reduced by the recent introduction of psychiatric utilization review committees which monitor the criteria for admission and for extended care. This has led to improved management. Naturally, longer periods of hospitalization are required to preclude premature discharge of high-risk patients.

THE USE OF MEDICATION IN THE TREATMENT OF SUICIDAL PATIENTS

Obviously, there are no drugs that are antidotal for suicide. There are, however, many drugs that have been used effectively to reduce the underlying psychopathology related to self-destruction. During the past quarter century, the introduction of pyschotropic drugs has inaugurated a new era for psychopharmacology. Modification of the molecular structure of existing medications has increased their potency, broadened their spectra, and decreased or eliminated side effects. Research into the synthesis of new drugs continues to be accelerated. Some drugs have even been combined in an attempt to bring about a synergistic effect. Triavil is a combination of amitriptyline (better known by its trade name, Elavil), a tryclic antidepressant, and perphenazine (trade name, Trilafon), a phenothiazine. Etrafon is another trade name for the same compound.

It is fascinating to note that some of the drugs that have proved to be most efficacious and enduring through the past two decades were discovered serendipitously. Chlorpromazine (Thorazine) was originally used by an innovative anesthesiologist to decrease autonomic nervous system responses to surgery. Its positive behavioral effect resulted in a trial use with schizophrenics in 1952. This drug, classified as a phenothiazine, has remained a valuable adjunct in the treatment of thought disorders (Davis and Cole, 1975).

Imipramine (a tricyclic antidepressant; trade name, Tofranil) was administered to schizophrenics to determine its antipsychotic properties. Although it failed in this regard, it was found to elevate mood and produce euphoria. It has since been prescribed as an antidepressant.

Cole and Davis (1975b) and Klerman and Hirschfeld (1978) consider the tricyclic drugs as the most effective in treating depression and the drugs of choice because of their wide range and the least risk of side effects. Klerman and Hirschfeld (1978) note:

> In general, for the patient with endogenous features, a trial on tricyclics is clearly indicated (p. 1405).

Slawson (1971) regards the tricyclic, imipramine (Tofranil), as a prototype antidepressant and found that one-third to one-half of selected patients benefit. Cole and Davis (1975b) estimate that 70 percent of depressed patients derive benefits from drugs.

Another class of drugs that have antidepressant effect, the monoamine oxidase inhibitors (MAO), resulted from clinical trials with iproniazid. This drug was known to have had a mood elevating and euphoric effect when administered to patients with tuberculosis. It was soon demonstrated that iproniazid inhibited the enzyme monoamine oxidase. Marplan, Nardil and Parnate are MAO inhibitors. Cole and Davis (1975b) suggested that this family of drugs acts much like aspirin in that it can have an antidepressive effect on depressive patients but will have little euphoric effect on normal subjects.

Psychotropic drugs are prescribed by psychiatrists, but any physician may use them, and there is evidence that internists, primary care physicians, family practitioners and others are prescribing a large range and variety of these drugs. Davis and Cole (1975) give some pause for reflection with the following statements:

A physician must be familiar with the side effects produced by the drugs he prescribes to his patients. Furthermore, in order to practice effectively, he must be acquainted with the side effects of all the psychotropic agents, since today these are some of the most frequently prescribed drugs. There is reasonable likelihood that many physicians will find themselves diagnosing and treating side effects produced by drugs prescribed by other doctors or taken on a patient's own initiative. Indeed, patients with puzzling psychotropic drug-induced side effects may present to general physicians, as well as to specialists of all kinds, from the anesthesiologist to the urologist, and will not always mention that they have been taking these drugs (p. 1933).

Some psychoanalysts, who are medically trained, elect not to prescribe drugs. If medication is indicated, they refer the patient either to a psychopharmacologist or to a psychiatric colleague who is experienced and knowledgeable in the area of psychopharmacology. The drug administrator sees the patient periodically and is in touch with the referring doctor who continues to treat the patient with psychotherapy. The nonmedical therapist does not prescribe drugs and uses this same protocol. Frequently, a referral may be initiated by a psychiatrist who prescribes drugs but does not wish to involve himself with a large psychotherapeutic project or effort. He may continue to serve as an administrator of medication but prefers to have psychotherapy performed by another clinician. Since the psychotherapist is more likely to have closer contact with the patient than does the drug administrator, he may be the first to notice the drug's effectiveness and any side effects. He may bring such observations to the administrator's attention, and he may also be in a position to suggest reductions in dosage or, in the case of negative responses, a change to another drug. For example, in the course of therapy he may elicit from a psychotic, depressed patient evidence of a bipolar component. A decision may then be made to give such a patient a trial on lithium carbonate.

Since so many patients who are referred, whether by a physician or a psychiatrist, are or have been on some drug regimen, a careful and detailed record should be made of the drug, the administrator, dosage, frequency of intake and quantity of drug that was prescribed, with specific inquiry about abuse and compliance. If the patient does not have this information, permission should be requested to obtain it.

Every physician is likely to have the *Physician's Desk Reference* (PDR), which contains generic and trade names of every drug that may be prescribed in the U.S. and includes indications, dosages, adverse reactions and hazards. It is updated yearly, and supplements are issued periodically to list changes and additions. Physicians refer to it as their Bible, and it should be in the possession of or available to every nonmedical therapist as well.

DRUGS, DOSAGES, DANGERS AND PRECAUTIONS

All drugs, regardless of their positive therapeutic effects, are potentially harmful and may be dangerous. At one time or another, all drugs have been misused or abused. Even sodium chloride, ordinary table salt, is known to raise blood pressure and may increase the risk of a cerebral accident in a hypertensive. All too many patients die from drugs, not just those purchased from pushers but also from medication legitimately prescribed by well-meaning physicians.

When drug therapy is indicated, this modality should be introduced in the context of a therapeutic interaction. It should not be administered coldly or indifferently. Nemiah (1975) noted:

> As a general rule, one should not institute a drug regimen until one has established a relationship with the patient, although on occasion the severity of the symptom may be an indication for the early use of medication. Many patients' symptoms will respond rapidly to psychotherapeutic techniques alone, and drugs should never be allowed to become a substitute for the relationship with the doctor. Indeed, the elevation of mood secondary to the action of medication will often make the patient more accessible to psychotherapy (p. 1263).

Although programmed research, adventitious discoveries and clinical progress have resulted in some very useful medications, the products are far from being universally effective, and there are patients who have been successively treated with almost every existing psychotropic drug; their hospital charts give the appearance of a drug inventory. The antipsychotics and antidepressants may alter or block physiologic functions with a galaxy of autonomic nervous system changes. Constipation, dry mouth, urinary retention, impotence and blurred vision are common. Davis and Cole (1975) note that extrapyramidal and central nervous system changes may occur, as well as endocrine, allergic, skin and eye responses. Reversing these changes is not always simple. When a patient presents in an emergency room with a parkinsonian syndrome these days, the physician would be wise to check for drug side effects.

The monoamine oxidase inhibitors made a rather dramatic debut when it was found that iproniazid use could lead to hepatic necrosis in some cases. Although the affected group was comparatively small, the mortality rate of those who developed liver disease was reported to be about 25 percent, and the drug was withdrawn. Very few instances of liver pathology have been linked to other MAO inhibitors. However, the MAO inhibitors do have their fair share of side effects. Such symptoms as nausea, vomiting, stiff neck and occipital headaches may be precursive to a hypertensive crisis that can cause intercranial bleeding in some patients. This has been ascribed to the effects of tyramine, which is present in well-ripened cheeses. Fava beans, epinephrine, amphetamine, ephedrine, yogurt, beer, wine, and chicken livers may also produce such an episode. It goes without saying that a physician who prescribes these drugs should warn the patient of the dangers. Some do so verbally, while others give a printed list of all the items and make sure that a reliable member of the family is cautioned and alerted to what may occur. Prompt treatment is indicated when the side effects appear.

It is small wonder that patients and their families often complain about pharmacotherapy. Even those who experience relatively minor side effects have been known to comment that the cure is worse than the disease. This is untrue and unrealistic. When a patient is schizophrenic, perhaps catatonic, or suffers from severe or even moderate depression that interferes with life and work, the value of psychotropic medication should not be underestimated. We must be mindful of risks and seek measures to reduce them. However, there is a risk factor in living, showering, crossing streets, eating (both at home and in restaurants), using salt and breathing polluted air. It therefore behooves us not to discard but, rather, to monitor and improve psychotropic agents. In the spirit of the times, the *New Yorker*, in the September 11, 1978, issue, contains a cartoon of a man who is carrying his head into a doctor's office. The doctor calmly surveys the head and matter of factly states in the caption, "My, my, Mr. Kessler. That certainly is a nasty side effect you've got there."

Secunda (1978), participating in a symposium at the 11th annual meeting of The American Association of Suicidologists, in New Orleans, discussed some of the serious problems and issues inherent in psychotropic drug treatment. Most of his admonitions and suggestions reflect and reiterate current attitudes in the field of psychopharmacology. Secunda's comments can be summarized as follows: A physician who prescribes antipsychotic and antidepressant drugs would be best off to limit himself to a few drugs in each classification (e.g., phenothiazines, tricyclics, MAO inhibitors, etc.), learn their pharmacological actions, dosages and side effects rather than to use a large variety of drugs with which he has only a nodding acquaintance. Large quantities of a drug should not be made available to the patient. Drug administration should be supervised, particularly when the patient is severely depressed or confused. A responsible relative can take charge of the drug and give the patient his daily allotment. Since noncompliance is frequent, it can be reduced by prescribing a full dose to be taken at bedtime. In this way, the patient is more likely to benefit with a good night's sleep and not have to repeat a lower dosage three or four times a day. Many studies have shown that patients forget or refuse to take their medication when daily dosage is divided. The antipyschotic and antidepressant drugs are longlasting and not absorbed all at once, therefore a full dose is usually not contraindicated. Although the physician may start off conservatively with a low dosage or use the low dosage as a trial, a poor response should not be construed as a failure. Often, increasing the dosage may produce the desired therapeutic effect. Conversely, starting off with a high-level dosage may produce side effects or poor results but these may be reversed by tailoring the dosage.

Although often done, prescribing a combination of drugs, such as contained in Triavil or Etrafon, may be unwise in some cases. Using an antidepressant such as Elavil at a relatively low dosage and combining this with a tranquilizing agent that merely reduces anxiety can have a paradoxical effect. The depressed patient may not be getting enough antidepressant effect from the Elavil, but the anxiety secondary to the depression may be somewhat diminished. This may give the illusion that the patient is better. However, the depression may reach greater proportions, and the danger of suicide may increase in some patients. In a severely depressed patient, it is wisest to target the medication to the depression.

The so-called "minor tranquilizers"—Miltown, Librium, Valium, Serax—have little or no effect on depressed states and are primarily useful for reducing anxiety. They are apparently more effective than the barbiturates and far less dangerous. With the exception of meprobamate (Miltown), no suicides have been attributed to taking the other minor tranquilizers that contain chlordiazepoxide and its analogues (Cole and Davis, 1975a). It cannot be stressed enough that alcohol potentiates most drugs, with a resultant synergistic interaction.

Another drug that is being used with varying degrees of success is lithium carbonate. Lithium carbonate is a salt, but it is not a replacement for a deficiency of lithium. It is now prescribed in mania, and it has been found to be effective when bipolarity exists, that is, when the patient gives evidence of both depressive and manic cycles. The drug has also been used for depression when there is a manic potential. Sometimes the use of the drug is even predicated on the fact that other members of the family have demonstrated episodes of mania or euphoria. Blood levels are required frequently when Lithium is prescribed. Its advantages are that it can serve a prophylactic function and prevent episodes of depression or diminish the impact of and take the edge off depressive episodes (Klerman and Hirschfeld, 1978) . Lithium should not be prescribed when there is an impairment of renal function or cardiovascular disease or, for that matter, for anyone who requires dietary restrictions or who is required to use diuretic drugs. Secunda (1978) and Cole and Davis (1975b) seem inclined to adopt a conservative wait and see attitude while further research is in progress.

Although a majority of patients subjected to drug therapy improve, it is unfortunate that very few improve immediately. With an optimal dosage, improvement may require two to three weeks. This is little help to a therapist with an acutely suicidal patient.

ELECTROCONVULSIVE THERAPY AND THE SUICIDAL PATIENT

There is no modality of psychiatric treatment that elicits such dread and apprehension as shock therapy, which is a misnomer for electroconvulsive therapy. Forty years after it was introduced, electroconvulsive therapy (ECT) still carries a stigma exceeded only by that associated with suicide. Furlong (1972) discussed the mythology of electroconvulsive therapy. Most psychiatrists who treat patients with both modalities—drugs and ECT—would probably agree that there are fewer complications and side effects from ECT than from the antidepressant drugs. There is no pain associated with ECT, and the only specific contraindication would be if the depressed patient had a brain tumor. Even patients with previous or recent myocardial infarctions and pregnant women have been successfully treated (Kalinowsky, 1975) .

It is current practice to treat the patient with antidepressant drugs first because bringing up the topic of ECT initially is much like planting a bomb. Even in the most severe depressions, depressions with marked agitation, and involutional melancholia, the patient and the family often reject the use of ECT as a first choice. Hospitalization and drugs are far more acceptable, and patients and their families often insist that there be no ECT. Although it would be more logical to interrupt a devastating depression with ECT and then prescribe drugs, most psychiatrists prefer not to offend the patient and the family and also do not wish to give the impression that they are overly eager to "rush" the patient into ECT. Kalinow-sky (1975) succinctly states, "There is one all important factor in favor of ECT: the danger of suicide" (p. 1974). This view is con-firmed by Klerman and Hirschfeld (1978) and others. Kalinowsky goes on to discuss the imminence of suicide as a definite indication for immediate ECT, particularly for patients who are ambulatory. He remarks that even in hospitals there may be some suicidal risk and the incidence may be higher than it was in the past due in part to the fact that hospital life has become less restrictive.

Kalinowsky (1975) makes some very persuasive arguments for ECT. He reiterates that there are no pathognomonic indicators of suicide and that patients who are on antidepressant medication may give the impression that their depression is comparatively mild and that they are, therefore, unlikely to take a suicidal course. He suggests that all psychiatrists have made serious misjudgments on this score, with the result that many seemingly improved patients have suffered a fatal outcome.

Other considerations for ECT revolve around prolonged suffering and economic hardship. The antidepressant drugs are rarely effec-tive immediately, and it therefore becomes necessary to wait the two to three weeks for improvement, which is not always forthcoming. Some patients require three to five weeks (Klerman and Hirschfeld, 1978). Such a long wait in the case of a suicidal patient represents a risk. Even after clinical improvement, when the patient is less de-pressed, reactivation may still ensue. In the meanwhile, considerable expense is incurred, and if the antidepressants fail and another course is adopted, then the time spent in the hospital was for naught. For the patient who seeks to return to work in order to maintain his family, ECT may be the most effective expedient.

The standard procedure for the administration of ECT is to apply electrodes to both hemispheres—bilateral stimulation. How-ever, a unilateral approach, where only the nondominant hemi-sphere is stimulated, has proved to be advantageous in that memory impairment and confusion can be reduced. Prior to ECT, the patient is carefully examined, and an electrocardiogram is done routinely. Patients are usually treated in the morning, before breakfast, so that there is no food in the stomach, and psychotropic drugs are withheld. The premedication is generally done by an anesthesiologist, who administers a short-acting barbiturate to anesthetize the patient, and then administers a muscle relaxant. These drugs can be given by injection or by the drip method. Curare, the muscle relaxant that was initially used to reduce the possibility of fractures when the patient convulsed, has been superseded by curare-like synthetics. Currently, the drug of choice is succinylcholine, which is safer. The muscle relaxant causes loss of the patellar and other reflexes. Electrical stimulation is initiated when the patient is paralyzed (Kalinowsky, 1975). The tonic and clonic phases simulate the grand mal of epilepsy, but without the dramatic convulsions of the latter. In order to determine whether the patient has responded to the electric stimulus, it is necessary to watch the feet. A slight plantar flexion verifies the tonic phase, and some ten seconds later a wiggling of a toe or some other motor response confirms the clonic phase. Another indicator of convulsion is gooseflesh. In the absence of these responses, it is unlikely that the patient has convulsed, and another treatment is indicated. These comparatively minor motor reactions are attributable to the muscle relaxant.

Following the treatment, the patient remains in an apneic state; oxygen is administered, and normal respiration is resumed. A short time later, the patient is ready to resume normal activity.

Slawson (1971) stated:

> The last factor is electric-convulsive therapy, which should always be considered as a possible form of treatment in the seriously depressed and suicidal patient. It is the treatment of choice for the actively suicidal patient. It is often ignored or forgotten because it is distasteful to staff, family, and patient. By and large this aversion is irrational and based on ignorance. Because electric-convulsive therapy is so effective (better than 85 percent good response in selected cases), it certainly deserves serious consideration (p. 452).

The word "selected" that Slawson uses has great significance with regards to this chapter. Psychotherapy, hospitalization, drug therapy, and ECT will not be helpful to every patient. For some patients, any or all of these forms of management could be ineffective, and yet for others they can be lifesaving. There are many patients who, despite their suicidality, lethality and plans for self-destruction, can and do enter into a therapeutic alliance without any medication, and respond. They cooperate in a psychotherapeutic approach, develop a transference, and ultimately work through their problems. There may be reactivations and exacerbations in the course of their treatment, but after a period of time such patients are able to make a reasonably good adjustment. There are, however, people whom one sees in a suicidal crisis who are highly unlikely to meet the prerequisites necessary to become involved in or to benefit from psychotherapy. They may be acutely psychotic; they may be suffering too much anguish to listen and too determined to follow through with their deadly course. Their mood fluctuations may be so large and erratic that their impulses ignite at the slightest provocation; also, their response to intrapsychic and external forces may be unpredictable. They may be dependent on alcohol or other drugs and unable to accept the dictates of reality, or they may be so rigid that they angrily refute the possibility that there could be an improvement by permitting another human being to participate in their lives. Individuals who are mute or smile in the face of their dilemma, regardless of their underlying psychopathology, whether they be schizophrenic, depressive or whatever, augur a poor prognosis by their negativism and denial. There are those who cry out for help but actively or passively negate intervention. Outpatient psychotherapy for them would have little or no impact, and their management requires custodial care, drugs or ECT. Although their active plans for self-destruction may be aborted temporarily, many refuse aftercare subsequent to hospitalization. Every effort must therefore be made to motivate and induce them to continue with treatment and not to regard a transient remission as a sign of resolution.

If the patient is not to be followed by the same therapist, it is good practice to introduce the next therapist while the patient is still hospitalized. In this way, a new therapeutic alliance and a positive transference may be effected, and feelings of anger over the loss of the first therapist can be contended with. It is conceivable that a considerable number of patients who are referred to another therapist for posthospital treatment harbor deep feelings of resentment and rejection. One often hears their bitter rationalization, "I didn't want to start all over again with someone else."

Another constructive move is to involve the family while the patient is still hospitalized. Informing and alerting the family about the myths, the prodromal signs and the need for continuation of treatment can be influential and serve as therapeutic reinforcement.

It is not possible to make an a priori determination about the management of an attempted suicide. This must be decided on an individual basis, with due consideration of the specific problems, the dynamics, the personality structure and the needs of the patient. Improvisation may be required. It is not unusual for a patient to run the gamut—to respond to psychotherapy initially and then regress, do well on drugs and then exacerbate, require hospitalization and ECT and then respond once again to medication and psychotherapy.

CHAPTER 10

CLINICAL STUDIES

PREAMBLE

There have been many complaints about the lack of information related to therapeutic management in suicidology. Some have contended that although primary, secondary and tertiary intervention are now familiar words, clinical implementation is still a vague area. This allegation has, in part, been answered by pointing out that the suicidal patient presents with such lability, or potential for lability, with a potentially lethal outcome, that the process is not unlike defusing an explosive. There may be more than one time-clock attached to the human explosive, and the process of defusing—treatment—may detonate a mine field and trigger off any number of catastrophic repercussions. However, a human being should not be compared to a bomb—a human being is much more complex and therefore far less predictable.

Psychotherapists are in the unenviable position of being forced to improvise. If one approach fails, they must be ready with another, and still yet another ad infinitum, until a disposition is effected. There is no time for theoretical consideration—or of how Freud, Stekel, Menninger, Alexander, Shneidman, Litman or Farberow would handle the situation.

Recently, during the lull that followed a dinner party, four psychotherapists adjourned to a side room with their cognac and cordials. A lone internist joined them. Everyone was tired but relaxed. After a few pleasantries, a psychiatrist who had the reputation of being quite erudite gained the attention of all with a terse announcement, "I saw an interesting patient today. Suicide. I've used this technique at least four times and it has always worked." It was shop talk but everyone looked up politely. "The problem is not unusual. A suicidal patient locks himself in a room and refuses to come out. What do you do?"

Everyone remained properly silent since it was obvious that the question was rhetorical.

"Early this morning I received a call from a woman whose husband had locked himself in the bathroom and refused to come out. I had seen this man a few times, and there were some suicidal vibes. My method was simple. I told her to knock on the door, tell him that I was on the line and that I wanted to speak with him. When he refused, I told her to knock on the door again and inform him that if he didn't come out immediately, I had instructed her to call the police; that they would break the door down, and that they could confine him in a hospital for observation. He came out at once, and although he was angry, he agreed to be seen. When he came into my office he was quiet, everything seemed to be under control. I know some of you will say that it's coercive, but it's worked for me. What do you think?"

There was a brief silence marked by a few sips, and then another therapist mentioned that he had used this same procedure. "I think my patient's wife waited too long. She estimated that her husband had locked himself in the bathroom for about a half-hour, but it might have been longer. When she asked him to come to the phone, he didn't answer. I told her to call the police. When they broke the door down, he was lying in the bathtub with wrists and throat slashed. He was dead by the time he arrived at the hospital."

After some reflection, another member of the group spoke up. "She called you too late, a half-hour too late. Maybe it would have been too late anyway. I've also had some experience with this kind of problem and I used a similar approach. I could hear the conversation. She told him that she had called me and that I was on the line, and he said, 'Fuck him.' Then he came out and spoke with me . . ."

"What happened?" the first, erudite psychiatrist asked.

"He picked up the phone and said, 'Doc, I'll see you later.'"

There was a pause.

"Did he see you later?" the erudite psychiatrist enquired.

"No . . . he told his wife he was going to dress and asked her to leave him alone. He walked into the bedroom, took a .38 Smith and Wesson from a drawer in the night table and fired it into the roof of his mouth."

"This man knew the trajectory," the internist marveled. "How did you get the details?"

"I did postvention with his wife. She was the dyadic figure and he hated her venomously. I treated her for a year—longer—and in the end I got half my fee."

"Why?"

"I had the thought that if she saw a lawyer and told him about my advice I'd be up the creek. Maybe if he wasn't pressured he would have sulked for a while, and all might have been well. Maybe I let him down. She was very guilty afterwards, very guilty. I think I saved her life but not his. I haven't heard from her for a while. She has a job, and she seems better, but I still have twinges and I'm still a little worried . . ."

The fourth therapist spoke up, "A few years ago, I had a female patient who locked the bedroom door on her husband, and we had good reason to feel that she might kill herself. When he called me, I told him to keep up a conversation with her, to stay at the door and to keep talking and that I would call the police. By the time the police arrived, she had already opened the door, and when he got rid of the police, they had sex. She refused to continue therapy, probably because I called the police, but her husband indicated that everything was okay. Perhaps I saved her life by having him keep talking to her until she saw the light. But she could have been dead by the time the police came. A razor blade was on her bedroom bureau."

There was a somber silence and a few deep sighs were audible. The internist broke in, "You shrinks are all too preoccupied with death. If you had to practice medicine, you'd starve. Talking of toilets, I had a patient who locked himself in, and his wife called me. She told me he'd been there for at least a full hour and he kept telling her to get the hell away. She wanted to know what to do. I told her to leave him alone and not bother him."

No one said a word.

"Aren't you going to ask why I gave her this advice?" the internist asked.

The erudite psychiatrist shook his head wearily. "We know. He was suffering from constipation and you did not wish to remove him from his throne."

There was no laughter and all dispersed quietly.

Perhaps suicidologists are sensitive about disclosing their clinical techniques and procedures because generalizations are rare, and universalities are nonexistent. What works well with one—or with six—may have no effect or a negative effect on the next patient who appears to have a similar problem. Although all psychotherapy carries heavy responsibility, the imminence and the factor of unpredictability that lurks behind the ambivalence of the suicide make it extremely difficult to be specific about therapeutic protocol. The patient's ambivalence provides some leverage, but it is complicated by unpredictability. Even the same patient may respond positively two or three times to a therapeutic maneuver, and yet the next time, for reasons that seem inexplicable, self-cessation can ensue. Therapists are not only reluctant but sometimes embarrassed to reveal some of the things that they did or said in order to prevene or intervene. Although this is not an apologia for the paucity of clinical material in treating the suicidal patient, it helps explain the lack of clearly demarcated routes, procedures or processes that possess those magic qualities that scientists esteem—namely, reliability and validity.

Suicidologists must bring up more clinical case material and accept the challenge to demonstrate the multitude of improvisations that may be useful in saving lives. Physicians do not hesitate to detail and to recount empirical and pragmatic measures, and there is no reason why psychotherapists should be inhibited.

THE CLINICIAN'S ROLE IN CRISIS INTERVENTION

Emergency situations create and foster confusion and chaos. Many years ago, Kurt Goldstein, a neurologist and psychiatrist, aptly described the course of initial mild anxiety on one end of the continuum that may expand gradually to the other end and erupt in catastrophic behavior. During World War II, it became routine to engage people sequestered in bomb shelters in specific tasks—rolling bandages, attending the wounded, even singing—so that everyone, young, old, or infirm, had a task and a role. The thesis was that if individuals know what they can do and do it, their structured behavior serves as a preventative or antidote for decompensation. Unstructured behavior is associated with catastrophic behavior.

In a crisis, the clinican must be able to impart to the patient and to others that his own role and his identity are well integrated and intact. The confidence that he generates and inspires must be based on reality grounds—namely, that he knows what he can do and that he can communicate with and teach the patient and significant others what they can do. This is neither omnipotence nor omniscience but, rather, a calculated way of transforming the crisis into a problem(s). The emergency is thus reduced to tangibles that can be sorted out, explored and, it is hoped, resolved. MacKinnon and Michels (1971) indicate that if the crisis is converted it enables the patient to make use of his own resources and his adaptive functions.

Unfortunately, this lucid technique does not always work, particularly if the patient is psychotic, deriving large secondary gain from his life-threatening stance, or is obstinate in his plan to end his life. The patient may respond briefly, but a few minutes or an hour later may realize that he had attempted to cope with and to resolve these same problems for years with no success. There can be a brief remission, then more ambivalence followed by reactivation. The clinician who senses that the outcome of his best "know what to do" techniques is equivocal would be well advised to reinforce them with hospitalization.

Wahl (1971) places considerable emphasis on the clinician's role as a magical ally. He teaches his residents the necessity of giving the patient the feeling of being involved in a very special and highly unique interaction. In a sense, he is suggesting that residents and, of course, suicidologists must provide restitution to the suicidal patient—warmth, sympathy, understanding and absolutely no disapproval or implication that the patient's character is defective. Wahl counsels, ". . . rather this is very much like working in a department store: the customer is always right" (p. 452).

One might say that Wahl is an advocate of regressing the patient to an oral level where the cardinal role of the therapist is to provide succor. He suggests that if the clinician lacks the ability to show warmth, deep involvement, dedication, and concern for the patient —the capacity to give and to love—he should learn to role-play it, to simulate. He goes on ". . . no single thing can save more lives in the course of your professional life than the ability to make the patient feel profoundly and immediately understood." Wahl, is, in fact, encouraging and developing a transference relationship concomitant with a therapeutic alliance. In short, the cry for help is answered by a loving, nonmoralistic figure who demonstrates both great interest and deep concern. At this point the focus is not on modifying behavior and identifying unconscious, intrapsychic factors, but rather on neutralizing the volatility that possessed or impelled the patient to act out. To quote Wahl (1971):

> The remedy for the passion of acting out of the suicidal person is dispassion and compassion. Explanation produces dispassion and diffuses the suicide by pointing out to him all the things that were going on, such as his legitimate but baffled rage, which underlay what he did. Do not deal with the secondary gains, which are wishes to get attention and interest. Indicate to the patient that his position is predominantly right. As I said, your task is to keep the patient alive. You can reform him later . . . (p. 453).

This approach lends itself to patients who have attempted or are on the verge of suicide. By playing the role of the magical ally, the therapist is a rescuer, a lifeguard, who knows what he can do and gives promise that he can teach the patient what to do, all the while laying the groundwork for a trusting and caring relationship in order to keep the patient alive.

Some clinicians might take issue with this approach and might object to simulating warmth and indicating that the patient's position is predominantly right. Magical allies, whether they be doctors or politicians, invariably have a lot of explaining to do when their mistatements and untruths ricochet later on. However, the proponents insist that all is fair in love and in the prevention of death.

Although every clinician has his own unique technique of developing rapport and an alliance that has served him well, it is nevertheless appropriate to review this matter. Treatment begins when the patient and therapist meet. The patient may not be disposed to shake hands or engage in pleasantries or amenities. However, even the most disturbed patient can detect a negative attitude. There is always an initial impression, even though many patients deny a recall of the first meeting. This initial impression can be vital for the future of the relationship and lifesaving for the suicidal patient.

Abrupt, curt, impassive, matter-of-fact, unctuous or sanctimonious behavior is contraindicated. The clinician should address the patient by surname, and it should be prefixed by Mr., Mrs., Miss or Ms. Only children or very young people should be called by their first names, and when in doubt with adolescents, the polite form should be used. Some doctors have double standards for private patients as against clinic patients. Others feel that in a crisis familiarity serves as a catalyst or that their authoritarian position entitles them to drop minor formalities. Many are jarred if the patient has the effrontery to treat the familiarity as an invitation and calls them by their first name.

The clinician should introduce him or herself, and should project a feeling of warmth rather than a cold or impersonal note. If the patient has been previously seen by another or others to whom his response was poor, there is all the more reason to create a positive interpersonal note.

The wisest procedure is to see the patient alone. The clinician should provide a soundproof office; there is nothing more unnerving than to sit in a waiting room and be exposed to audible or semi-audible conversation. It is virtually impossible to confide in a therapist under such conditions, particularly when the patient might wish to discuss confidential material and is afraid he can be overheard by a relative or friend in the waiting room. Although it is wisest to see the patient alone, if the patient is accompanied and is fearful, then it is advisable to begin with his companion present. After a few minutes, the patient may agree to speak with the therapist alone and can be assured that his companion will be called in later. In some instances the patient is initially seen alone but remains mute, and then the wisest approach is to call in the individual who accompanied the patient. If the patient begins to respond and does not require the presence of the escort, the other may be requested to wait outside. In the case of an incoherent, confused, psychotic patient, the only available information may come from the person who accompanied him. The individual who accompanied the patient should never be seen first. Such a person may be seen with the patient, but having a discussion with such an individual prior to seeing the patient has a destructive effect on rapport, alliance and transference. A companion who feels that it is necessary or essential to see the clinician should be given this opportunity after the patient has been seen and has given his permission.

The same protocol should be followed in the hospital. Patients should not be interviewed in a room that does not provide privacy. If the patient is in a double room, the other occupant should be politely asked to leave. If this is not possible or feasible, the interview should be held in another room or office that affords privacy. The scrupulous attention and sensitivity to the needs of others establish the clinician from the very beginning as a humanistic but structured person who demonstrates his concern and respect and merits confidence and trust. Many disturbed and confused psychotic patients are later able to recall the thoughtfulness extended to them. Those who are less perturbed are motivated to regain their self-esteem and to enter into the therapeutic alliance.

CLINICAL ILLUSTRATIONS

The following vignettes are intended to provide a representative picture of clinical management in the context of a frame of reference. There is also the attempt to include a variety of phases and stages of life-threatening behavior. It is important to recognize that, even if any number of clinicians use the same approach, outcomes would still differ. Both the patient and the therapist bring their personalities and their respective expectations and demands into the therapeutic interaction. There are many therapeutic techniques, and the examples cited here are intended to stimulate and encourage improvisation that is based on dynamic understanding. Some of the illustrations are lengthy and detailed, others are comparatively brief. One complete therapeutic account might require a volume. In accord with reality and with respect for the informed reader, outcomes are not restricted to fairy tale endings. Dialogue is close to verbatim and was taken from notes made after the sessions.

Insulation, Isolation and Alienation

The suicidal patient is often withdrawn and self-immersed. Attempts to initiate, foster or maintain relationships may have failed. Sometimes there has been a loss of meaningful and significant others. Grief, loneliness and inflexibility are invariably intertwined, with depressive affect; guilt, hopelessness and helplessness gradually engulf and inundate, with resulting despair; inertia, retardation, apathy and futility can bring about further regression. A meaningless vegetative existence ensues and becomes chronic. Life has lost all meaning and there is a longing for eternal peace. Even the smallest expenditure of effort is torture. There is no respite and no gratification. The zest for life is dissipated and the individual lives in a sea of ennui. The inexperienced, well-meaning others find themselves thwarted when their intervention efforts are met with disinterest, suspicion, distrust and rejection.

Such patients are not necessarily old, homeless or without families. Because they are turned off, they turn off others; they negate, nullify, subvert, sabotage until they exhaust the patience of significant others. At this point, they are completely isolated, alienated, insulated and ready to end their lives.

In a different category are those individuals who have always lived a solitary existence, craving for love and affection all the while. However, their character structure is such that they cannot display warmth, cannot reciprocate, and when they are loved and in the position to realize their fantasies, their small resources and their misperceptions and/or distortions make it impossible. They are then in a worse position because their fantasies brought them some measure of hope for attainability. The unconscious as well as the conscious recognition that they are incapable of loving unmasks the fraudulent fantasies. Denial may be impossible. The inability to feel and to show warmth is crippling, and if pyschopathological defenses prove inadequate, the archaic fury against a nongiving, dyadic figure of the past is turned inward to a destruction on the self.

Case 1: Mr. and Mrs. A

Mr. A, age 38, married two years, childless, was referred by a surgical resident who sutured him in the emergency room after a suicide attempt in which he slashed his wrists. The patient came for psychotherapy only because his wife insisted on it and accompanied him to three sessions.

Tall, thin, spectacled, skeletal in appearance, he was withdrawn, uncomfortable and sparse of speech. When he did speak or answer a question, his affect was flat. He tried to be polite, but there was a retarded aspect, and every guarded sentence required time to censor and a considerable effort in order to verbalize. His voice was often inaudible, and he gave the impression of a neatly attired wraith talking softly to himself, not intending to be heard by anyone. Even his misery was too valuable to share, too precious to disclose. Any relationship, and particularly an evaluation, might rob him of his nothingness, perhaps reveal that his emotional constriction was perpetual sentry duty over an empty vault.

History-taking required a number of sessions. The day prior to the suicide attempt, his wife had told him that she was fed up with him and was planning a divorce. Her reasons were clear and had been incessantly repeated for two years. He had been unable to consummate the marriage. She wished to have children, and there was no hope in sight. She denounced him for their loveless marriage, and for some months had stopped calling him by his first name, scornfully referring to him as "Mr. Faggot."

When she announced that she was leaving him, he felt immensely relieved. Now he could once again reexperience his lonely tranquility. She had berated him constantly and he described her as a "scold."

An attempt was made to reconstruct the events that led to his suicide attempt. On that fateful evening, his wife did not prepare supper, glared at him when he came home, and coldly told him she was going out with her sister-in-law, her best friend. He immediately darted into the bedroom, his usual practice when she had visitors; he was painfully shy. He heard the sister-in-law's greeting clearly. "Where is your boy?"

"Hiding. What did you expect?"

"Did you give him the news?" The rest of the conversation was in whispers but he overheard derisive laughter.

He sat on the bed for a while after they left but couldn't remember how long. He denied any thoughts, fantasies or the wish to kill himself, but in robot-like fashion he went to the kitchen, wrapped a glass in a dishtowel, broke the glass against the edge of the sink and cut both wrists. He sat down and watched the bleeding. He made no effort to stop it but dabbed at the wounds with the dishtowel. He had no idea when his wife would return or, for that matter, whether she would ever return. Sometimes she slept over at her sister-in-law's house. He was able to recall that the blood trickled slowly. He insisted he did not think about his wife, or about death, and that he was not in pain. He could not explain why he had not used a knife, but after a long silence merely stated that it had not occurred to him. He had no idea how much time elapsed before she returned, but it was later determined to be about two and a half hours.

When his wife came home, he appeared to be in a trance. She took the situation in stride, recognized that he was not at death's door, and after a makeshift wrapping of both his wrists with towels she called a cab. They lived no more than three or four blocks from a large metropolitan hospital.

His cuts were superficial, and the resident estimated that he had lost less than one unit of blood. Luckily he had not severed an artery, and the toughest job was probing for glass fragments before suturing. He was seen briefly by a psychiatric resident, who decided not to hospitalize him but suggested further outpatient evaluation. The surgical resident spoke to Mrs. A briefly but authoritatively before they left and instructed her not to leave her husband alone and to arrange for an appointment with a therapist as soon as possible.

In spite of Mr. A's reticence and hesitation, he answered questions in a logical and relevant manner. His sensorium was clear and he was well oriented. There were no delusions or hallucinations, no tangential thinking, and no bizarre behavior aside from the brief psychotic episode of the suicide attempt. His work history as a state civil service employee was good. He never missed work. A comment of approval was made about his excellent record, and for the first time he made eye to eye contact. There were no illnesses, other than childhood diseases, no surgery or accidents. Physical examination two years before, prior to his marriage, was negative. Again, he made eye to eye contact. During the session he did not express, nor was it possible to elicit, suicidal ideation, fantasies or plans. However, he was able to recall that during the past year he had fleeting thoughts of jumping out of his fourth floor apartment on two occasions, that this was frightening but had been quickly dismissed. He made the comment, "I don't really know how to commit suicide." Toward the end of the session he appeared less constricted, and his answers required less forethought. He agreed to further sessions. When the contract was mentioned, he assented, again with eye to eye contact.

The tentative diagnosis of personality disorder, schizoid type, with depressive features was later confirmed. The dyadic figure on the basis of the material elicited was his wife. He grudgingly agreed that she should be called in to discuss the situation.

Mrs. A had anticipated that she would be seen together with her husband, and she was upset when she was asked to wait, although she was assured that the therapist would speak with her later.

Mrs. A was a short, markedly obese woman with closely cropped hair made up in tiny wringlets that accentuated a large face marked with cystic acne. She seated herself without looking at her husband and stated matter-of-factly that she had no idea why her husband had attempted suicide. She paused briefly and then continued with a lucid account of two miserable and humiliating years of marriage that she punctuated by crying.

Mr. A's eyes were averted, and he said not one word in his defense. She loved him when she married him; he was kind and considerate. She worked, kept a neat home and catered to his every need. She worked in a civil service job as a typist, bought few clothes and her demands were small. She wanted him to show her some affection, some recognition for the many little things that she did to please him, and above all else, she wanted to have children. She was the oldest of eight children in her own family, and when she married at the age of 28, she hoped to have a family. She described him as "not being there." He was silent, and it was impossible for her to carry on any dialogue with him. He ignored her, and any attempts to develop closeness proved futile. When their marriage could not be consummated, she went to see an obstetrician who suggested that Mr. A be seen by a urologist. He refused at first until she threatened to leave him. This was after the sixth month of marriage. The examination was negative but the urologist suggested a sex therapist. Again, he refused to go, but she made the appointment and he accompanied her. A plan of treatment was outlined by the sex therapist based on a behavioral approach. They were given assignments for mutual pleasuring—encouraged to hug, kiss, and embrace in order to achieve some relaxation that could lead to the experience of warmth. It was all for naught. Throughout the entire marriage he had never kissed her on the lips. When she tried to kiss him, he withdrew; when she placed his hands on her breasts while they were in bed, he pulled away with the explanation that he was tired. Every seductive attempt on her part proved futile. He would go to bed, turn away and go to sleep.

She hadn't mentioned a word of her unhappiness to anyone other than her sister-in-law to whom she felt close and who became her confidant. They were Roman Catholic, and the sister-in-law suggested that she speak with her parish priest. The priest made a home visit and arranged an appointment for them to be seen by a colleague who did counseling. Mr. A refused, and she went to the first session alone. Another appointment was made, and again he refused to go. On her third visit with the priest-counselor, separation and divorce were discussed. It was explained to her that she would have no difficulty in obtaining a canonical divorce on the basis of the facts that the marriage had not been consummated and that he had no wish to procreate. Since she was depressed, she had continued to see the counselor on a weekly basis but terminated her contact with him about six months ago. She was becoming increasingly resolute about leaving her husband.

He kept his eyes averted while she was speaking and showed no emotion. Her voice became scornful. "Pull up your socks, they're hanging down to your ankles." He obeyed clumsily. Her voice rose. "Why did you do this? You don't love me, you don't care for me, you never take me out, and you never talk to me. You're an invisible man." She looked up at the therapist. "Do you know why he did it, Doctor?"

"Not fully, but he must have been very unhappy."

"Unhappy about my leaving? Isn't that what he wanted?" She appeared incredulous.

"Perhaps he needs you even though the marriage is unhappy."

Her mouth opened as if about to make a retort, but she remained quiet. There was a plaintive look in her eyes. Perhaps the statement about her being needed struck a chord. She wished to be wanted, and there was the impression that the hope for maintaining the marriage still lingered. She agreed to stay with him "for a while," and the next appointment was made.

She came with him for the next two sessions, and each time they were seen separately at first, and then conjointly. Mr. A haltingly provided additional material but invariably gave the impression that it was a huge effort. He was an only child, and his father, a construction worker, died after falling from a scaffold. Mr. A could not remember him except from pictures in the album. His mother never remarried and worked as a bookkeeper for a law firm. In addition to being a compulsive housekeeper, she also involved herself in politics since some members of the law firm were part-time elected officials. She was very pious and went to Mass every morning. She was cold, undemonstrative and very demanding of Mr. A during his childhood. She showed him no love and no warmth. He could never remember her kissing or hugging him. She was extremely critical, and everything that he did was subject to her review. His mother was vitriolic, taunted and teased him about his inadequacies. He had no memory of approval. From his account, she was the prototype of the schizophrenogenic mother.

He was sent to parochial school, and his mother hoped that he would have a call to make the church his vocation. He was clumsy, inept, had no friends, and apparently had great difficulty in keeping up with the others, both academically and in sports.

He referred to his mother as a "scold," just as he had described his wife. He admitted that he hated her, wished she was dead so that he could be adopted by another family.

He was a solitary child, and when it came time to become an altar boy, he proved to be unacceptable. He could not remember exactly why, but suspected it might have been due to the fact that he was frequently late. The Sisters of the school complained that he was nonresponsive, very quiet, and not making suitable progress. His conduct was excellent, but the other children made him a target and he was often embarrassed and bullied.

His mother did not hesitate to use corporal punishment for minor infractions, which were usually related to his poor conformance. He recalled periods of severe constipation and visits to the doctor about this problem. Although his mother did not administer enemas, she frequently dosed him with laxatives. He was enuretic until about four. He suffered from sleep disturbance during his grammar school days, and then later this turned to hypersomnia. He dreaded getting up in the morning, and his mother would awaken him with a tirade about his laziness and his inertia.

He had a difficult time of it in high school because his mother demanded that he choose a college preparatory course. Teachers advised her that he was not college material, but she insisted that he continue in spite of his poor grades. He was even more unhappy in high school than in grammer school, and he was emphatic about the fact that he had no friends. Mathematics and other required courses were incomprehensible. He was in terror of being asked to present material before the class. He recalled that two summers were spent in makeup work; also, his mother was called on one occasion, and it was suggested that he be kept back a year. She was enraged, and was so cajoling to the principal that he somehow managed to receive his diploma.

He had no interest in girls. To enable him to earn extra money, his mother arranged a job for him at the local supermarket, where he was assigned the task of stocking shelves and bagging.

After his graduation from high school, his mother, who had by then given up on his entering the priesthood, insisted that he go to college. Since he was not qualified for admission to a four-year college, she managed to enroll him at a community college where the prerequisites were minimal and for which he was eligible as a state resident. His marks were so poor that he withdrew to work full-time at the supermarket doing the same work that he had performed as a high school student.

He had no hobbies and no recreations. His only relief from the struggle of existing was daydreaming in the quiet of his room, often interrupted by his mother who came to check up on him and to belittle him. He was unable to give a clear account of his fantasies. It was doubtful as to whether he had read a single book in his life. When he was offered a better position with more responsibility at the supermarket, he felt overwhelmed and refused.

As a result of his mother's persistent efforts and her political ties, he was appointed and ultimately tenured as a clerk in state civil service. His mother had died suddenly about ten years previously after a brief hospitalization. He had never taken the trouble to ascertain the cause of her death but thought that it was either cancer or a heart attack. He demonstrated no overt signs of a grief reaction, and after his mother's death he rented a room close by from a widow, his mother's friend, where he resided for the eight years prior to his marriage.

During the conjoint portion of the third session, this premarital period of eight years came up in the discussion, and Mr. A made a rare spontaneous utterance. It was almost a whimsical whisper. "That was the happiest time. It was so good." He glanced up, frightened at the ecstatic slip.

For a minute or two Mrs. A was stunned and regarded him with hurt and bewilderment. "You were happiest before I married you?" Then it appeared that she was about to explode, but tears came to her eyes instead, and she quietly repeated, "You were happiest before I married you when you lived alone with that old lady?" Could it be that she had suddenly realized that it was she who had married him and that he had merely been a passive participant, an innocent bystander?

She sobbed with a heartrending little cry accompanied by hyperventilation. Then it ceased abruptly. "Now I know what to do." She made the remark slowly, calmly and emphatically.

The therapist sighed. The signal was all too loud and clear. The dyadic figure was transmitting a message that required careful exploration. Mr. A was invited to wait outside so that his wife could be seen alone, and the next patient was cancelled.

Mrs. A composed herself. When offered some Kleenex, she refused politely. "I don't need any. Besides, it won't help. I know what to do."

She was evasive at first and insisted that she now knew that she had to divorce her husband and that was what she meant by her remark. She wasn't angry with him anymore. She felt very sorry for him. He was basically a nice person. The therapist felt that this explanation was glib, contrived, and he continued to probe. Finally she admitted a plan for self-destruction. At first she refused to reveal it except "that it won't be as stupid as his. Mine will work." She was persuaded to be specific and after a lengthy silence mentioned that her plan was to go to the roof of her apartment building and jump.

She appeared somewhat relieved that the plan had been elicited and went on to discuss her predicament, with intermittent sobbing. She had felt demeaned all her life, and her mother in periodic fits of anger and disdain had told her that she would never be married, that no man would put up with her.

Mrs. A described her appearance as a child in great detail. She was short, obese, ungainly, and myopic, she couldn't see well without her glasses, which she abhorred, but she wore them only at work. Hirsutism and acne had their onset at adolescence. Also, she was maloccluded, and her classmates nicknamed her "Teeth" or "Teethy." She was the oldest child, and since puberty her mother had encouraged her, then cajoled her, to enter a novitiate and become a nun. After graduating from high school and working briefly for Blue Cross and an insurance company, she passed the typist exam for civil service, and it was there that she met her husband. She had never been out on a date before, but she perceived Mr. A as equally inadequate and attached herself to him tenaciously. His timidity and helplessness made him an easy target. She followed him everywhere relentlessly. She sat beside him in the lunch room, then brought sandwiches for both to avoid the lunch room. She invited him to the movies and offered to pay her own. After two years of this court-ship, she proposed, and although she was never really sure that he had accepted, they were married. She was fully conscious of what she had done. It was a desperate attempt on her part to attain a heterosexual status, and she had interpreted his sotto voce criticism that he had been snared—lassoed into the marriage—correctly.

She began to cry. It was the cry of a guilty, penitent little girl. "I shouldn't have done it to him, but I thought I had something to give him." This time she accepted the Kleenex. "What do I do now?"

"Let's examine your options."

"I can kill myself and the whole mess will be over."

"Mess?"

"I'm a mess. My marriage . . . is a mess . . . and life is a mess."

"Perhaps there's something that you can do about it. Have you considered treatment?"

She looked up with blurred eyes.

"You think that would help me?"

The "yes" was emphatic.

"I've thought of it for years. I've also thought of plastic surgery, contact lenses . . . getting rid of the hair on my face . . ."

"We both know how you feel about yourself. It is essential to do something about it now."

Her response was positive and it required little effort for her to realize that therapy was her best option. She gave her firm promise that she would not make a suicidal attempt. Since she had been in treatment before, it was suggested that she discuss the matter with her previous therapist and that she could resume with him. She said that she had called him after her husband's suicidal attempt and that he had suggested that she continue with conjoint therapy. Her rapport had been enhanced when he mentioned that he was a former student of and had been supervised by the therapist.

The next step was to insure a period of safety and stability before attempting to separate, to free them of their reciprocal psychic malignancy. Their marriage was a sham and attempts to maintain it could well invite tragedy for both.

Mr. A came back in and was told that his wife had also agreed to treatment. The discussion was then centered on their being alone in their apartment, and a suggestion was made that someone be with them for the next few days. Mrs. A felt sure that her sister-in-law would stay and that Mr. A could sleep on the sofa. He shifted uncomfortably. It was obvious that this arrangement didn't please him. It might even increase the risk for him. She sensed his discomfort. "I think that we can handle it alone." She turned to him. "I promise not to give you a hard time." He nodded.

Mr. A came to his next session alone for the first time. He mentioned that he felt better, but overtly he appeared tense. After a long silence, he asked, "Will my wife be all right? I mean, will you be able to help her?" This was answered affirmatively.

"Why are you so concerned?"

"I mean, will she be all right without me?"

The therapist tensed. "What do you mean?"

"If I left . . . left her . . . would she be all right?" He looked anxiously at the therapist.

"What is your plan?"

He hesitated for a moment. "I'm thinking of leaving her."

"Leaving her? How?"

"Moving out . . . finding another place to live."

The therapist sighed with relief. Mr. A's story unfolded. His wife had ceased harassing him, and he felt much better but realized it couldn't last—that he could never meet her needs and demands. Instead of her leaving him, it occurred to him that it would be easier if he left and she remained on in the apartment. His concern about her masked his wish for the therapist to assume responsibility for her welfare. He had even taken her hint of a previous session and had been to see his former land-lady. She was willing to take him back—apparently delighted to do so. He promised to continue to help pay for his wife's apartment—anything to get away from the constant humiliation. Also, he wished to terminate treatment. All he needed was peace and freedom from retribution on her part. The therapist sighed again; Mr. A was not suicidal and was in-genious enough to remove himself from the untenable situation.

When Mrs. A came for her session she matter-of-factly announced that her husband had already moved out of the apartment.

Mrs. A's analytically oriented treatment extended uneventfully for more than two years. There were transient periods of depression that were accompanied by self-destructive fantasies and ideation, but there was no acting-out and she adhered faithfully to the schedule and the goals that were set up. Her treatment was no different from that of any patient with such a personality configuration. Mrs. A was characterologically dis-turbed, with large pregenital components and some minor hysterical fea-tures. Her psychosexual development had not as yet achieved the status and defensive system of the hysteric. Her voracious orality was mani-fested by intense receptive needs, compounded by omnipotence and nar-cissism. Her early deprivations stimulated her to devour and usurp. Cumu-lative failures resulted in depressive episodes with paranoid overtones. Anal erotic and sadistic surges were clearly evident. She was amazed at the insights that emerged from this sector. Her cystic acne, her myopia, the malocclusion, her obesity and ugliness were all equated with mani-festations of anality. She unconsciously perceived herself as oozing with feces, and during one of her intermittent bouts with diarrhea, vaguely diagnosed as mucous colitis, she informed her puzzled gastroenterologist that she was not surprised because she was "so shitty." Her and her hus-band's confused identities made it impossible at first for her to even at-tempt to play out a meaningful heterosexual role.

Mrs. A's therapy was not intended to be a substitute for psychoanalysis, and she was not cured. Perhaps the term "cure" in the context of psycho-therapy—bring about a complete remodification of personality—is mis-leading and might more appropriately be applied to treatment of ham. However, fruitful and positive strides were made. Mrs. A initiated separa-tion and divorce proceedings with church sanction. She lost weight, changed her hairdo and her attire, adjusted to contact lenses, went to another dermatologist and was considering a dermabrassive procedure. She was promoted to secretarial status at work, became involved in evening courses and for the first time felt at ease interacting with peer figures. She joined a church-sponsored group for divorced people and began dating actively. Toward the termination of her treatment, she became engaged to a widower who was ten years her senior and a partner in a real estate business. She was highly gratified that her parents, particularly her mother, were impressed and pleased with her prospects for remarriage.

She reported an amusing event a few months before her treatment was concluded: In reading the marriage listings in the local paper, she noted that Mr. A had applied for a license to marry his landlady.

Case 2: Mrs. C

Mrs. C, aged 64, married 44 years, was referred by Dr. L, an internist whose office was in the same building. He had treated Mrs. C and her family for 30 years. According to Dr. L, Mrs. C had consulted him frequently for functional problems through the years, and he described her as a hysterical personality who required a good deal of reassurance. The past five years she had suffered from mild hypertension, and now she was not responding well. He had been treating her conservatively with a diuretic. The reason for the referral was a change in her personality, which he had at first considered to be postmenopausal, and a severe depression that had not yielded to minor tranquilizers. He also related the elevation of diastolic pressure to the considerable stress that she was encountering with her husband. Her latest complaint was precordial pain, and Dr. L had just done an EKG which proved to be negative. He had not ruled out angina. It was an early Saturday afternoon, and there was a note of urgency in his voice. She was outside in his waiting room after the examination, and he offered to come with her to the therapist's office to introduce her.

It became apparent immediately after the introduction why Dr. L was so concerned and why he wished to share the responsibility for this agitated, depressed woman. The next 90 minutes were painful for both the patient and the therapist. She found it extremely difficult to sit still, and she writhed with psychic agony, rubbing her hands and shifting her position constantly. She appeared gaunt, haggard and very troubled. Her greying hair was disheveled and looked uncombed. History-taking proved to be an ordeal since her mouth was dry and she wanted to leave. She had not wanted the consultation and had told Dr. L so, but he had been insistent, and she wished that he "hadn't dragged me here." Throughout the session she expressed deep concern that her husband would be very angry about the consultation. It became clear that she required his permission before she could take any course of action whatsoever. Every few minutes she repeated, "I have to go now. Please call a cab."

In spite of the lack of a therapeutic alliance, the following facts were ascertained. She was anorectic and had lost about 10 pounds over the past month; she was suffering from insomnia and chest pain. Medication that Dr. L had prescribed wasn't helping her. She was very vague about the onset of her depression. At first she stated it was about five years ago, then that it was 10 years ago, and finally that it may have started even before then. At first she thought it was related to the menopause, and her gynecologist had prescribed replacement hormonal medication. Subsequently she gained a good deal of weight and was feeling worse, so this medication was discontinued "years ago"—she was vague about time. She had been going progressively downhill, and at the present time she was at her lowest ebb. When asked about suicide, she remained silent. The question was repeated and again she remained silent. The question was repeated, and again she remained silent but made the comment "No one can help me. I belong in a garage." Her last comment was picked up immediately.

"What did you mean that you belong in a garage?"

She said nothing and stared blankly.

"I don't belong in the house anymore . . . I should be in the garage . . ."

It was a lame explanation.

"Do you intend to kill yourself in the garage?"

She began to cry but didn't answer. An attempt was made to discuss her relationship with her husband. All that could be ascertained was that he was a good man, was very successful in his business and had provided her "with every luxury." Surprisingly enough, she described him as very giving and very generous. They had three children; two sons, one in his early forties and one about 39, were involved in the father's business. A daughter in her mid-thirties was married and lived in another state. Her husband's behavior to her had changed, and again she was very vague about why or when, but thought it may have been about 15 years ago. She thought that it might have been related to her menopause. "He's a good man, but I think he hates me now. He's disgusted. The children have all gone along with him. They treat me as if I wasn't there . . . as if I was dead." .

She could not be prevailed upon to discuss changes in her children's attitudes in any detail. Hospitalization was brought up. She dismissed this by getting up and again made the comment, "I belong in the garage."

Her husband was contacted after she had been asked to remain in the waiting room, and he was both surprised and angry. He could not understand why Dr. L had not informed him about the consultation, and why it was carried out behind his back. The therapist stressed the seriousness of the situation, the danger of suicide and the need for immediate hospitalization. It was suggested that he drive over at once. He was abrupt and angrily ordered that a cab be called for his wife. The therapist insisted that she should not be sent home alone and that he should pick her up. He refused to do so because of his "back problem," but grudgingly agreed to come in on Monday to discuss the situation. He offered to send his older son to pick up Mrs. C. In view of his refusal to permit hospitalization, it was stressed that Mrs. C should not be left alone and that precautions should be taken against the possibility of self-destruction. Mr. C terminated the conversation with, "I suppose I owe it to Dr. L to come in to see you on Monday, but I can tell you that I know her a lot better than you do."

About 10 minutes later, her son, a stocky, balding middle-aged man took his mother's arm and escorted her out. An attempt to speak with him about the situation was met with the terse comment, "I'm in a hurry . . . I was there when you called, and my father will see you on Monday." He made it clear that picking up his mother was a chore and an imposition.

Mr. C arrived on Monday promptly at the appointed hour. He was a tall man in his mid-sixties, immaculately and expensively attired. He strode briskly into the room but showed no inclination to shake hands. He seated himself and abruptly inquired, "What is it that you have to tell me?"

Mrs. C's condition was discussed in terms of her depression, her agitation, her desperation, and the great lethal potential. The need for immediate hospitalization was emphasized. He glared at the therapist and glanced at his watch. "Is that what you called me down here for?" Needless to say, Mr. C possessed a unique, provocative quality that made him an ideal candidate for a negative countertransference.

"Dr. L asked me to see your wife immediately, and I felt that it was essential to speak with you. However, if you are not satisfied with my recommendations, I would strongly suggest getting another opinion. I thought that you might be able to cast more light on the situation so that something could be done to help your wife in this crisis."

He looked at his watch again. "I'm a busy man, and to cast more light on my wife's problems would probably cost me at least a quarter of a million dollars for my time. As far as her crisis is concerned, it started from the time that I first saw her. She has an eternal crisis. I called Dr. L after I spoke with you on the phone, and he insisted that I come in to see you. I respect him and didn't want to tell him to go to hell. That's why I'm here. Since I am here, for better or for worse, I'll give you just a little illumination." He spoke with a cold, controlled anger and proceeded to give the following account:

When he married his wife, she was a beautiful young girl who had many suitors. Her parents were extremely wealthy, and all-giving. They treated her like "a fragile princess." Since Mr. C was independently wealthy, and already managing his own father's business, his prospective father-in-law readily accepted him. Mrs. C was naive about sex, but her passion knew no bounds, that is, until she got into bed. Then she was frigid, and coital pain was so severe that a gynecologist was consulted subsequent to a passionate but sexless honeymoon. Her hymen was surgically perforated by the gynecologist in the hope that this would make sexual relations less frightening and less painful. This did not solve the problem. In addition to her inability to consummate the relationship, she showed no inclination to cook or involve herself in household chores. She was eventually prevailed upon to see her first psychiatrist, but after three months of treatment there was no improvement.

As Mr. C became increasingly engrossed in his bitter memories of the events of four decades, he forgot about the time. Although he was often circumstantial, his biting account was cogent and pertinent.

He paused for breath and then continued. When he had demanded an appointment with the psychiatrist, the latter was reluctant to meet him without his wife's being present but finally acceded. He recalled the interaction with the doctor vividly, and it had a familiar ring as he repeated the dialogue: "What is wrong with my wife?"

"She's still a little girl who has to learn to grow up."

"What's the disease called?"

"It's not really a disease—it's a functional disorder."

"I kept asking the bastard what it's called. I warned him I wouldn't pay him if he didn't tell me. He wrote it down on a pad and I kept it for years and then threw it out—'psychoneurosis.' I asked him why she screamed and he wrote underneath, 'dyspareunia and vaginismus.' What do you do about it? 'It requires long and intensive psychotherapy,'" he mimicked the pyschiatrist in a high falsetto. "Will making her pregnant help? 'In some cases maybe, but it is not recommended and not advisable. It could worsen her in other ways.'

"I decided to get rid of him, and since my wife didn't like him either because he didn't talk to her, it was no problem. Here I was, married to this beautiful girl—all my friends envied me—and she was driving me crazy. She would kiss me, caress me, put on her sexy clothes, take off her sexy clothes, and moo and coo like she was going to blow a fuse. I could play with her for an hour, masturbate her until she was hitting the roof—then all of a sudden she'd begin to scream." He mimicked again, "'You are hurting me. I'm dry. Please stop . . . please. I can't stand it anymore.' Then she'd cry like mad and I felt that I was a rapist.

"I loved her. I didn't want to divorce her—it would have been a disgrace. I thought about it for weeks, and finally I decided to make her pregnant. She liked to drink before dinner, so I mixed her a drink one night that would have put a horse to sleep. Even then she screamed—but that's how my older son was born. You met him. That's how the other two kids were born.

"You wanted information about her, and since I have to pay you for two visits anyway, I may as well get it off my chest. The first doctor was right; she has required long and intensive treatment ever since. Maybe 10 doctors, maybe 15, through the years. They were all highly recommended, and she thought they were all marvelous until they tried to get down to business with her. She bought new clothes for every pyschiatrist. It took her two hours to make up, even to go shopping for food. I had to take her. A dinner party took even longer. Every man she met turned her on. She loved to dance. I was jealous, and I gave her a hard time about that. But I figured she wouldn't screw anyone—I heard her screams every time I tried. Then I had a hard time getting it up. The bitch had made me impotent."

His voice became harsher. "She was a lousy housekeeper. She'd stay in bed till 11 or 12, and when she tried to cook a meal it tasted like crap. There were no dishwashers in those days, so I washed the dishes, and sometimes she wiped.

"When she became pregnant with my older son she went crazy. She had two or three doctors. She was in a hospital for a while then. I went to see her psychiatrist, and he told me she was still a little girl. The first one was right. She's still a little girl, and she will be one until she croaks. He advised me to hire a housekeeper, and I've had maids and housekeepers ever since. Did she tell you that we have one now? She never did a goddamn thing in the house. I'd be living in a shithouse without help.

"She never brought the kids up, except for buying clothes and toys—gifts. They all know her well. The boys are with me. My daughter married at 18, when she started college, and the first thing she did was to move to California. She comes home maybe twice a year, and when she calls, she calls me at the factory. None of them can stand their mother.

"About 10 or 15 years ago, she started off with the menopause crap. More doctors. As far as I'm concerned, her menopause started when she was born.

"I didn't divorce her. She had nowhere to go. I put up with her. We've had separate bedrooms for years.

"Her committing suicide makes me laugh. Every time she blows her nose, she sees a doctor. If she dies, it will be from x-rays. She has had x-rays of her stomach constantly. I like Dr. L because he stopped that. She'll kill everyone before she commits suicide. As for the garage—she hasn't had a car for at least eight years. I put my foot down there. She was having accidents at least twice a week. She doesn't have car keys. The only thing she can do in the garage is water her horse." He stood up; the session was over.

Four days later, on Friday at 4 a.m. there was a call from Dr. L at home. He had just completed the formality of signing Mrs. C's death certificate. She had taken her husband's car keys from his bureau while he was asleep, turned the motor on, and became asphyxiated by carbon monoxide. It was interesting that Mr. C had awakened, heard the motor running and found his wife in the garage. He did not call the police department or an ambulance; he called Dr. L, and it was Dr. L who called for the police, and he arrived while the medics were attempting to resuscitate her. He pronounced her dead. Mr. C was described as calm, and he had asked Dr. L if he could ascribe the cause of death to a heart attack while his wife was starting the car.

Every clinician conducts his own private inquest. What more could have been done to prevent this death? Did the therapist work hard enough to promote an alliance? Should the therapist have insisted that Dr. L, who had a relationship with Mrs. C, be present during the last phase of the introductory session to reinforce hospitalization? Should the younger son and the daughter in California have been alerted? Did Mr. C arrange to leave his car keys in such an accessible place? Why did he waste time in calling Dr. L instead of summoning an ambulance? Why did Dr. L wait so long to request a consultation? Would it have been helpful if the therapist had confronted Mr. C with his death wish toward his wife?

THE PROBLEM OF UNIDENTIFIED PSYCHOTIC AND ORGANIC STATES IN SUICIDAL ATTEMPTS

Patients who present after a suicidal attempt or during a suicidal crisis may prove difficult to evaluate at that time and are frequently diagnosed as depressed. This should be a tentative or preliminary diagnosis. The patient may well be depressed, but psychotic and/or organic features may be overlooked because of the imminence of a lethal outcome. The underlying syndrome may not be uncovered even after hospitalization until further studies, tests, the patient's behavior or the clinician's interaction and acumen serve to disclose and identify extensive pathology that may or may not be related to depression. Patients who have made repeated suicidal attempts are initially labeled as depressed, appear to respond, are discharged, often return after another attempt, and continue to be labeled as depressed. For many of these patients the depression masks a Pandora's box, and only when the dynamics become manifest is it possible to contend with their repetitive need to self-destruct. Because of the prevalence of depression among presuicides and suicide attempters, the link has been so firmly established that even experienced clinicians cling to their initial impression and may be reluctant to explore other possibilities. Old charts from the same or other hospitals often provide stale diganoses of a depressed state, and it is assumed that reenactments are corroborative of the initial diagnosis. The sensitive clinician would do well to make each session or interaction with the patient a new venture and not hesitate to make a differential diagnosis and reevaluate the patient.

Case 3: Mr. D

Mr. D was a 23-year-old college senior who was admitted after a suicide attempt and had ingested every drug he could lay his hands on. These medications had been prescribed for his parents and included nitroglycerine, digitalis, thyroid, hydrodiuril, Dalmane, Nembutal, and Valium— followed by a beer chaser.

He had made a suicide attempt three years previously with a barbiturate, and the diagnosis of depression had been made during a few days' stay at a community hospital. Outpatient treatment was recommended, and he was seen weekly for a few months and then monthly. For the past two years he had seen his therapist infrequently on a followup basis, estimated to be about a half a dozen times a year. His parents recalled that he suffered from episodic periods of depression that were touched off when he was subjected to stress. The father insisted that the first suicide attempt was an accident and theorized that the patient had wished to fall asleep, was confused, and took too many pills from the bottle. He was adamant in insisting that his son's problems were all due to "a drug kick that began when he was a sophomore in high school." Both parents had been ambivalent about treatment and felt that brief hospitalization had been sufficient. The father was a biochemist with a good knowledge of medical protocol, but he was very defensive about psychic disturbances and attempted to ascribe his son's predicament to upset and confusion resulting from pressure at college. He repeatedly brought up the negative physical findings, the negative neurological examination, the EEG and the CAT scan as conclusive evidence for his thesis.

Mr. D was seen by the therapist after his second suicidal attempt, and he was followed during hospitalization. The initial diagnosis made by the resident on admission was again the carry-over of "depressed state." The patient was withdrawn, sulky and uncooperative. In the first phase of treatment, he often pretended to be asleep to avoid interaction. He gave indication of apathy and psychomotor retardation. Sometimes he yawned for ten minutes to ward off questions and in this passive-aggressive manner indicated his pseudo indifference and disinterest. In short, he gave surface indications that he wished to be left alone. This behavior was not inconsistent with a depressed state; however, the therapist was inclined to include epilepsy and schizophrenia in a differential diagnosis.

Patience and persistence were rewarded by a therapeutic alliance and transference; but during the early void his mother, an obsessive-compulsive personality, was able to provide helpful data regarding his early life and developmental history that brought forth the matter of the differential diagnosis. He was hyperkinetic as a child—stubborn, negativistic —and was very difficult to socialize. Her attempts to socialize him resulted in temper tantrums that persisted to date. He made a poor adjustment in school. A pediatrician examined him repeatedly but found no evidence of minimal brain dysfunction. He hated school, was disobedient and was often aggressive with playmates. Complaints about his destructive behavior abounded; curtailing privileges and disciplinary action only led to more release of primary process affect. Other children refused to play with him because of his erratic bursts of fury. During adolescence, he was a loner, isolated from his peers. The mother stressed that parental demands were not harsh or overbearing, but the importance of school achievement had been emphasized. She seemed proud that some of her structure had rubbed off and that her son had been able to continue with school in spite of his difficulties.

During adolescence his hyperkinesis was manifested by constant activity—cycling, running, skiing—but rarely with others. Any interaction invariably led to aggressivity. His frustration-tolerance was extremely low, and he would blow up at the slightest provocation. His mother often found him in his room staring into space, daydreaming. When she suggested that he do his homework or a chore, he became frenzied and "tore his room apart." His grades were low and he was sent off to a prep school. On one occasion the school counselor voiced his concern and told the parents that the patient's abrupt personality changes—his violent behavior—made the counselor fearful that he might hurt other students or injure himself. He was involved in numerous accidents, and by age 18 every extremity and most of his ribs had been fractured. However, there had been no injuries to the skull.

The mother made an astute observation: Whenever she was solicitous, kind, loving or caring, he reciprocated. She considered him to be a very feeling person and that "he was basically a good boy." He was very dependent on her. However, after a loving interlude, he would suddenly become violent. She intuitively felt that the hostility was directed toward her, "but he would go off into a fit and wreck things in the house instead." Shortly thereafter he would quiet down, act dazed, find it difficult to believe that he had indeed been responsible for what had transpired, and would behave in a contrite manner with marked withdrawal. The mother commented, "At times like that he seemed to be in another world."

It was interesting to note that similar behavior occurred with a surrogate figure during his second hospitalization. He became attached to a nurse on the team that had been assigned to him. Erotic affect that he could not control surfaced, and he asked her if she had ever been raped. Then, after some wild laughter, he made an attempt to rampage. This was foiled, but he remained markedly excited, and in the middle of the night made another attempt to act out.

He had had no experience with girls whatsoever, and he made every effort to avoid them. Any sexual excitation in school and college mobilized overwhelming hostile impulses toward the female who had stimulated the upheaval. In this disorganized state he had three options: to destroy the female, to destroy objects that were associated with or valued by her, or to destroy himself. When his inadequate controls proved ineffective, he made use of the second alternative, but on at least two occasions he had used the third and attempted suicide.

His mother's expressed concern about her own safety was justified because prior to his most recent suicide attempt he become so menacing toward her that she barely had time to call the police. Meanwhile, he had gone back to option two, broken all the glassware in the living room, looked perplexed, began to sob uncontrollably, and ran up to his room. When his father arrived, they found him and their empty medicine bottles and the beer can on his night table. Finally they recognized the need for intervention.

In the matter of differential diagnosis, the therapist was impressed by the epileptoid outbursts of rage subsequent to the accumulation of erotic and aggressive urges. This explosive type of behavior was suggestive of an epileptic equivalent.

Another neurological examination, EEG, and a CAT scan were ordered, and the father was very pleased when the results proved to be negative and organicity could not be demonstrated. He now theorized that his son became very frightened when the police came, was afraid that charges would be made against him, and on this basis made a suicidal attempt. However, two days later a corrected report came in from the neurological service indicating that there were definite signs of temporary lobe pathology that had been overlooked on first reading. The patient was indeed epileptic.

In the course of treatment during his hospital stay, young Mr. D corroborated the second tentative diagnosis of schizophrenia beyond the slightest doubt. As he began to reveal himself, it was evident that he had been hallucinating and delusional for years. He carried on conversations with extraterrestrial people, had been on space ships, and even pointed out some of his sightings to the therapist from the hospital window. It seemed remarkable that he had managed to go undetected through college. Perhaps this is dubitable testimony to large universities, where many psychotics can remain undetected. He learned by rote but had not the remotest conception of what he was studying. He could not remember the names of his courses and had great difficulty in recalling the names of any of his professors. His thought disorder was replete with personalization, depersonalization and derealization. When the professor wrote something on the board, he often perceived this as a personal message directed at him that had derogatory implications, and he felt that this was done to confound or insult him. This even applied to equations in a math course. Every time he attempted to memorize an equation, he became consumed with anger. A number of times a day he would examine himself in front of a mirror and ask himself questions. "Is that you? You don't look like that. Who the hell are you?" He often awakened feeling that he was in another world, everything seemed strange and unbelievable. At such times he often screamed and responded to his milieu as to a nightmare. Only when his mother or a familiar voice answered was it possible for him to test reality.

His affect was markedly inappropriate, and while talking about some of his unearthly experiences or during periods of silence he would burst into wild laughter. It was a private joke that he could not share with anyone. Sometimes he pointed his finger toward the window while he was laughing; at other times the laughter would merge with feelings of depression, and his eyes filled up with tears for no apparent reason. In his early stay at the hospital, he would spend hours lying in bed—immobile, unresponsive and completely removed from reality. This alternated with periods of excitement and resulted in motoric manifestations. On one such occasion, he threatened to jump out of the window. Even in a brief conversation, his tangentiality was pronounced. The picture was one of schizophrenia with a mixture of simple, hebephrenic, paranoid and even catatonic features. When asked why he had attempted suicide, he let out a loud guffaw.

The patient responded well to a phenothiazine and was discharged after six weeks. He continued with psychotherapy twice weekly and then requested that the sessions be increased. However, the intensification of treatment at this time was deemed to be unwise and premature. The approach with him had been cautious and conservative. The emphasis was not on attempting to develop closeness, which might frighten him and reactivate his problems, but rather to enable him to develop a nonthreatening and understanding relationship, to enable him to test reality and to cope with the real world more effectively. Because of the antipsychotic medication, he no longer hallucinated, and the delusions and inappropriate affect had appreciably lessened. He graduated from college and is employed by a relative in a position where he is tucked away carrying out routinized office work. However, there are opportunities for him to advance. He is still unable to relate to women, lives at home, but tends to be less solitary and seems to be reaching out. His destructive behavior has ceased, and if he were evaluated at this point, one might regard him diagnostically as a personality disorder, schizoid type. He may be a candidate for a dynamic approach in the future.

Case 4: Mrs. E

Mrs. E, a 50-year-old nurse, had been hospitalized three times for depression. The first admission was precautionary, initiated by her threats to commit suicide. The second two were subsequent to suicidal attempts when she ingested large quantities of a minor tranquilizer. Although she was a nurse, she was apparently unaware that one cannot kill oneself with Valium alone. She had previously been diagnosed as a decompensated obsessive-compulsive. Much of her concern appeared to be localized about her 19-year-old daughter, who had numerous accidents, numerous boyfriends and was "living a fast life." Previous psychotherapy and antidepressant medication had failed to ameliorate Mrs. E's depression. Her psychiatrist felt that a new evaluation of the underlying forces might be helpful. Mrs. E was resistant and noncommunicative. She wanted "out" so that she could find a better way of destroying herself and saw no reason why she should continue to be hospitalized.

In spite of her reluctance to see another doctor, she yielded to persuasion and developed sufficient rapport to bring forth the following material in three sessions: She was divorced 20 years ago from an alcoholic husband who had been abusive, and he "dropped dead" the day the divorce was finalized. Since that time she had been involved with three men, and each one of them had died suddenly. In every case she had an argument, an altercation or misunderstanding with these men just prior to their deaths. There was no question that she considered herself a harbinger of death.

It also emerged that she felt that the dead could communicate with the living. When she closed her eyes while lying in bed, she went into a hypnogogic state and hallucinated. Her dead mother appeared most frequently and demanded that she join her. The patient would argue and sometimes plead with her mother not to make this demand. When she made a suicidal attempt, it was invariably due to a command that came from her mother, and at such times she felt compelled to obey. At other times she behaved like her mother and treated her daughter as her mother had treated her. She had taken care of her mother prior to the latter's death.

On one occasion she was stumbling down the hospital corridor and could barely stand up, and was escorted back to her room. She began to cry, scream and moan, with a galaxy of symptoms that simulated those of her mother, who died a lingering death due to cancer. At such times, she was particularly furious with her daughter for neglecting her. There were times when she was reasonable, but she would suddenly revert to psychotic behavior. When an old woman was admitted to the floor, the patient had a serious exacerbation and insisted that this woman was her mother, who had come back to haunt her.

During her relatively brief periods of remission, she became euphoric and mildly elated. At such times she was very helpful to the staff and supportive to some of the other patients. Her doctor and the staff considered her to have made improvement during such periods. However, her moods fluctuated, and when she became depressed she refused to leave her room even to go to the dining room to eat with the others.

Since she did not discuss the psychotic intervals and had been noncommittal beyond revealing a depressed state, her thought disorder had been concealed, not only through her early hospital stay but for many years. Even prior to her mother's death, she had been convinced it was possible to communicate with the dead.

The psychiatrist who had requested the consultation assumed a more active approach in addressing her psychotic problems, and her diagnosis was changed from a reactive depression to a schizo-affective disorder. She was discharged some two months later with a marked lessening of hallucinations and delusions. Her psychiatrist had strongly advised her to continue with treatment and medication. At this point she terminated with him, and about a month later he reported that he had received a letter of inquiry about her from a state hospital. It was his opinion that she was fighting all attempts to neutralize her psychotic defenses and her prognosis was poor. A long-term hospitalization for this woman appeared inevitable.

SUICIDAL ATTEMPTS DURING ACTIVE PSYCHOTHERAPY

Therapeutic alliance/transference has been stressed as essential to the intervention process. A good alliance may lead to transference; positive transference may contribute to the alliance. The combination of both in concert is desirable. Unfortunately, the patient, and sometimes the therapist, may be unable to effectuate conditions under which the interaction will have a therapeutic effect. The confused, psychotic patient, hallucinating and delusional, disorganized, and consumed with suspicion and rage, cannot be expected to meet requirements in short order. The transference may be fragmented and distorted. The therapist who is poorly trained may feel threatened. Even well-trained therapists who develop negative transferences or who fail to recognize an alliance or transference that appears to be positive on the surface may overlook or misinterpret the patient's motivation for a suicidal attempt.

A depressed therapist, who may be suicidal himself, is hardly capable of contending with a patient who is ensnared in the same web. A sensitive patient may pick up the prodromal lethal nuances expressed by the therapist and utilize them as a catalyst. Such a relationship is for all practical purposes a folie à deux. Under such conditions the therapist becomes a self-destructive partner, and the question arises as to who will make the attempt at suicide first. Perhaps this explains why there are so many reports of patients who commit suicide subsequent to the suicide of their therapists. It is a fact that being a member of the healing professions does not provide immunity against the vicissitudes of life.

The therapeutic alliance may be illusory; the patient may appear to be complying and may be overtly cooperative but is really playing for time in order to complete his self-destructive plan. Sometimes the therapist may be beguiled by the appearance of cooperative behavior and fail to recognize this stratagem. In some instances the therapeutic alliance may continue for an extended period, during which the patient maintains his ambivalence by adopting a wait-and-see attitude. The slightest provocation, such as the change of time for an appointment, the therapist's taking a vacation, the patient's misperception of the therapist's motives, or some stress from the milieu, could be enough to destroy the alliance. Such an unsteady alliance in conjunction with a shaky transference may continue for varying periods. Not infrequently the patient requires and/or demands that the therapist satisfy archaic needs and play out the role of the dyadic figure. Neither the patient nor the therapist may be fully aware that the seemingly apparent and impressive progress is a far cry from resolution.

The patient who has been provided with some restitution may still require prolonged supportive care, and there can be no criticism of the therapist who understands what is transpiring and offers supportive relationship therapy. However, sustained care need not necessarily be the function of a professional; a sympathetic Samaritan or volunteer might be equally effective. Physicians and lay people alike have often voiced their suspicions of a professional who employs a befriending approach that goes on for years and the patient appears to be very much the same—that is, he holds his own and maintains himself, but the deeper issues remain unresolved.

Case 5: Mr. L

Mr. L, a 33-year-old assistant professor of sociology, had been hospitalized after ingesting a massive overdose of a phenothiazine and a tricyclic drug and spending three days in the Intensive Care Respiratory Unit. The psychiatrist, Dr. S, a highly respected senior professional, requested a consultation to help determine what had brought about the suicidal action. The patient had been in treatment with him for about ten years, with a diagnosis of paranoid schizophrenia. During this period he was seen three to five times a week. Although there had been numerous crisis, he had responded to medication in combination with supportive and some insight therapy. The therapeutic alliance had been excellent; the patient was motivated, kept his appointments promptly, and was cooperative except for short regressions that were quickly ameliorated. His transference had been "positive," and although there were brief periods during which the patient was delusional and hallucinating and considered terminating therapy and going off to live with an older sister, the relationship was warm and trusting, and Dr. S felt that many significant problems had been worked through. The patient had never been in better shape, and Dr. S was puzzled by the suicide attempt.

When the patient entered therapy, he was 23 and had completed two years of college but had withdrawn because of his severe pathology. He had no friends, was not interested in his courses, and had no goals. Although he was independently wealthy, he worked for three years at the checkout counter of a large book store and lived alone. After a few years of therapy, he returned to college, but his first semester grades were so low that he was asked to leave. A year later, with more assurance, he completed his studies with excellent grades and went on to graduate work in sociology. He proved to be so promising that he was assigned to do some research prior to receiving his doctorate. Upon the award of his Ph.D., he was offered an assistant professorship and had accepted this appointment two weeks before his suicidal attempt. As a matter of fact, he had seen Dr. S a few hours prior to his attempt. He had told Dr. S that he was planning to spend the day at the university library to prepare lectures for the first semester, due to begin in two months.

Dr. S summarized the situation: "Here is a brilliant guy. He still showed paranoid tendencies, and he probably will for the rest of his life. But he was doing beautifully; his dissertation is being published as a book, he is respected by everyone he comes in contact with, he has a beautiful apartment, he's wealthy and doesn't have to depend on his salary and even has a few acquaintances now. Girls are out, but that's understandable and perhaps even that can be worked out eventually. I've never had a better relationship with a psychotic patient in 35 years. I could have hospitalized him a dozen times, but each time I was able to carry him through. If he were my own son, I couldn't have given him better treatment." The last sentence gave ample cause for an analyst's ear to perk up.

The patient was lying in his bed somnolent, with his eyes half-closed. He showed no response to the introduction, but after a few minutes of silence, he looked up. "What do you want?" His voice was hoarse, probably from the effects of tubal incubation.

"Dr. S asked me to see you, to talk with you."

He opened his eyes and glared, then sat up. "I've seen enough doctors. I'd rather be left alone." Then as an afterthought, "How do I know that Dr. S sent you? How do I know you're a doctor?" His hoarseness was tinged with some alarm, and he threw off the blanket and stood up. He was markedly overweight and looked older than his years.

"Show me your identification." He moved up closer and studied the picture on the therapist's identification badge. This did not satisfy him, and he searched the night table for his glasses. "Where did they hide them?" He walked over to the bureau and found them lying there. He again peered at the badge, sat down briefly on the bed and then slipped into a cotton robe.

"How do I know that you haven't been sent over by the university—and the FBI? How do I know that this isn't a torture house?" He was manifestly paranoid, his sensorium was cloudy and he was disoriented. Above all else, he was frightened and trembled as he asked questions that related to punishment and torture. He was reassured, Dr. S's name came up a few times, and he was assured that Dr. S would be in to see him and would continue to see him. "I hope he comes soon. I didn't know that they'd let him in this place. I'd like to see him as soon as possible." It was apparent he did indeed have warm feelings for and trust in Dr. S.

An attempt was made to determine the events preceding his suicide attempt, but his recall was poor. He remembered going to the university library, and there he heard voices discussing his imminent detention, arrest and persecution. Two members of the sociology faculty came into the room and then "they ran out . . . not to be seen with me." Reality testing pointed up his distortions. He felt that he had been encouraged to write a dissertation in a specific area in order to incriminate himself, and that he had received the doctorate and the faculty appointment in order to set him up as a target for persecution. He felt that the university, the government, and other groups had been keeping him under surveillance. He was convinced that his telephone had been tapped and had the phone removed from his apartment. People with hidden microphones were recording his every word. They were about to pounce on him just prior to his suicidal attempt.

It is testimony to the effectiveness of pharmacotherapy that the patient became much more reasonable and rational a short time after drug administration. His terror was markedly reduced. Dr. S had been in to see him and had reassured him that he was not in a torture chamber. No longer in a hospital johnny, he was dressed in trousers and a shirt. He mentioned Dr. S a few times and expressed his feelings of gratitude. "He's the best person in my life. He means well. He's always pushed me to do more things and to try to get ahead. . . ." His voice trailed off.

"He pushed you?"

The patient hesitated. "He never really pushed me, but I wouldn't have gone back to college if it hadn't been for him. He was always pleased when I did well. My mother always wanted me to go to college . . . to be educated and to get ahead in life."

As he talked, it became clear that Dr. S was equated with his mother and that his relationship with his mother was a very ambivalent one. He was the youngest child and the only boy. One sister, five years his senior, lived abroad, and his other sister, seven years older, lived in a neighboring state; both had gone to college. He had been an extremely solitary child and spent his time alone daydreaming and reading. His mother goaded him to become involved in sports and other activities. The mother was the central controlling figure in his life, and when he talked about her, his ambivalence was reflected by love and hostility. He was bitter about her nagging and her insistence on feeding him. Memories of the past came forth vividly, and he recalled that up until he was 12 or 13 she would spoon feed him and insist that he finish everything on his plate.

He reverted to Dr. S: "Dr. S told me I could speak to you in confidence. I told him years ago that I used to put on my mother's clothes. I guess I was a sissy. Did he tell you anything about that?"

In his early life, the patient had played a passive-aggressive role. He was very docile and was constantly fearful that he would be attacked by the other children at school or that the teacher would scold him. His peers badgered him because of his inability to interact with them or to participate in sports. His mother also pressured him to engage in sports, but she confused him because she was constantly concerned that he would hurt himself. He was not allowed to ride a bicycle or do some of the things that were consistent with being virile. He often felt that she wanted him to be a girl. As a result of the contradictions, he was in a double-bind; he couldn't be a girl and he felt too frightened to be a boy. He distorted the feedback from Dr. S to imply that he could legitimatize his dual identity.

His father was an ambitious, vain, wealthy industrialist, who demonstrated little interest in the family. His contacts with the patient were relatively infrequent. He found fault with his young son in every area and was verbally abusive. However, the patient could not remember that his father had ever inflicted any corporal punishment upon him. One of the few things he felt certain about was that he did not wish to emulate his father or to make him his model. Although his father never struck him, he was always fearful that if he were punished it would be dreadful, devastating, and deadly. The father died of a cerebral accident when the patient was a sophomore in high school, leaving the family a large fortune. The mother died of cancer three years later during his freshman year in college. The patient showed little grief reaction to their deaths.

After three sessions, it became clear that the patient's therapeutic alliance was fraudulent and that he pretended to be motivated in order to please Dr. S, just as he had reacted to his mother, and thus was able to maintain his feminine identification. In the transference, Dr. S was the mother surrogate, and although the patient was projecting, he attributed his scholastic success and attainment to Dr. S, just as he had previously done with his mother. Dr. S with his supportive effort had been extremely helpful, but the surface positive transference veiled and facaded hostile affect. The closer Mr. L came to assuming the responsibility for playing the male role, the greater the anger at Dr. S. The transference had shifted, and Dr. S became father, an arrogant bully who dictated a course that would lead to annihilation. At that point he felt betrayed; Dr. S had failed to transform him into a female and failed to provide him with a male identity. The disguised dual identity could no longer be maintained.

If this patient had been presented to a staff meeting prior to the attempted suicide, Dr. S would have been complimented for his skill in bringing about such a marked transformation. It was, however, manifest that therapy had made it increasingly impossible for Mr. L to regress and resort to archaic behavior now that he was an accredited college professor. In order to remove himself from a struggle in which he felt doomed, he chose his last resort—suicide.

Dr. S, a sophisticated clinician, found the consultation helpful. Psychotherapy with a paranoid schizophrenic represents an ordeal that cannot be ameliorated by the wave of a magic wand. He continued to treat Mr. L through his hospitalization but then decided to relinquish his commitment. At Dr. S's request, the consultant agreed to continue therapy with Mr. L. The patient was prepared for the transition for some weeks and entered into the relationship with a reasonably good rapport. There had been a remission of his delusions and hallucinations, although there was little doubt that he was still vulnerable. His warm feelings toward Dr. S were displaced, and soon he was attempting to use the same old tactics to acquire another protective mother.

The early sessions were designed to set the scene, and he would recount events in his early life in a circumstantial manner—events that he had reported before in his previous therapy. The foremost theme was his involvement with mother, and there was no doubt that she had given him conflicting signals. In his own words, "She wanted me to be a girl and to act like a boy." She curbed his autonomy effectively, except in scholarly pursuits. She was extremely proud of his grades, boasting to friends, relatives and neighbors about his intellectual prowess. She prodded him to go out and play with the other children but imposed a series of prohibitions that made this virtually impossible. Some of these memories were humorous, others were pathetic.

He regarded his father as a humbug, controlled by his wife and attempting to play an authoritarian role by assuming a pugnacious and ferocious stance; hurling dishes at the walls, throwing food on the floor, and describing fights with employees and competitors that the patient suspected were fictitious. As long as Mr. L could revive the past in dreams and fantasies and continue to relive it and to reenact it, he was able to maintain a measure of equilibrium.

In order to bring him into the present, Mr. L was encouraged to discuss his adult problems and activities. It soon became obvious that much of his day was spent in a series of obsessive-compulsive rituals that duplicated his early life. When he opened his eyes in the morning, he invariably glanced at the photograph of his deceased mother on the mantelpiece, and then proceeded to get ready for work just as he had been readied by her to go to school. His breakfast consisted of the same foods that she had prescribed, which he hated. He still hated the prune juice administered because of constipation and the cereal with milk that he was obliged to finish. The introject of his mother gave him directions. If there was the slightest drizzle, he had to put on his rubbers, and if he didn't put them on it was necessary for him to go back to his apartment and put them on to avoid punishment. He never showered, but a few nights a week he took a bath, just as she had dictated. He attempted to take showers but felt uncomfortable afterwards and was compelled to take the bath. A number of times he had considered drowning himself in the tub but had not mentioned this to Dr. S.

Travelling to school had always been an unhappy experience because he was afraid someone might accost or insult him. Since he felt powerless in a fight and any provocation would be extremely humiliating, he was in constant dread. Even as an adult he harbored the same fears; some adolescents might laugh at him, or some of his peers might talk about him in a derogatory or denigrating manner. He sighed with relief when he arrived at the university. Lunch time again brought forth the fear of a fantasied provocation. The slightest titter, laughter or whispered discussion was personalized. Delusions of reference persisted throughout the day. During psychotic episodes, the hissing of the radiator produced auditory hallucinations. The fantasies of being insulted and attacked would expose his lack of virility, but there was also great excitement because of the wish to be female. These same dynamics also applied to any closeness. A warm interaction or familiarity could have the same effect. He was, in fact, attempting to live or exist as a male with a secret female identity. However, when it became imperative to renounce the feminine identity and the attendant fantasies, he was reduced to helplessness. A conglomerate of sinister adversaries would now swoop down upon him, rape, torture and destroy him. His previous therapy had brought him to a level where he was forced to accept risks that he could not tolerate. His most recent exacerbation of paranoid schizophrenia, with delusions of being brutally tortured and murdered, revived the fantasied archaic antagonists that not even a Goliath could contend with.

When he tried to reinitiate his former therapeutic relationship, he was encouraged to reality test, examine options, and then make his own decision. For example, he had some transitory chest pain and he questioned whether he should see a physician, and if so, who. The alternatives were obvious. There was an infirmary at the university, and he could be seen there, or he could consult a physician whom he had seen periodically during his treatment with Dr. S. In order to get mother's blessing, he next wanted the therapist's opinion as to whether his pain was severe enough to require medical attention. This query was met by silence. His response to this was, "If you thought it was serious enough then you would tell me to go see a doctor." Again, silence. "Whenever I had pain, Dr. S always suggested that I see a doctor."

"Who has the pain?"

"Me."

"Who should decide whether you should see a doctor?"

He was silent and disgruntled, and looked at his watch.

In the next session he was less garrulous. The spontaneous anecdotal material did not come forth. After a few minutes, he noted that he was still having the chest pain but hadn't done anything about it yet. "I suppose you don't care."

"I do care, but what do you want me to do about it?"

He appeared a little puzzled. "The least you could do is to tell me to go see a doctor."

"Who has the pain?"

The dialogue continued for a while, but it became clearer to him that he must make the decision, take the small risk, and not use the therapist as a surrogate of mother.

The past was not excluded but was de-emphasized, and the effort was on utilizing it but not to reenact it or to dwell on it. For example, "The faculty is having a Christmas party and they've asked me to contribute. I don't intend to go, but I gave the money anyway so that they won't think I'm cheap. I remember a Christmas party that I had to go to when I was eight, and my mother got me all dressed up, and it was awful . . ."

"Sometimes it's difficult for an eight-year-old child to go to a party where he's afraid that he'll be uncomfortable. Let's get back to this party. You must know some of the people who will be there. Why don't you want to go *now?*"

Later in the dialogue, to avoid the implication of pressure, Mr. L was given the opportunity to discuss his options and rationale. "If I go, it means I'll have to drink."

"Drink what?"

"Liquor. I don't drink liquor. It makes me sick."

"Does everyone at the party have to drink liquor?"

"They think you're queer if you don't drink."

"Who are the people who will think you are queer if you don't drink liquor? Who can tell whether you are drinking liquor or ginger ale?"

Balint (1972) and Ornstein (1972) and others have used focal psychotherapy in a highly specific way. The analyst appreciates that the archaic problems are there but orients his therapy about the present. The past is taken into account, but the patient is not encouraged to develop an intense transference. It is a time-limited approach, and psychotic patients such as Mr. L are not ordinarily considered to be good candidates for this technique. However, this man was so involved with repeating the past and utilizing it as a rationale for not contending with the present in a realistic way that it was deemed expedient to utilize it.

An attempt was also made to establish a male model for Mr. L. He perceived all males as aggressive, dangerous, threatening and stupid, and the only interactions that he had with males were under structured conditions. He had no friends, only acquaintances. The only male he considered to be nonferocious, kind and thoughtful was Dr. S. Then, as an afterthought, "I suppose you, too, but . . . you are different . . . you are not helpful, but you are helpful at the same time." He smiled. "Every time I do something, you make sure that I'm the one who is doing it. After I leave I try to think of ways to blame you, but it ends up that I'm the one who is doing it."

Mr. L is learning to differentiate his former shallow alliance that was based on his passivity and his wish to please from his present more honest and open working alliance. He is beginning to recognize that he must make decisions for himself, even when such decisions might cause anxiety. He is now less likely to use projection and to blame the therapist. This is due to a more objective understanding of the therapeutic collaboration. There are some signs of an embryonic relationship with a male figure. He is better able to bring up current issues and to utilize new coping techniques that carry some risk. In the past it was impossible for him to express anger towards his therapist. Now he is increasingly able to voice disagreement and hostility without fear of retribution. His dreams are replete with repressed homosexual wishes and fantasies, but his struggles with homosexuality are far less disguised and he is able to talk about them more openly without a galaxy of regressive defenses. There is abundant evidence that his ego is stronger and more flexible. However, he appreciates the fact that his therapy is far from over. Although relationships with men are improved, he still finds it impossible to interact with females other than his sisters. Treatment is still in progress, and it is not inconceivable that unforseen variables may once again result in an exacerbation. It might be discrete to resort to the familiar "prognosis is guarded."

Similar approaches are probably used by numerous psychotherapists. This modality, which is a psychoanalytic variant, is not intended to serve as a model for treating paranoid schizophrenia.

Sub-intentioned Suicide

Case 6: Dr. F

Dr. F, a 55-year-old dental surgeon, married, with three children, was referred by a cardiologist who had been treating him for hypertension. It finally became necessary to use medication to control his blood pressure, but even with hypotensive drugs it still fluctuated markedly. The cardiologist, who was well aware of his great tension, finally succeeded in referring him for psychotherapy.

It was difficult for Dr. F to arrange for appointments because he started the day at 7 a.m. and often did not leave his office until 7 p.m. He did not stop for lunch and described his office as "a factory." He employed two assistants, four nurses, three secretaries and a bookkeeper. His practice was voluminous. In addition, he spent a few hours a week teaching at a dental school "for prestige purposes." His weekends were spent mountain climbing, motorcycling and long-distance swimming. "I live young." His most recent hobby was scuba diving, for which he had bought expensive equipment.

Dr. F made no bones about the fact that he was unhappily married. He had known his wife for about a month while he was in dental school, and in spite of parental objections, they were married by a justice of the peace. "My marriage was on the rocks from the beginning. I hardly see my wife and I'm rarely home. She doesn't bother me and I don't bother her, so I've left things as they are. I can go wherever I want and do whatever I please. As long as she's content, I'm leaving things as they are. I give her all the money she wants and it's more convenient to be married than to be divorced."

He spoke with a staccato pressure of speech and kept crossing and uncrossing his legs. He made it abundantly clear that he knew he was under stress and that his colleagues and his physician had repeatedly warned him to cut down. He found this impossible, with the explanation, "If patients are referred to you, and you refuse to see them immediately, you lose not only the patient but the referral source. I live high. I spend money like water, I'm too young to quit, and I just don't have enough money anyhow."

He did not feel that he required psychotherapy and anticipated that he would merely get a lecture on how to modify his life. He was obviously in a hurry to have the consultation over with, and every now and then he would ask, "Is there anything else that you want to know?" The invariable answer was, "Yes."

In the two sessions that this patient was seen, there was a veritable flow of self-destructive, acting-out behavior. He sometimes had relations with two, three, or more women in the course of a night. Prostitutes and mistresses galore proved to be an avocation that he hadn't mentioned when he talked about his hobbies. He included a wide variety of sexual orgies in his repertoire. His need to prove his virility was incredible. Since he felt assured that what he was saying was in confidence, he brought this material up with a euphoric pride. Who else could practice a profession, be exceptionally skillful and competent and yet at the same time be a Casanova incarnate? After work and sometimes during the late afternoon, he drank. He vaguely described his intake as six to ten drinks. He boasted that he was a habitue of the leading hotels in the city and that he could get a room "at the drop of a hat even if a convention was there." He was overweight but made no effort to take dietary precautions for his hypertension. He also confessed a penchant for gambling at Las Vegas, where his credit "was good." He estimated that he owed about $50,000, but showed little concern and was sure that he could pay it within the next two or three weeks, "before the bone-breakers get to me."

He demonstrated embarrassment only once, when he mentioned that he required gingivectomies because of poor dental hygiene. He obviously did not have enough time to brush his own teeth regularly.

He denied being depressed. With a straight face, he announced that it was impossible for him to find time for treatment because of his busy schedule. He was manifestly hypomanic and slowly destroying himself, insisting all the while that he was having a wonderful time.

The possibility of using lithium carbonate was considered, but his hypertension contraindicated its use.

Dr. F terminated after the evaluation but called for an appointment about three months later. He was depressed. During the intervening period, he had developed a contact tremor that interfered with his work. His physician had prescribed Inderal—propranalol hydrochloride—an adrenergic blocking agent. Dr. F was convinced that this drug, in combination with the hypotensive medications, was making him impotent. Parkinson's disease was excluded, and his physician suggested that since the tremor was on a psychogenic basis, psychotherapy might be helpful and that the Inderal might be dispensed with if the underlying psychic aspects that produced his tremor were reduced. This had motivated him to return.

This time he provided a more detailed history. He was an only child and was born nine years after his parents were married. His father, a dentist, was a tall, light-complexioned man, and his mother was also tall and fair, slim, with light auburn hair. He was short, dark, with black hair. Although he might have been younger, he recalled that at about 11 or 12 he strongly suspected that he was "different" and had been adopted, a suspicion that was belatedly confirmed by his parents. It was his mother who "made a speech about it," and his father had "piously" reiterated, "we both love you."

His mother adored him in his early childhood. His father, however, was kind but diffident. They were austere but not in concert, and they maintained a cool, proper relationship and never quarreled in his presence. He never saw any signs of warmth between them and could not recall them ever embracing or kissing, even on birthdays or other festive occasions.

After being told that he was adopted, he felt depressed and isolated, but in his sophomore year in high school be became actively involved with "a hip group" at the expense of his grades. He drank beer, then hard liquor, got drunk at parties and impregnated a girl. His parents were dismayed, but "my father managed to get me off the hook." The following year he was sent off to a prep school in another state. He recalled being furious with his father after being told of the adoption and feeling extremely uncomfortable with his mother, avoiding her whenever possible. Being sent away reinforced his feelings of rejection. These feelings had not changed for four decades.

Although his grades fluctuated at prep school, he was accepted by an Ivy League college, "not my father's alma mater," he noted with satisfaction.

The Second World War was in progress, and he enlisted after his sophomore year without consulting his parents. Again, they were furious. Their plans for his future had been carefully laid out. He was to be a dental surgeon, and his father had insisted that he enroll in a basic science program in college. His enlistment shocked them and thwarted their aspirations. He did not consider that it was the possibility of his death in combat that upset them. After accelerated basic training, he was assigned to an infantry unit and readied for shipment to the Pacific.

His account of the ensuing events was reminiscent of Dostoevsky's death commutation when an emissary of the Czar arrived as the firing squad was preparing for the execution. Dr. F, then just plain Private F, had assembled his possessions about to embark when he was ordered to report to his commanding officer. "F, I have just received orders that you are to report within 48 hours to the University School of Dentistry. You are not going with us. Good luck."

Private F stood dumbfounded; it was his father's alma mater. He must have arranged it somehow. In saying goodbye to his parents he had signed some papers, but he couldn't for the life of him recall an application to dental school. He burst into tears. The CO was touched, put his arm around F's shoulder and gave him a hug. "We need dentists, live dentists. Good luck, son."

He laughed as he told the story—and then he sobbed, "I hated my father. I wanted to die. God knows what he did to save me; I only had two years of basic science. I hated him even more afterwards. He kept me from going with my buddies. Now I had to live up to his expectations. Look at me—I'm a drunken, screwed-up louse—sick and broke." This was the first time that his ego-syntonic state was not in evidence. Until then he had felt that his acting-out was justified and saw nothing wrong with his behavior.

During this three-month depressive period, Dr. F had shown little inclination to act-out—he couldn't. However, he was able to work, but at a reduced pace. He was less effective but more reflective. A few times he resorted to self-destructive tactics by failing to take his medication, and he became even more alarmed when his impotence persisted. He found it difficult to accept the fact that depression per se could cause impotence and related his loss of libido solely to the drugs. His expectations from the psychotherapy were unrealistic. He regarded it as a magical means to restore his potency and cure his psychopathology.

Although Dr. F's previous hypomanic state with bipolarity was highly suggestive of an affective disorder, the therapist considered him to be characterologically disturbed, a personality disorder with cyclothymic and paranoid features, the latter precipitated when he felt that he had been "set up." Suspicions that he was being taken advantage of occurred after large gambling losses, litigation, or rejection by a mistress who cheated on him. His inadequacy as a male, his dubious heterosexuality, and his lifelong rivalry with his father had persisted.

He had married a dark-haired "Mediterranean girl" whom he impregnated while he was in dental school. His initial attraction to her stemmed from the fact that "she looked Italian." He had the fantasy that his natural parents were Italian.

Dr. F proudly proclaimed that he had never sponged off his parents. The government had paid his tuition, and he managed to win money at gambling. After graduation, he had been commissioned a dental officer and also had the opportunity to begin specialty training as a dental surgeon. After completing his training, he "blew" what money he had in one week of gambling and felt compelled to accept his father's offer to join him in practice. He was unable to tolerate the association and opened his own office. His father was willing to give or loan him the money, but he refused and asked only that his father co-sign a loan for his equipment. He could have taken over his father's practice, but he insisted that "I can't stand being told what to do; I have to be my own boss."

He was, in fact, oral and voracious in his demands, but all the while he had to be in charge. His constricted emotional state, his negativism, precluded the expression of love. He aspired to be the immortal hero, ever the victor. Decompensation and disruption of his narcissism, omniscience and omnipotence revealed the terrible self-hatred that had persisted throughout his life. He no longer fell into a sub-intentioned category. He was fully aware that he wished to die. He owned a shotgun and had a narcotics license.

The active precipitants were that his father had suffered a stroke and had called to inform him that his mother was being hospitalized after mammography had revealed a mass that was suspected to be a neoplasm. To make matters worse, Dr. F had decided to terminate treatment. Nothing could help him. His threat was explicit: "If you can't live like a man, there's no sense in being alive."

There was a brief silence, and the therapist attempted to formulate an approach. Hospitalization was out; he would resist. There were no ancillary figures who would have the slightest influence on him. He would reject community resources. He regarded his physician as a nincompoop, so he was out. He required immediate restitution, and this meant a confrontation. He was disillusioned with treatment and the therapist. The magic was ineffective. His cry for help sounded like an ultimatum. There was no choice but to confront him in the attempt to offer him restitution.

"You stated that if you can't live like a man, there's no sense in being alive." The therapist's voice rose, "Have you ever lived like a man?" Dr. F appeared startled but remained silent. "From what you've told me, you've been battling and revolting against your parents and the entire world. You want everything your way, and no matter how much you get it's not enough. You want to be loved and admired but you're unwilling to give a bit of yourself to anyone. When you can't have your way and score, which is your definition of being a man, you fold up and get depressed. Don't you feel that your parents need your help now?"

Dr. F paused and wet his lips. "I don't like to be talked down to and to be bawled out like a child."

"Maybe you still are a child. You've been successful professionally, but in other ways you're an angry child who can't run the world his way."

Dr. F sat still, made no attempt to refute or to leave.

"When did your father call you about your mother's condition?"

"Yesterday."

"Did you go to see her? Did you call her?"

"No."

"What hospital is she going to?"

"I don't know."

"What would a man do under such circumstances?"

He remained silent.

"When did your father tell you that he had a stroke?"

"Two weeks ago. I expected it. He mentioned that he was having small strokes."

"Do you understand the message he was giving you?"

"They're both sick."

"Yes, but he didn't just call you for that. He called you for your help. What do you intend to do?"

He fidgeted. "What am I supposed to do, cry?"

"What does a man do? What do you do when a patient hemorrhages?"

"It's not the same thing."

"That doesn't matter right now. I know you have old gripes about your father and your mother. That can be worked out later. It's easier working it out with a man—an adult. What can you do about being a man now?"

"I know what you're trying to get me to do . . . call them, see them . . ."

"I'm trying to get you to accept a man's commitment and responsibility.

How is your mother going to get to the hospital if your father has been having CVA's?"

He sat quietly for a minute or two, then walked to the door. Just as he was about to leave, he popped his head back in. "When is my next appointment?"

The confrontation or sermon on virility had a positive effect. Dr. F took weeks off from his practice and was in frequent contact with his parents. He proved helpful and supportive. His mother required a radical mastectomy and radiation later. He also arranged for a consultation with a neurologist and a cardiovascular specialist about his father's transient cerebral ischemia.

His wife is now becoming involved in psychotherapy, and there is some slight hope of reviving the marriage. Dr. F regained his potency when his depression was ameliorated. The Inderal was discontinued when his contact tremor ceased. However, about three months after the events described above, Dr. F suffered a mild myocardial infarct but recovered uneventfully, returned to work on a more realistic schedule, and continues with treatment. There are still old problems and new issues that call for resolution. The positive changes did not occur abruptly and they appear to be dramatic only when they are viewed in perspective. Many laborious hours of intensive interaction were required to bring about modifications. A serious characterological disturbance does not disappear nor is it easily dissipated in a man who is in his mid-fifties. He is still frequently tense, uptight, and dysphoric. However, the outstanding subintentioned, self-destructive and manic features that characterized his life style are markedly reduced. In the course of a recent session, he made an amusing remark, "If I hadn't become impotent, I would have been dead." The therapist was inclined to agree.

SOMATIZATION, MASKED DEPRESSION AND SELF-DESTRUCTION

The substitution of somatic complaints for a typical or classical depression is the bane of the physician and the psychotherapist alike. The disposition of such patients is a collaborative responsibility and concern. It is an area where there is a merging of science, art and intuition, where multidisciplinary participation is essential and where misjudgment or mismanagement may result in fatal consequences.

When the patient presents with a functional disturbance and does not demonstrate a classical depressive syndrome, he is ordinarily reassured and dismissed by the physician with a minor tranquilizing agent. Unresponsive patients may be referred to a specialist for further study, or any number of laboratory studies and procedures may be performed. For the physician with an inflexible adherence to organicity, explorative laparotomies, invasive procedures and/or surgery, may be the logical, scientific approach. Unfortunately, the referral of such a patient to a psychiatrist or psychologist does not necessarily produce a correct diagnosis and appropriate treatment. In the absence of a depressive or a psychotic syndrome, even the sophisticated therapist may exclude or negate the possibility that severe somatization may have a psychic origin and that the ensuing anguish, unrelenting pain and despair can result in suicide. Masked depression is often given short shrift in the training of physicians and psychotherapists.

Case 7: Mrs. G

Mrs. G, aged 45, complained of chronic abdominal pain of three years' duration. There were no cognitive distortions, and she did not demonstrate a depressive or psychotic syndrome. She was a teacher but had been forced to take a leave of absence for a year and finally had to resign. She held a graduate degree and certification in learning disabilities and managed to tutor a few dyslexic students to supplement her husband's income as a school custodian. He was her second husband; her first husband had died in an automobile accident 11 years before.

The persistent pain had become so severe that two weeks previously, when she couldn't fall asleep, she quadrupled her dosage of Percodan, a narcotic. She slept through the next day and was groggy but was not hospitalized. She did not require medical care and denied making a suicidal attempt, but when she saw her physician the following week she told him about her overdose. He had previously questioned her about suicidal ideation and fantasies and she had denied any such thoughts. She explained her overdose simply as a wish to get some sleep. However, at this point her physician insisted on a consultation and referred her to the therapist.

She was an intelligent, likeable woman—open, thoughtful, not aggrieved section. Her doctor thought that she may have had adhesions and after evaluation by a general surgeon, an exploratory laparotomy was performed, but the findings were negative. More surgery was suggested but was postponed. During this recital she spoke quietly and calmly and gave no evidence of anger or depression. Mrs. G had the utmost confidence in her physician. He had treated her and her family for at least 20 years. He had been thoughtful and thorough and had explored the possibility "that it might be pyschosomatic." He had suggested that she be seen for evaluation a few years ago, but she had refused. However, recently she had been referred to a cardiologist because her pain was sometimes in the substernal area, and her doctor considered the remote possibility of abdominal angina, but the cardiologist ruled it out. Finally, her physician persuaded her to make an appointment to see the therapist: "He told me that one more doctor can't possibly do any harm."

She was an intelligent, likeable woman—open, thoughtful, not aggrieved and philosophical. "We all have our crosses to bear, and we have to learn to live with them. Many people have been helpful to me. My doctors have all tried their best, and I'm grateful. I trust people, and even though I've just met you I know that you'll try your best, too."

She was encouraged to bring up background material and responded with no prompting: She came from a middle-class family, went to a state college after high school, and majored in education with a minor in psychology. While working as a teacher, she continued with her education and earned a master's degree in the field of learning disabilities. She met her husband when she was in college and he was studying law. After he graduated and passed the bar, they married. They were happy together. He didn't care to work in a large law office so they moved to a suburban area, where he opened an office and began to practice. They both worked and although his practice did not flourish, they were content.

Her first son was born with a cleft palate when she was 28. They decided to have another child quickly because she felt that she was "getting beyond childbearing." The second son was delivered a short time prior to her thirtieth birthday, and he appeared to be normal. They had been upset about the cleft palate and were happy that the second child showed no abnormalities or birth defects.

A few years later, much to their dismay, their pediatrician made a diagnosis of epilepsy in the younger son, which was confirmed in a university hospital. The son, now 14, had not responded well to medication and also suffered from intellectual deficits that made it impossible for him to attend the local public school. Mrs. G attempted to tutor him but finally recognized that using euphemisms did not alter his condition and he required highly specialized education. Her second husband refused to pay for a private school and wanted the youngster sent to a state school. She refused to accept this, and the money that she earned as a learning disability tutor was used to pay the tuition at a private school. The oldest son had surgery for the cleft palate but was dull normal. If and when he graduates from high school, he will be able to perform only a menial job.

She dabbed at her eyes, and the therapist offered a tissue. "I am not crying; every now and then my eyes itch. I have a salve but I use it only at night because it blurs my vision. That's the least of my problems." She paused briefly and then continued. "It was just about 11 years ago that my first husband, John, developed some trouble walking and complained about headaches and his vision. Our doctor examined him and sent him to a neurologist who tried to tell us gently that John had a brain tumor. I remember some of the terms; they were not unfamiliar. I am a learning disability teacher so I could sort of put things together. I had read about it—ataxia, diplopia, excruciating headaches and God knows what else. He told us both that John must go into the hospital immediately for further tests. John drove back with me to our house. His mother had been babysitting while we went to see the doctor. I wanted to drive her home. He hadn't spoken a word since we heard the news, and he said, "No, I'll take her home, I have to tell them that I'm going into the hospital. I won't alarm them." She kept rubbing her eyes, but there were no tears.

She continued calmly: "I told him to stay with the kids, I would drive his mother home, and he could talk to his family about going into the hospital tomorrow. He said no, and I didn't want to argue with him. He drove his mother home, but he didn't tell her the truth. He told her that he was all right. He didn't even go into the house but just dropped her off outside. On his way home he drove into a telephone pole. The car went out of control. The doctor told me that he must have died instantly."

The calmness dissolved, her whole body tightened up and she clutched her abdomen with both hands. "It's killing me. I can't stand it anymore. The pain—it's horrible. Please, get me some water. I can't stand it!"

"You felt that your husband killed himself?"

Her taut abdomen seemed to bulge. She removed her clutching hands.

First came a wail, then a piercing sound like a siren, and then a scream that subsided into uncontrollable sobbing. Her abdomen reacted spasmodically. It was like an epileptic attack. This went on for a minute or two, followed by crying—loud uncontrollable crying. The therapist was shaken. She didn't want any water. For lack of anything to say, he remained silent. Her eyes were closed but tears were streaming down. The therapist continued to remain silent. The abdominal spasms quieted down, and she accepted some tissues.

When she opened her eyes, she was still hyperventilating, but this too quieted down. "Yes, I'm certain that he killed himself; I've known it for 11 years. I could have prevented it . . . I shouldn't have let him take his mother home . . . I should have known . . . Maybe they could have operated on him and saved his life." Suddenly she calmed down.

"Do you have any pain in your belly now?"

"I don't know. I was just holding on to it. No, I don't have any pain now. John kept talking about another baby. I would have tried it again."

Gradually she regained her composure. She apologized for what she termed an outburst. "I never dreamed I could behave like that." Her control was such that she was able to continue for a few minutes longer with additional material. Her husband had a $10,000 insurance policy on his life. The company investigated, but the cause of death had been declared an accident and they had no cause to challenge it.

Mrs. G was a victim-survivor of her husband's suicide, and in a sense her treatment constituted tertiary intervention that was long overdue, as well as primary and secondary intervention. It would be equally correct to term her problem as a delayed grief reaction that had been masked by somatization.

She agreed to further therapy and followed through. There were many interesting aspects related to her depressed state. The agony in her abdomen symbolically represented childbirth. On that fateful day, while driving home from the neurologist, she had fantasized that even if John were to die, she might be impregnated and still have a normal child. Her guilt was enormous because she felt that she should never have permitted him to drive alone after he had been given what was tantamount to "a death certificate."

In the following sessions, other aspects of her problems were investigated. About four years before, she attended a Christmas party at the school where she had taught and became involved with the school custodian whom she had known for some years. He was a divorced alcoholic, .

but her self-esteem was low and she, too, apparently had had too much to drink. Her loneliness and her desire "to be a woman and also to have a normal child" resulted in an affair and then marriage. This alliance also represented an expression of anger toward her former husband. "He should have taken the chance that brain surgery, or whatever, might be helpful." Instead, he had deserted her by dying. Her revenge was to marry the school custodian.

The severe abdominal pains had their onset three years ago, but for a while she was unable to reconstruct any events in her life that might be related to her abdominal pain. Some months later the reconstruction was clarified. She was about a month late with her period and there were many fantasies that she was pregnant again. Her second husband, the alcoholic school custodian, demanded that she have sexual relations with him. He was drunk, and when she refused, he drove off angrily. She had fantasies and wishes that he would kill himself. Then she had fantasized that if he died it would be her fault because she had refused to have relations with him. In the middle of the night, she began to menstruate, and the fantasy of having another child was punctured. She had not conceived, and since her second husband was totally incompatible with her life-style, she was left with a void. She couldn't sleep and was preoccupied with death wishes toward her second husband and toward herself. At this point there was an acute onset of abdominal pain—labor pains.

The situation was repeated the night she overdosed. Her husband was drunk, and again she refused to have sex. He stormed out of the house, and she had death wishes about him, with a large reactivation of the abdominal pain. Then she took the overdose of Perkodan. It was a suicide attempt. She wanted to die, and her simplistic explanation that she merely wanted to sleep represented a denial of her self-destructive impulses.

Her treatment was successful in that she had a remission and was free of the abdominal pain and the itch. At this point, she divorced her second husband and abruptly terminated treatment.

Both husbands had failed to provide her with a child that would reinforce her femininity. When she perceived her first husband as terminal, he became useless and her previous death wishes came true. Even before John became ill, she wished that he would die, starting when she found out that her second son had epilepsy.

Although the immediate goal to alleviate the depression underlying her somatization was achieved, the therapist regretted that a deeper analysis was not possible. She was too precipitous about leaving, and the impression that she was still vulnerable persisted. The termination of therapy made it possible to retain her fantasy of having another child.

TERMINAL ILLNESS AND SELF-DESTRUCTION

Society's general abhorrence of suicide was discussed earlier. There is, however, one exception that may be countenanced and regarded as justifiable; when an individual is terminally ill, suffering severe pain, and the "magic" of modern medicine is ineffectual, suicide becomes more acceptable. Under such circumstances, it appears to be more logical and less paradoxical. It can readily be understood that an individual in such circumstances may choose to give up life because all of the available means to make life bearable and liveable have been exhausted. Far less guilt is felt by those significant others who have watched the growing anguish and have made every attempt to contend with an unrelenting Thanatos. Relatives and friends have been known to pray for the patient's demise. "I hope he dies in his sleep so he can finally have peace." "Why doesn't the doctor give him something to get it over with?" In such situations death wishes can be openly discussed and are regarded as an expression of love rather than hate. The patient who commits suicide may be commended for his courage and good judgment in terminating his life. "He had guts. He knew the end was near. Now he has peace." The bereaved are far less likely to feel stigmatized and may openly discuss the suicide without remorse. In short, the self-destructive act in a terminal illness can be well rationalized and mitigated.

There is a movement now under way to give physicians the right to end life if an individual requests it and a medical board agrees that the patient's condition is hopeless. The extended life span has resulted in a vast increase in the number of individuals who linger on for protracted periods with degenerative and/or neoplastic diseases. The question arises as to whether there is a double standard for suicide in cases of terminal illness. Another cogent question is why most individuals with terminal illness elect and fight to live on to the very last breath. Despite horrendous pain, some may experience a new dimension. During the last period of their lives, they may be able to express warmth and affection, interact with others on another level, and view the world from an entirely different perspective.

Physicians, and even psychotherapists, have in the past been notoriously remiss and derelict in learning to deal with the dying. Fortunately, this attitude is changing. Prevention, intervention and postvention can and should be utilized. Physicians and therapists should not restrict themselves to "curing" and neglect or desert those who can no longer benefit from their scientific ministrations and therapeutic armamentaria. Growing interest in thanatology is evidenced by the increase in the research, clinical and technical literature and is providing the public with information about humane programs for those who are about to die. Perhaps the fact that all of us must eventually die is a truism that has yet to be psychically synthesized.

It might be appropriate at this point to touch briefly on the thrust of the many studies that relate intrapsychic pathology, stress and unconscious self-destructive impulses with physical disease. Hans Selye, who devoted his life to a study of the immune system and won a Nobel Prize for his research, discussed the malignant effect of severe stress in terms of the individual's capacity to cope and contend with and withstand this stress. In the first stage, there is an alarm reaction wherein the body mobilizes its defenses. In the second stage, there is an attempt at adaptation, and the full resources of the body are evoked in its defense. The last stage of exhaustion occurs when such defenses prove to be futile, and this leads to death.

Selye, in an interview (Wixen, 1978), is quoted: "Some people have described cancer as a disease that is somewhat like the body's way of rejecting itself." In the same interview, Selye went on to state, "All I can say as a scientist is that the great majority of physical illnesses have in part some psychosomatic origin. What happens is that when extreme stress hits, especially for a prolonged duration, certain predictable events take place. It's as if the body were a chain and its weakest link breaks down."

It is moot whether self-destructive influences-can initiate diseases that have a terminal outcome and whether they reactivate old suicidal impulses, or serve as a catalyst during a period when the body's defenses are at an extremely low ebb. Not all people with terminal illness are death-driven, and many may live on for varying periods of time, and the quality of their lives during this final stage can and may be very satisfying. Physicians are often amazed, puzzled and sometimes a bit embarrassed when their dire prognoses of imminent death prove to be wrong. At such times they are quite likely to use terms like "spontaneous remission," "chemotherapeutic success," etc.

Dr. Selye is a living example of a man who is vital while living with terminal disease. This 71-year-old man developed reticulosarcoma six yeers ago (Wixen, 1978). The fatality rate for this type of cancer is 99.5 percent, and Dr. Selye, who was quite familiar with the prognosis for this malignancy, felt certain that he was going to die. His lifelong emphasis was on adaptation, and he decided that rather than wait for inevitable death he would try to extract as much from life as he could. He mentioned that after his interview with Wixen he was leaving for Houston, then Montreal, and then for a nine-day lecture tour in Europe.

Dr. Selye is fortunate in that he has the inner strength to make an adaptation to life and to impending death. Those countless others who would give up and succumb require help from outside sources and desparately need primary and secondary intervention.

Case 8: Mrs. H

Mrs. H, a 52-year-old married woman with two young children, was seen in consultation at the request of her physician. During Mrs. H's routine yearly physical, her internist had found evidence of a brain lesion. She was hospitalized immediately, and the diagnosis was confirmed. The primary malignancy was in a lung and had metastasized, was widely disseminated and had spread to the brain. Surgery, chemo, and radio therapy were of no avail because of the insidious progress of her cancer. The consensus of the oncology department was that continuing chemotherapy would only compound her suffering. The patient and her husband were informed that her life expectancy at that time was about two to three months at the most. Both she and her husband knew that she suffered from a malignancy, but they had not expected that the end would come so soon. Her pain was increasing steadily, and her response to narcotics was becoming increasingly poor.

The consultation was requested to determine whether hypnosis might be helpful as an analgesic, and also whether talking to a professional therapist might ease her anguish. Mrs. H's internist, a perceptive and sensitive man, saw her daily and spent many hours providing her with support. It was his opinion that she would not have to be bedridden if her pain could be relieved or reduced and that she could be ambulatory for this last period of her life.

Mrs. H, a gracious lady, was highly cooperative. Her warm transference toward her internist was displaced to the therapist. In spite of her pain, she was able to provide a halting summary of her life. She was a college professor and prior to her hospitalization was acting chairman of the department. She had married at age 33, and her husband, a sensitive artist, was the most meaningful figure in her life. They had two children, a daughter aged 13 and a son 11. The children were astute and suspected that she was seriously ill, but they had not been told of her impending death. There were many things that she wished she could do before she left "the vale of tears." She had discussed suicide with her internist, but this was virtually impossible because she was bedridden. In a jocular way that was not jocular, she had asked if he could help her out. Her ego strength was amazing, perhaps in part due to the fact that she had been in analysis in her late twenties. She suggested that treatment had made it possible for her to marry. There were long periods when she appeared to be well oriented and her sensorium was clear, but at times there was evidence of expressive aphasia, which she referred to as "blocking."

She readily agreed to a hypnotic approach, was placed in a relaxed state and went into a trance without the slightest difficulty. In the very first session, a deeper state was instituted, and it was possible to bring about analgesia. She sat up, stood up, and then walked about. After posthypnotic suggestion she felt exhilarated as she walked about the room, free of pain. "It's so good to be alive again."

Mrs. H insisted that her husband, who was in the waiting room, join us and witness her walking around. He came in and was overjoyed to see her up and about. It was a warm summer day, and since she was wearing only a nightgown, her husband helped her on with a light bathrobe. She walked back and forth across the room exultantly and then pirouetted like a model. Roguishly she removed her wig and revealed a totally bald head. The therapist had not realized that she was wearing a wig. Apparently radiation treatments had resulted in alopecia totalis. "It's hot and I might as well take this nasty thing off."

She was seen frequently and taught autohypnosis. It was possible to bring her into deeper states. A week later she was discharged from the hospital and was able to resume some of her activities at home. She had made it quite clear that she had no intention of committing suicide and that there were many, many things that had to be taken care of.

She discussed her imminent death with her children and they all cried together. There were warm occasions when the family went out to dinner, and on two occasions they went on a picnic. She spent a good deal of time with her children and taught her 13-year-old daughter the rudiments of cooking. They had pleasant experiences when she taught her how to bake a cake and a pie. They laughed and they cried together. She showed her son how to make his bed and how he might help his sister in maintaining their home.

During this period she developed episodes of bursitis and was briefly hospitalized three times. Butazolidine and Indocin were given to reduce the inflamatory process but produced side effects and were discontinued. Her discomfort was again relieved by hypnosis. It was now comfortable for her when she came for therapy to sit in an upholstered chair rather than on a straight chair buttressed by a pillow that she brought along. During this time it was possible for her to have an older brother and a 72-year-old father who was convalescing from a coronary occlusion spend some time with her. Every day and every hour were eventful.

She gradually became progressively aphasic, and edema of the brain caused greater disorganization. Her doctors found it difficult to believe that she was still alive. She died in her sleep nine months after her first contact with the therapist.

Following her death, her husband spent a number of sessions voicing his grief. He also expressed his gratitude for having had the opportunity to talk with his wife about so many things they had never discussed before, and was intensely grateful that they had been able to communicate their deep love.

During the course of Mrs. H's illness, the entire family had been seen on a number of occasions, and her therapist had suggested that it might be helpful for the children to be seen by a child psychiatrist who had also been consulted. At the time, both Mr. and Mrs. H felt that this would "disrupt" the family. After Mrs. H's death, the 13-year-old daughter had assumed the mother's role and was cooking and keeping house; the son was also adapting well. The deceased mother often was the subject of conversation, and it was regarded as "normal" to talk about her and their love and warmth for her. During this time, both children were followed by a child psychiatrist. Both are making satisfactory adjustments.

Mrs. H's life was not saved, but the freedom from pain certainly enabled her to live out the last period as an effective human being. Time, as well as space, is relative. Who can say how much she accomplished and how much she lived out during that brief time? The therapist who shares in such an experience would agree that the terminally ill should not be abandoned.

It is very difficult to conclude a book on suicidology on a cheerful note. Even guarded optimism must be tempered by the ever-rising incidence of self-destructive behavior. Perhaps, in spite of world turbulence and increased inner turmoil, we are approaching a time when we shall be willing to give due recognition to the agony of fellow human beings who feel so helpless and so overwhelmed that they are impelled to resign from life.

A colleague who read the manuscript asked, "After having written this book, what in your opinion is the greatest single obstacle to a more effective approach against this needless self-inflicted slaughter?"

The author's unhesitating reply was, "Indifference." Perhaps more of us can and will reach out.

APPENDIX

Numerous references have been made in this book to the American Association of Suicidology (AAS), and it is appropriate to identify this multidisciplinary group of professionals and others which is concerned and involved with the prevention of suicide and self-destructive behavior.

The American Association of Suicidology owes its inception to Edwin S. Shneidman, Ph.D., and was founded by him subsequent to the first Annual National Conference on Suicidology, which was held at the University of Chicago in 1968.

The membership reflects a multidisciplinary approach to the research, education, training and service required to contend with suicide and self-destructive behavior. Individuals who are seriously concerned about suicide and life-threatening behavior are eligible for one of three classes of AAS membership. The Association encourages professionals and nonprofessionals alike to work in concert in a large variety of programs and projects designed to lessen the toll of self-destruction. An eclectic attitude provides for a number of ways to attain this objective.

Annual meetings in various parts of the United States draw large attendance and make it possible for the membership to keep abreast of the newest research findings, theoretical concepts and the application of techniques in coping with suicide and self-destructive behavior. The annual meetings also provide for workshops in which particular problems can be explored intensively by smaller groups. The exchange of ideas is not restricted to the views of a few of the foremost specialists, and ample opportunity is provided to ensure the participation and the contributions of the membership.

The Association publishes an official journal, *Suicide and Life-Threatening Behavior*. A newsletter about current organizational activities, *Newslink,* is published three times a year.

Since 1974, the AAS Task Force has been involved in developing standards and procedures for the accreditation of Suicide Prevention

Centers. A directory of Suicide Prevention Centers is updated annually and provides relevant information about Suicide Prevention Centers in the United States.

The American Association of Suicidology also makes use of multiple educational resources on a regional level, providing workshops, symposia, programs for volunteers, and speakers for groups interested in self-destructive behavior. A wide variety of printed material, tapes and films are available.

Information about membership may be secured from Ms. Sandra A. Lopez, Executive Secretary, American Association of Suicidology, P. O. Box 3264, Houston, Texas 71001.

The *Suicide Prevention Training Manual* of the American Association of Suicidology, 1978, represents a significant additional resource and instrument in the armamentaria against self-destruction. Copies of the manual can be purchased for $9.00 by writing to: Mr. Clem Hallquist, AAS Public Relations, P. O. Box 7, Gwynedd, Pennsylvania 19436.

REFERENCES

ABRAHAM, K. *Selected Papers on Psychoanalysis.* New York: Basic Books, 1953.

ADLER, A. *Problems of Neurosis.* London: Routledge & Kegan Paul Ltd., 1929.

ADLER, A. Suicide. *Journal of Individual Psychology,* 1958, 14:57-61; translated from *Selbstmord, Internationale Zeitschrift für Individualpsychologie,* 1937, 15:49-52.

ADLER, A. In P. Friedman (Ed.), *On Suicide.* New York: International Universities Press, 1967.

ADLER, A., et al. Über den Selbstmord Inbesondere den Schuler-Selbstmord. (Suicide, especially among students.) *Diskussion des Wiener Psychoanalytischen Vereins.* Wiesbaden: J. F. Bergmann, 1910.

ALLPORT, G. W. *The Use of Personal Documents in Psychological Science.* New York: Social Science Research Council, 1942.

ALVAREZ, A. *The Savage God: Study of Suicide.* New York: Random House, 1972.

ARIETI, S. *Interpretations of Schizophrenia.* New York: Robert Brunner, 1955.

BACHRACH, A. J. Some factors in the prediction of suicide. *Neuropsychiatry,* 1951, 1 (4): 21-27.

BALINT, M., ORNSTEIN, P., and BALINT, E. *Focal Psychotherapy: An Example of Applied Psychoanalysis.* London: J. B. Lippincott, 1972.

BARRACLOUGH, B. M., NELSON, B., and SAINSBURY, P. The diagnostic classification and psychiatric treatment of 25 suicides. In N. L. Farberow (Ed.), *Proceedings of the Fourth International Conference for Suicide Prevention Center.* Los Angeles: Delmar Publishing Company, 1968.

BECK, A. T., DAVIS, J. H., FREDERICK, C. J., PERLIN, S., POKORNY, A., SCHULMAN, R., SEIDEN, R., and WITTLIN, B. Classification and nomenclature. In H. L. P. Resnick and B. Hathorne (Eds.), *Suicide Prevention in the Seventies.* Washington, D.C.: U.S. Government Printing Office, 1972.

BECK, A. T., RESNICK, H. L. P., and LETTIERI, D. J. *The Prediction of Suicide.* Bowie, Maryland: Charles Press Publishing, Inc., 1974.

BELLAK, L. (Ed.). *Schizophrenia: A Review of the Syndrome.* New York: Logos Press, 1958.

BENDER, L. and SCHILDER, P. Aggressiveness in children. *Genetic Psychology Monographs,* 1936, 18:410-526.

BENDER, L. and SCHILDER, P. Suicidal preoccupations and attempts in children. *American Journal of Orthopsychiatry,* VII, 1937.

BENNETT, A. E. Suggestions for suicide prevention. In E. S. Shneidman and N. L. Farberow (Eds.), *Clues to Suicide.* New York: McGraw-Hill Book Co., 1957.

BERGLER, E. Problems of suicide. *Psychiatric Quarterly* (supplement), 1946, 20:261-275.

BERNARD, V. Some interrelationships of training for community psychiatry, community mental health programs and research in social psychiatry. In *Proceedings of Third World Congress of Psychiatry.* Montreal, Canada: McGill University and University of Toronto Press, 1961, Vol. 3.

BERNFELD, S. Selbstmord (Suicide). *Z. Psychom. Pädag.,* 1929, 3:355-363.

BETTELHEIM, B. *Love Is Not Enough.* Glencoe, Ill.: Free Press, 1951.

BETTELHEIM, B. *The Empty Fortress.* New York: Free Press, 1967.

BIBRING, E. The mechanism of depression. In P. Greenacre (Ed.), *Affective Disorders.* New York: International Universities Press, Inc., 1953.

BILLINGS, J. H. ROSEN, D. H., ASIMOS, C., MOTTO, J. A. Observations on long-term group therapy with suicidal and depressed persons. *Life-Threatening Behavior*, 1974, 4(3):160-170.

BLACHLY, P. H., DISHER, W., RODUNER, G. Suicide by physicians. *Bull. Suicide*, December 1968, 1:1.

BLACHLY, P. H., OSTERUD, H. T., and JOSSLIN, R. Suicide in professional groups. *New England Journal of Medicine*, June 1963, 268:1278-1282.

BLEULER, E. *Dementia Praecox or The Group of Schizophrenias.* New York: International Universities Press, 1950.

BOGARD, H. M. Follow-up study of suicidal patients seen in emergency room consultation. *American Journal of Psychiatry*, 1970, 126:1017-1020.

BOISEN, A., JENKINS, R. L., and LORR, M. Schizophrenic ideation as a striving toward the solution of conflict. *Journal of Clinical Psychology*, 1954, 10:389-391.

BOJAR, S. Psychiatric problems of medical students. In B. B. Blain and C. C. McArthur (Eds.), *Emotional Problems of the Student.* New York: Appleton-Century-Crofts, 1961.

BRAUN, M. Suicide in psychiatrists. *Journal of American Medical Association*, 1973, 233(1):81.

BROMBERG, A. A psychological study of murder. *International Journal of Psycho-Analysis*, 1951, 32:1.

BROSIN, H. and EARLY, L. W. *Psychiatry and Medical Education.* American Psychiatric Association, 1952.

CAMUS, A. *The Myth of Sisyphus.* Justin O'Brien (trans.). London: Hamish Hamilton, 1945.

CAVAN, R. S. *Suicide.* Chicago: University of Chicago Press, 1926.

CHORON, J. *Suicide.* New York: Charles Scribner & Sons, 1972.

CHOWDHURY, N. and KREITMAN, N. A. A comparison of para-suicides (Attempted Suicide) and the Telephone Samaritan Service. *Applied Social Studies*, 1971, 3:51-57.

CHRIST, J., BROWNSBERGER, C. N., and SOLOMON, P. In: Solomon and Patch (Eds.), *Handbook of Psychiatry.* Los Altos: Lange Medical Publications, 1974.

COHEN, A. S., FREIDIN, R. B., and SAMUELS, M. A. *Medical Emergencies: Diagnostic and Management Procedures from Boston City Hospital.* Boston: Little, Brown and Co., 1977.

COLE, J. O. and DAVIS, J. M. Minor tranquilizers, sedatives and hypnotics. In: A. M. Freedman, H. I. Kaplan, and B. J. Sadock (Eds.), *Comprehensive Textbook of Psychiatry*, Vol. 2. Baltimore: Williams & Wilkins, 1975a.

COLE, J. O. and DAVIS, J. M. Antidepressant drugs. In: A. M. Freedman, H. I. Kaplan, and B. J. Sadock (Eds.), *Comprehensive Textbook of Psychiatry*, Vol. 2. Baltimore: Williams & Wilkins, 1975b.

COMSTOCK, B. S. Suicide events and indications for hospitalization. *Proceedings Tenth Annual Meeting*, American Association of Suicidology, Boston, 1977.

COOPER, P. R. Medical treatment facility liability for patients' suicide and other self-injury. *Journal of Legal Medicine*, Jan. 1975.

CRAIG, A. G. and PITTS, F. N. Suicide by physicians. *Diseases of the Nervous System*, 1968, 219:763-772. In: *JAMA*, Vol. 228, No. 3, April 15, 1974.

CSERR, R. Why a psychiatric hospital: Indications and contraindications. *Charles River Hospital News*, May 1978, V. 1 (2).

CURPHEY, T. J. The role of the social scientist in medicolegal certification of death from suicide. In: N. L. Farberow and E. S. Shneidman (Eds.), *The Cry For Help.* New York: McGraw-Hill Book Co., 1961.

CURPHEY, T. J. In the question of suicide. *Roche Medical Image and Commentary.* New York: McGraw-Hill Book Co., 1961.

DANTO, B. L. Message from the President Elect. *ASS Newslink,* Feb. 1978, 4:1.

DATSUN, P. G. and SAKHEIM, G. A. Prediction of successful suicide from the Rorschach Test, using a sign approach. *Journal of Projective Techniques,* 1960, 24:355-361.

DAVIS, J. M. and COLE, J. O. Antipsychotic drugs. In: A. M. Freedman, H. I. Kaplan, and B. J. Sadock (Eds.), *Comprehensive Textbook of Psychiatry,* Vol. 2. Baltimore: Williams & Wilkins, 1975.

DESOLE, D. E., SINGER, P., and ARONSON, S. Suicide and role strain among physicians. *International Journal of Social Psychiatry,* 1969, 15:294-301. In: *JAMA,* Vol. 228, No. 3, April 15, 1974.

DEUTSCH, F. *The Psychosomatic Concept in Psychoanalysis.* New York: International Universities Press, Inc., 1953.

DEUTSCH, F. Body, mind and art. *Daedalus, Journal of American Academy of Arts & Sciences,* Winter 1960, 38-42.

DIGGORY, J. C. Predicting suicide. In: A. T. Beck, H. L. P. Resnik, and D. J. Lettieri (Eds.), *The Prediction of Suicide.* Bowie, Maryland: Charles Press Publications, 1974.

DORPAT, T. L. In: *Suicide.* Published by the American Association of Suicidology, Winter 1975, 5:4.

DORPAT, T. L. and BOSWELL, J. W. Evaluation of suicide intent. (Unpublished paper, 1959).

DORPAT, T. L. and BOSWELL, J. An evaluation of suicidal intent in suicide attempts. *Comprehensive Psychiatry,* 1963, 4:117-125.

DORPAT, T. L. and RIPLEY, H. S. A study of suicide in the Seattle area. *Comprehensive Psychiatry,* 1960, 1:349-359.

DORPAT, T. L., RIPLEY, H. S., and LEIDIG, R. A study of suicide in Seattle. (Unpublished paper, 1959).

DOUGLAS, J. D. *The Social Meanings of Suicide.* Princeton, New Jersey: Princeton University Press, 1967.

DUBLIN, L. I. *Suicide: A Sociological and Statistical Study.* New York: Ronald Press, 1963.

DUBLIN, L. I. and BUNZEL, B. *To Be Or Not To Be: A Study of Suicide.* New York: Random House, 1933.

DURKHEIM, E. *Le Suicide.* Paris. Libraire Felix Alcan, 1897. *Suicide.* Glencoe, Ill.: Free Press, 1952.

DURKHEIM, E. *Suicide: A Study in Sociology.* London: Routledge & Kegan Paul, Ltd., 1952.

EISSLER, K. R. *The Psychiatrist and the Dying Patient.* New York: International Universities Press Inc., 1955.

ERIKSON, E. H. *Childhood and Society.* New York: W. W. Norton, 1950.

ERIKSON, E. H. The problem of ego identity. *Journal of the American Psychoanalytic Association,* 1956, 4:56-121.

ERIKSON, E. H. Identity and the psychosocial development of the child. In: *Discussion on Child Development,* Vol. 30. New York: International Universities Press, 1958.

ERIKSON, E. *Identity: Youth and Crisis.* New York: W. W. Norton, 1968.

EYSENCK, H. J. *Psychology and the Foundation of Psychiatry.* London: H. K. Lewis, 1955.

FARBER, J. L. *Theory of Suicide.* New York: Funk & Wagnalls, 1968.

FARBEROW, N. L. Personality patterns of suicidal mental hospital patients. *Genetic Psychology Monographs,* 1950, 42:3-79.

FARBEROW, N. L. The suicidal crisis in psychotherapy. In: E. S. Shneidman and N. L. Farberow (Eds.), *Clues to Suicide*. New York: McGraw-Hill Book Co., 1957.

FARBEROW, N. L. Bibliography on suicide and suicide prevention. Washington, D.C.: National Clearing House for Public Health Information, 1969.

FARBEROW, N. L. Use of the Rorschach in Predicting and Understanding Suicide (unpublished paper). American Psychological Association Convention. Honolulu, Hawaii, 1972a.

FARBEROW, N. L. Vital process in suicide prevention; group pyschotherapy as a community of concern. *Life-Threatening Behavior*, 1972b, 2 (4):239-251.

FARBEROW, N. L., BREED, W., BUNNEY, W. E., DIGGORY, J. C., LETTIERI, D. J., MAY, P., MURPHEY, G. E., and SULLIVAN, F. Research in suicide. In: H. Resnik (Ed.), *Suicide Prevention in the Seventies*. Rockville, Maryland: NIMH, 1973.

FARBEROW, N. L. and McEVOY, T. L. Suicide among patients with diagnoses of anxiety and depressive reaction in general medical and surgical hospitals. *Journal of Abnormal and Social Psychology*, 1965.

FARBEROW, N. L. and SHNEIDMAN, E. S. (Eds.). *The Cry For Help*. New York: McGraw-Hill Book Co., 1961a.

FARBEROW, N. L. and SHNEIDMAN, E. S. A survey of agencies for the prevention of suicide. In: N. L. Farberow and E. S. Shneidman (Eds.), *The Cry For Help*. New York: McGraw-Hill Book Co., 1961b.

FARBEROW, N. L., SHNEIDMAN, E. S., and LEONARD, C. (Eds.). Suicide among schizophrenic mental hospital patients. In: *The Cry For Help*. New York: McGraw-Hill Book Co., 1961.

FARBEROW, N. L., SHNEIDMAN, E. S., and LEONARD, C. V. Suicide among general medical and surgical hospital patients with malignant neoplasms. *Medical Bulletin*, 9, Veterans Administration, 1963.

FEDDEN, H. R. *Suicide: A Social and Historical Study*. London: Peter Davies, 1938.

FEDERN, P. Selbstmordprophylaxe in der analyse. (Suicide prophylaxis in analysis.) *Z. Psychoan. Pädag.*, 1929a, 3:379-389.

FEDERN, P. Die diskussion uber "Selbstmord," inbesondere "Schuler-Selbstmord" im *Wiener Psychoanalytischen Verein* im Jahre 1918. (The discussion on "Suicide," in particular "Suicide of School-children" in the Vienna Psychoanalytic Group in 1918.) *Z. Psychoan. Pädag.*, 1929b, 3:333-344.

FENICHEL, O. *The Psychoanalytic Theory of Neurosis*. New York: W. W. Norton & Company, Inc., 1945.

FOX, R. The recent decline of suicide in Britain; the role of the Samaritan prevention movement in suicidology. In: E. S. Shneidman (Ed.), *Suicidology: Contemporary Developments*. New York: Grune & Stratton, 1976.

FOX, R. Talking down suicides. *Community Care*, Nov. 1, 1978a.

FOX, R. What are the arguments for and against the claim that the Samaritans are largely responsible for the falling U.K. suicide rate? In: *Answers to Suicide* (presented to Chad Varah by the Samaritans on the 25th anniversary of their founding). London: Constable, 1978b, pp. 113-124.

FRANKL, V. Selbstmordrophlaxe und jugendberatung. (Prevention of suicide and youth counseling.) *Münch. Med. Nschr.*, 1929, 76:1675-1676.

FRANKL, V. Arstliche Seelsorge. *Medical-Pastoral Counseling*. Vienna: Deuticke, 1952.

FRANKL, V. *From Death Camp to Existentialism*. Boston: Beacon Press, 1959.

FREEDMAN, A. M., KAPLAN, H. I., and SADOCK, B. J. (Eds.). *Comprehensive Textbook of Psychiatry*. Baltimore: Williams & Wilkins, 1975.

FREEMAN, W. Psychiatrists who kill themselves: A study of suicide. *American Journal of Psychiatry*, 1967, 124:846.

FREIDIN, R. B. In: A. S. Cohen, R. B. Freidin, and M. A. Samuels (Eds.), *Medical Emergencies: Diagnostic and Management Procedures from Boston City Hospital.* Boston: Little, Brown, 1977.

FREUD, A. *The Ego and the Mechanism of Defense.* London: Hogarth Press, Ltd., 1937.

FREUD, S. *The Origins of Psychoanalysis,* Vol. 6. New York: Basic Books, 1954.

All references to Sigmund Freud are from S. Freud, *Standard Edition of the Complete Psychological Works.* London: The Hogarth Press, Ltd., (1953-1965).

FREUD, S. Mourning and melancholia. (Originally published in *Zeitschrift für Psychoanalyse,* Band IV, 1917.) Standard Edition, Vol. 14.

FREUD, S. Thoughts for the times on war and death (1915). Standard Edition, Vol. 14.

FREUD, S. *Beyond the Pleasure Principle.* Standard Edition, Vol. 18.

FREUD, S. Psychogenesis of a case of homosexuality in a woman (1920). Standard Edition, Vol. 18, pp. 147-172.

FREUD, S. *The Ego and the Id* (1923). Standard Edition, Vol. 19, pp. 289-300.

FREUD, S. *Civilization and Its Discontents* (1930). Standard Edition, Vol. 21.

FRIEDMAN, M. and ROSENMAN, R. H. *Type A Behavior and Your Heart.* New York: Knopf, 1974.

FRIEDMAN, P. (Ed.). *On Suicide* (New York: International Universities Press, 1967, English translation of the Minutes of the 1910 meeting of the Vienna Psychoanalytic Society, with a brief introduction by the editor.)

FROMM-REICHMANN, F. *Principles of Intensive Psychotherapy.* Chicago: University of Chicago Press, 1950.

FURLONG, F. W. The mythology of electroconvulsive therapy. *Comprehensive Psychiatry,* 1972, 13:235.

GARMA, A. Psychologie des selbstmordes. *Imago XXIII,* 1937.

GERO, G. An equivalent of depression: Anorexia. In: P. Greenacre (Ed.), *Affective Disorders.* New York: International Universities Press, 1953.

GIBBS, J. P. Suicide. In: R. K. Merton and R. A. Nisbet (Eds.), *Contemporary Social Problems,* 2nd ed. New York: Harcourt, Brace & World, 1966.

GIBBS, J. P. *Suicide.* New York: Harper & Row, 1968.

GIBBS, J. P. and MARTIN, W. T. *Status Integration and Suicide: A Sociological Study.* Eugene: University of Oregon Press, 1964.

GLOVER, E. Notes on the psychopathology of suicide. *International Journal of Psychoanalysis,* 1922, 3:507-508.

GLOVER, E. Some observations on suicidal mechanism. *Psychoanalytic Review,* 1928, 15: 89-90.

GLOVER, E. *The Techniques of Psychoanalysis.* New York: International Universities Press, 1955.

GLOVER, E. *On the Early Development of the Mind.* New York: International Universities Press, 1956.

GOLDSTEIN, K. *The Organism.* New York: American Book Company, 1939.

GORDON, J. E., LINDEMANN, E., IPSEN, J., and WARREN, W. T., JR. An epidemiological analysis of suicide. In: *Epidemiology of Mental Disorders.* Gilbank Memorial Fund, 1950.

GORWITZ, K. Case registers. In: S. Perlin (Ed.), *Handbook for the Study of Suicide.* New York: Oxford University Press, 1975.

GRAY, J. A. M. *Lancet,* 1977, 11:1339.

GREENACRE, P. (Ed.). *Affective Disorders.* New York: International Universities Press, Inc., 1953.

GREENSON, R. R. *The Techniques and Practise of Psychoanalysis.* New York: International Universities Press, Inc., 1967.

GREIST, J. and GUSTAFSON, D. et al. A computer interview for suicide-risk prediction. *American Journal of Psychiatry*, Dec. 1973, 130 (12).

GREIST, J. and GUSTAFSON, D., et al. Suicide risk prediction. *Life-Threatening Behavior*, (winter 1974), 4.

GRINKER, R.*Neurosis psychosis and the borderline states. In: A. M. Freedman, H. I. Kaplan, and B. J. Sadock (Eds.), *Comprehensive Textbook of Psychiatry*. Baltimore: Williams & Wilkins, 1975.

GRINKER, R. R. and HOLZMAN, P. S. Schizophrenic pathology in young adults. *Archives of General Psychiatry*, 1973, 28:168.

GUSTAFSON, D. and GREIST, J., et al. A probabilistic system for identifying suicide attempters. *Computers and Biomedical Research*, Vol. 10, 1977.

GUZE, S. B. and ROBINS, E. Suicide and primary affective disorders. *British Journal of Psychiatry*, 1970, 117:437-438.

HALBWACHS, M. *Les Causes du Suicide*. Paris: Librairie Felix Alcan, 1930.

HEBB, D. O. Alice in Wonderland, or psychology among the biological sciences. In: H. Harlow and C. Woolsey (Eds.), *Biological and Biochemical Basis of Behavior*. Wisconsin: University of Wisconsin Press, 1958.

HENDIN, H. Suicide in Denmark. *Psychiatric Quarterly*, 1960, 34:443-460.

HENDIN, H. Suicide: Psychoanalytic point of view. In: N. L. Farberow and E. S. Shneidman (Eds.), *The Cry For Help*. New York: McGraw-Hill Book Co., 1961.

HENDIN, H. Suicide in Sweden. *Psychiatric Quarterly*, 1962, 35:1-28.

HENDIN, H. The psychodynamics of suicide. *Journal of Nervous and Mental Disease*, 1963, 136:236.

HENDIN, H. *Suicide in Scandanavia*. New York: Grune & Stratton, 1964.

HENDIN, H. Psychiatric emergencies. In: A. M. Freedman and H. I. Kaplan (Eds.), *Comprehensive Textbook of Psychiatry*. Baltimore: Williams & Wilkins, 1967.

HENRY, A. F. and SHORT, J. F., JR. *Suicide and Homicide*. Glencoe, Ill.: Free Press, 1954.

HIRSCH, S. and DUNSWORTH, F. A. The psychiatrist and apparently imminent suicide. *Canadian Psychiatric Association Journal*, Vol. 18, 1973.

HOCH, P. H. *Differential Diagnosis in Clinical Psychiatry*. New York: Science House, Inc., 1972.

HODGE, J. R. Hypnosis as a deterrent to suicide. *American Journal of Clinical Hypnosis*, 1972, 15 (1):20-24.

HOLDEN, L. D. Therapist response to patient suicide; professional and personal. *Journal of Continuing Psychiatry*, May, 1978.

HOLLINGSHEAD, A. B. and REDLICH, F. C. *Social Class and Mental Illness*. New York: Wiley, 1958, pp. 244-248.

HORNEY, K. *Self Analysis*. New York: W. W. Norton & Company, Inc., 1942.

HORNEY, K. *Our Inner Conflicts*. New York: W. W. Norton & Company, Inc., 1945.

HORNEY, K. *Neurosis and Human Growth*. New York: W. W. Norton & Company, Inc., 1950.

JACOBZINER, H. Attempted suicides in adolescence. *Journal of the American Medical Association*, 1965, 191:7-11.

JACKSON, D. Suicide. *Scientific American*, 1954, 191:88-96.

JACKSON, D. Suicide and the physician. *The Prescriber*, March, 1955.

JACKSON, D. Theories of suicide. In: E. S. Shneidman and N. L. Farberow (Eds.), *Clues to Suicide*. New York: McGraw-Hill Book Co., 1957.

JASPERS, K. *General Psychopathology*. Chicago: University of Chicago Press, 1963.

JEFFREY, M. D. W. Samsonic suicide or suicide of revenge among Africans. *African Studies*, 1952, 2 (3):118-222.

JENSEN, V. S. and PETTY, T. A. The fantasy of being rescued in suicide. *Psychoanalytic Quarterly*, 1958, 3:327-339.

JONES, E. *The Life and Works of Sigmund Freud*, Vol. I, p. 5. New York: Basic Books, Inc., 1953.

JUNG, C. Seele und tod (The soul and death). In: *Die Wirklichkeit der Seele* (The Reality of the Soul) Zurich: Rascher, 1939.

JUNG, C. The soul and death, translated by R. P. C. Hull. In: H. Feifel (Ed.), *The Meaning of Death*. New York: McGraw-Hill Book Co., Inc., Blakiston Division, 1959.

KAHNE, M. J. Suicide research. *International Journal of Social Psychiatry*, 1966, 12: 117-186.

KALINOWSKY, L. B. The convulsive therapies. In: A. M. Freedman, H. I. Kaplan, and B. J. Sadock (Eds.), *Comprehensive Textbook of Psychiatry*. Baltimore: Williams & Wilkins, 1975.

KALLMANN, F. J. The genetics of psychosis. *American Journal of Human Genetics*, 1950, 2:385.

KAPLAN, M. and LITMAN, R. E. Telephone appraisal of 100 suicidal emergencies. *American Journal of Psychotherapy*, 1962, 16:591-599.

KESSEL, N. Self-poisoning. *British Medical Journal*, 1965, 2:1265-1270.

KETY, S. S. Biochemical theories of schizophrenia. *International Journal of Psychiatry*, 1965, 1:409.

KIEV, A. Cluster analysis profiles of suicide attempters. *American Journal of Psychiatry*, 1976, 133 (2):150-153.

KIRSTEIN, L., PRUSOFF, B., WEISSMAN, M., and DRESSLER, D. M. Utilization review of treatment for suicide attempters. *American Journal of Psychiatry*, Jan. 1975, 132:1.

KLERMAN, G. L. Major affective disorders. In A. M. Freedman, H. I. Kaplan, and B. J. Sadock (Eds.), *Comprehensive Textbook of Psychiatry*. Baltimore: Williams & Wilkins, 1975.

KLERMAN, G. L. and HIRSCHFELD, R. M. A. The use of antidepressants in clinical practice. *Journal of American Medical Association*, 1978, V. 240(13).

LABOVITZ, S. Variation in suicide rates. In: J. P. Gibbs (Ed.), *Suicide*. New York: Harper & Row, 1968.

LAFONTAINE, J. Anthropology. In: S .Perlin (Ed.), *A Handbook for the Study of Suicide*. New York: Oxford University Press, 1975.

LAING, R. D. *The Politics of the Family*. New York: Pantheon Books, 1971.

LAING, R. D. *The Facts of Life: An Essay in Feelings, Facts and Fantasy*. New York: Pantheon Books, 1976.

LEIGHTON, A. H. and HUGHES, C. C. Notes on Eskimo patterns of suicide, Southwest. *Journal of Anthropology*, 1955, 11:327-338.

LENNARD-JONES, J. E. and ASHER, R. Why do they do it? *Lancet*, 1959, 1:1138.

LESHAN, L. Psychological states as factors in development of malignant disease: A critical review. *Journal of National Cancer Institute*, 1959, 22.

LESHAN, L. A basic psychological orientation apparently associated with malignant disease. *Psychiatric Quarterly*, 1961, 35:314.

LESHAN, L. An emotional life-history pattern associated with neoplastic disease. *Annals New York Academy Science*, 1966, 125:780-793.

LESHAN, L. and WORTHINGTON, R. E. Some psychological correlates of neoplastic disease: Preliminary report. *Journal of Clinical and Experimental Psychopathology*, 1959, 16:2810-2888.

LESSE, S. The range of therapies in the treatment of severely depressed suicidal patients. *American Journal of Psychotherapy*, 1975, 29:308-326.

LESTER, D. Suicidal behavior, a summary of research findings. (Mimeographed. Buffalo, New York: *Suicide Prvention and Crisis Service*, 1970.)

LESTER, D. The myth of suicide prevention. *Comprehensive Psychiatry*, 1972, 13 (6):550-560.

LESTER, D. Demographic vs. clinical prediction of suicidal behavior. In: A. T. Beck, H. L. P. Resnik, and D. J. Lettieri (Eds.), *The Prediction of Suicide*. Bowie, Maryland: D. J. Charles Press, 1974.

LINDEMANN, E. Symptomatology and management of acute grief. *American Journal of Psychiatry*, 1944, 101:141.

LINDNER, R. M. The content analysis of the Rorschach protocol. In: L. E. Abt and L. Bellak (Eds.), *Projective Psychology*. New York: Alfred Knopf, 1950.

LINN, L. Clinical manifestations of psychiatric disorders. In: A. M. Freedman and H. I. Kaplan (Eds.), *Comprehensive Textbook of Psychiatry*. Baltimore: Williams & Wilkins, 1967.

LIPTON, R. *Death in Life; Survivors of Hiroshima*. New York: Random House, 1967.

LITMAN, R. E. Some aspects of the treatment of the potentially suicidal patient. In: E. S. Shneidman and N. L. Farberow (Eds.), *Clues to Suicide*. New York: McGraw-Hill Co., 1957.

LITMAN, R. E. Emergency response ot potential suicide. *Journal of Michigan Medical Society*, Jan. 1963, 62:68-72.

LITMAN, R. E. When patients commit suicide. *American Journal of Psychotherapy*, 1965, 19:570-576.

LITMAN, R. E. Sigmund Freud on suicide. In: E. S. Shneidman (Ed.), *Essays in Self-Destruction*. New York: Science House, 1967.

LITMAN, R. E. Psychotherapists' orientations toward suicide. In: H. L. Resnik (Ed.), *Suicide Behavior: Diagnosis and Management*. Boston: Little, Brown, 1968.

LITMAN, R. E. Controlled study of an anti-suicide program. *NIMH Grant*, 20628, 1974.

LITMAN, R. E., CURPHEY, T. J., SHNEIDMAN, E. S., FARBEROW, N. L., and TABACHNICK, N. D. Investigations of equivocal suicides. *Journal of American Medical Association*, 1963, 184:924.

LITMAN, R. E. and FARBEROW, N. L. Emergency evaluation of self-destructive potentiality. In: N. L. Farberow and E. S. Shneidman (Eds.), *The Cry For Help*. New York: McGraw-Hill Book Co., 1965.

LONG, R. H. Barbiturates, automatization and suicide. *Insurance Council Journal*, April 1959, 299-307.

McCULLOCH, J. W. and PHILIP, A. E. *Suicidal Behavior*. Oxford: Pergamon Press, 1972.

McGEE, R. K., BERG, D., BROCKOPP, G. W., HARRIS, J. R., HAUGHTON, A. B., RACHLIS, D., TOMES, H., and HOFF, L. A. The delivery of suicide and crisis intervention services. In: H. Resnik (Ed.), *Suicide Prevention in the Seventies*. Rockville, Maryland: NIMH, 1973.

McGEE, R. K., RICHARD, W. C., BERGUN, A. Survey of telephone answering services in suicide prevention and crisis intervention agencies. *Life-Threatening Behavior*, 1972, 2 (1):42-47.

McGUIRE, F. Psychosocial studies of medical students. *Journal of Medical Education*, 1966, 41:424-444.

MacKINNON, R. A. and MICHELS, R. *The Psychiatric Interview in Clinical Practice*. Philadelphia: W. B. Saunders, 1971.

MALINOWSKI, B. *Crime and Custom in Savage Society*. London: Kegan Paul, 1926.

MANDELBAUM, D. Social uses of funeral rites. In: H. Feifel (Ed.), *The Meaning of Death*. New York: McGraw-Hill, 1959.

MARIS, R. W. *Social Forces in Urban Suicide*. Homewood, Ill.: Dorsey Press, 1969.

MASSEY, J. T. *Suicide in the United States.* (PHS Publication 1,000, series 20, No. 5. Washington, D.C.: U.S. Department of Health, Education and Welfare, 1967.)

MAUSNER, J. S. and STEPPACHER, R. C. Suicide in professionals: A study of male and female psychologists. *American Journal of Epidemiology,* 1973, 98:436-445. In *JAMA,* Vol. 228, No. 3, April 15, 1974.

MAY, R., ANGEL, E., and ELLENBERGER, H. *Existence.* New York: Basic Books, 1958.

MEERLOO, J. A. M. *Suicide and Mass Suicide.* New York: Grune & Stratton, 1962.

MENNINGER, K. A. Psychoanalytic aspects of suicide. *International Journal of Psychoanalysis,* 1933, 14:376-390.

MENNINGER, K. A. Some clinical examples of indirect suicide. *Southern Medical Journal,* 1935, 28:356-360.

MENNINGER, K. A. Purposive accidents as an expression of self-destructive tendencies. *International Journal of Psychoanalysis,* 1936, 17:6-16.

MENNINGER, K. A. Organic suicide. *Bulletin of the Menninger Clinic,* 1937, 1:192-198.

MENNINGER, K. A. *A Man Against Himself.* New York: Harcourt, Brace, 1938.

MENNINGER, K. A. I. Psychological aspects of the organism under stress. II. Regulatory devices of the ego under major stress. *Journal of American Psychoanalysis Association,* 1954, 2:28-310.

MENNINGER, K. A. Foreward. In: E. S. Shneidman and N. L. Farberow (Eds.), *Clues to Suicide.* New York: McGraw-Hill Book Co., 1957.

MENNINGER, K. A., MAYMAN, M., and PRUYSER, P. *The Vital Balance: The Life Process in Mental Health and Illness.* New York: Viking, 1963.

MILLER, L. *Fourth International Congress of Social Psychiatry.* Jerusalem: AHVA Cooperative, 1972.

MILLER, M. Guest Editorial *AAS Newslink* 4, No. 1, Feb. 1978.

MILLER, M. H. Neuroses, psychoses and the borderline states. In: A. M. Freedman and H. I. Kaplan (Eds.), *Comprehensive Textbook in Psychiatry.* Baltimore: Williams and Wilkins, 1967.

MINKOFF, K. et al. Hopelessness and depression and attempted suicide. *American Journal of Psychiatry,* 1973, 130:455-459.

MINTZ, R. S. The psychotherapy of the suicidal patient. In: H. L. P. Resnick (Ed.), *Suicidal Behaviors, Diagnosis and Management.* Boston: Little, Brown, 1968.

MINTZ, R. S. Prevalence of persons in the city of Los Angeles who have attempted suicide. *Bulletin of Suicidology,* Fall, 1970.

MONK, N. Epidemiology. In: S. Perlin (Ed.), *A Handbook for the Study of Suicide.* New York: Oxford University Press, 1975.

MORIYAMA, I. and ISRAEL, R. Problems in compilation of statistics on suicide in the U.S. In: N. L. Faberow (Ed.), *Proceedings of the Fourth International Conference for Suicide Prevention.* Los Angeles: Delmar Pub. Co., 1968.

MOSS, L. M. and HAMILTON, D. M. Psychotherapy of the suicidal patient. In: E. S. Shneidman and N. L. Farberow (Eds.), *Clues to Suicide.* New York: McGraw-Hill Book Co., 1957.

MOTTO, J. A. Suicide attempt: A longitudinal view. *Archives of General Psychiatry,* 1965, 13:516-520.

MOTTO, J. A. Refinement of variables in assigning suicide risk. In: A. T. Beck, H. L. P. Resnik, and D. J. Lettieri (Eds.), *The Prediction of Suicide.* Bowie, Maryland: Charles Press Publishing Co., 1974.

MOTTO, J. A. and GREENE, C. Suicide in the Medical Community. *AMA Archives of Neurology and Psychiatry,* 1958, 80:776-781.

NEMIAH, J. C. Depressive neuroses. In: A. M. Freedman, H. I. Kaplan, and B. J.

Sadock (Eds.), *Comprehensive Textbook of Psychiatry*. Baltimore: Williams & Wilkins, 1975.

NEURINGER, C. *Psychological Assessment of Suicidal Risk*. Springfield, Ill.: Charles C Thomas, 1974.

NOTMAN, M. Suicide in female physicians. *Psychiatric Opinion*, 1975, 12:29-30.

O'CONNOR, W. A. Some notes on suicide. *British Journal of Medical Psychology*, 1948, 21:222-228.

OKUN, R. et al. In: The management of the pre-suicidal, suicidal and post-suicidal patient. *Annals of Internal Medicine*, 1971, 75:441-458.

ORNSTEIN, P. H. and ORNSTEIN, A. Focal psychotherapy: Its potential impact on psychotherapeutic practice in medicine. *Psychiatric Medicine*, 1972, 3:311.

PAGE, J. D. *Psychopathology*. Chicago: Aldine, 1975.

PARKES, C. M. *Bereavement Studies of Grief in Adult Life*. New York: International Universities Press, 1972.

PARKIN, D. and STENGEL, E. Incidence of suicidal attempts in an urban community. *British Medical Journal*, 1965, 2:133.

PATRICK, J. H. and OVERALL, J. E. Multivariate analysis of clinical rating profiles of suicidal and non-suicidal psychiatric patients. *Journal of Projective Techniques*, 1969, 33:138-145.

PAYKEL, E. S., HALOWELL, C., DRESSLER, D. et al. Treatment of suicide attempts: A descriptive study. *Archives of General Psychiatry*, 1974, 31:487-494.

PERLIN, S. *A Handbook for the Study of Suicide*. New York: Oxford University Press, 1975.

PITTS, F. N. and WINOKUR, G. Affective disorders, III: Diagnostic correlates and incidents of suicide. *Journal of Nervous and Mental Diseases*, 1964, 139 (2):176-181.

PITTS, F. N., WINOKUR, G., and STEWARD, M. A. Psychiatric syndromes, anxiety symptoms and responses to stress in medical students. *American Journal of Psychiatry*, 1961, 118:333-340.

POKORNY, A. D. Characteristics of forty-four patients who subsequently committed suicide. *AMA Archives of General Psychiatry*, 1960, 2:314-323.

POKORNY, A. D. A scheme for classifying suicidal behaviors. In: A. T. Beck, H. L. P. Resnik, and D. J. Lettieri (Eds.), *The Prediction of Suicide*. Bowie, Maryland: Charles Press, 1974.

POKORNY, A. D., TEMOCHE, RUGH, and MACMAHON. Suicide rates in various psychiatric disorders. *Journal of Nervous and Mental Disease*, Dec., 1964, 139.

PORTERFIELD, A. L. The problem of suicide. In: J. P. Gibbs (Ed.), *Suicide*. New York: Harper & Row, Publishers, Inc., 1968.

POWELL, E. H. Occupation, status, and suicide: Toward a redefinition of anomie. *American Sociological Review*, April, 1958, 23:131-140.

PREVENTION OF SUICIDE, *Public Health Paper No. 35* (Geneva, World Health Organization, 1969.)

RADO, S. Psychodynamics of depression from the etiological point of view. *Psychosomatic Medicine*, 1951, 13:51-55.

RADO, S. The problem of melancholia. In: *Psychoanalysis of Behavior*, Vol. 1. New York: Grune & Stratton, 1956.

REICH, W. Psychischer Kontact and Vegetative Stroemung. Copenhagen: Sexpol Verlag, 1935.

REIK, T. *The Compulsion to Confess*. New York: Farrar, Straus and Cudahy, 1959.

RESNIK, H. L. P. (Ed.). *Suicidal Behaviors, Diagnosis and Management*. Boston: Little, Brown, 1968.

RESNIK, H. L. P., DAVISON, W. T., SCHUYLER, D., and CHRISTOPHER, P. Videotape confrontation after attempted suicide. *American Journal of Psychiatry*, April, 1973, 130:4.

RESNIK, H. L. P. and HAWTHORNE, B. C. (Eds.). Summary and recommendations. In: *Suicide Prevention in the Seventies*. Rockville, Maryland: NIMH, 1973.

ROBINS, E., GASSNER, J., KAYES, J., WILKINSON, R. H. and MURPHEY, G. E. The communication of suicidal intent. A study of 134 consecutive cases of successful suicide. *The American Journal of Psychiatry*, 1959a, 115:724-733.

ROBINS, E., GASSNER, J., KAYES, J., WILKINSON, R. H., and MURPHEY, G. E. Some clinical consideration in the prevention of suicide based on a study of 134 successful suicides. *American Journal of Public Health*, 1959b, 49:888-899.

ROBINS, E., SCHMITT, E. H., and O'NEAL, P. Some interrelations of social factors and clinical diagnosis in attempted suicide. *American Journal of Psychiatry*, 1957, 114:221-231.

ROCKWELL, D. A. and O'BRIEN, W. Physicians' knowledge and attitudes about suicide. *Journal of the American Medical Association*, 1973, 11:1347-1349.

ROSEN, G. History in the study of suicide. In: *Psychological Medicine. A Journal for Research in Psychiatry and the Allied Sciences*. Oxford University Press, Vol. I, No. 4, Aug., 1971.

ROSEN, G. In: S. Perlin (Ed.), *Handbook for the Study of Suicide*. New York: Oxford University Press, 1975.

ROSS, M. Medical News. *Journal of American Medical Association*, 1965.

ROSS, M. The presuicide patient: Recognition and management. *Southern Medical Journal*, 1967, 60:1094-1098.

ROSS, M. Suicide among physicians. *Psychiatry Medicine*, 1971, 2:189-198. Also *Tufts Medical Alumni Bull.*, Vol. 34, No. 3, 1975.

ROSS, J. F., HEWITT, W. L., WAHL, C. W., OKUN, R., SHAPIRO, B. J., SLAWSON, P. S., and SHNEIDMAN, E. S. The management of the pre-suicidal, suicidal and post-suicidal patient. *Annals of Internal Medicine*, 1971, 75:441-458.

ROST, H. Bibliographie des Selbstmordes (Augsburg, 1927). In: N. L. Farberow, and E. S. Shneidman (Ed.), *The Cry For Help*. New York: McGraw-Hill Book Co., 1961.

RUDESTOM, K. Some cultural determinants of suicide in Sweden. *Journal of Social Psychology*, 1970, 90:225-227.

RUSK, H. and TAYLOR. *New Hope for the Handicapped*. New York: Harpers, 1946.

RUSK, H. *Rehabilitation Medicine*. St. Louis: Mosby, 1958.

RUTZ, P., VASQUEX, W., and VASQUEX, K. The mobile unit: A new approach in mental health. *Community Mental Health Journal*, 1973, 9 (1):18-24.

SAINSBURY, P. *Suicide in London*. London: Chapman & Hall, Ltd., 1955.

SAWARD, E. and SORENSEN, A. The current emphasis on preventive medicine. *Science*, 200, No. 4344, May 26, 1978.

SAWYER, J. B., SUDAK, H. S., and HALL, R. S. A follow-up study of 53 suicides known to a suicide prevention center. *Life Threatening Behavior*, 1972, 4:227-238.

SCHOFIELD, M. A study of medical students with the MMPI: III Personality and academic success. *Journal of Applied Psychology*, 1953, 38:47-52.

SECUNDA, S. Symposium—Update 1978: Understanding and Treating the Depresions: Proceedings of the Eleventh Annual Meeting, American Association of Suicidology, New Orleans, April, 1978.

SEIDEN, R. H. Suicide among youth, a review of literature 1900-67. Supplement to the *Bulletin of Suicidology*, December, 1969.

SHAPIRO, B. J., et al. In: The management of the pre-suicidal, suicidal and post-suicidal patient. *Annals of Internal Medicine*, 1971, 75:441-458.

SHNEIDMAN, E. S. Psycho-logic: A personality approach to patterns of thinking. In: J.

288 HANDBOOK OF SUICIDOLOGY

Kagan and G. Lesser (Eds.), *Contemporary Issues in Apperceptive Fantasy*. Springfield, Ill.: Thomas, 1960.

SHNEIDMAN, E. S. Orientations toward death. In: R. W. White (Ed.), *The Study of Lives: Essays on Personality in Honor of Henry A. Murray*. New York: Atherton Press, 1963, pp. 202-209.

SHNEIDMAN, E. S. (Ed.). *Essay in Self-Destruction*. New York: Science House, 1967.

SHNEIDMAN, E. S. Suicide, lethality and the psychological autopsy. In: E. S. Shneidman and M. Ortega (Eds.), *Aspects of Depression*. Boston: Little, Brown, 1969.

SHNEIDMAN, E. S., FARBEROW, N. L., and LITMAN, R. E. *The Psychology of Suicide*. New York: Science House, 1970.

SHNEIDMAN, E. S. Prevention, intervention, and postvention. *Annals of Internal Medicine*, 1971a, 75:453.

SHNEIDMAN, E. S. Perturbation and lethality as precursors of suicide in a gifted life group. *Life Threatening Behavior*, 1971b, 1:23.

SHNEIDMAN, E. S. *Deaths of Man*. New York: Quadrangle Books, 1973.

SHNEIDMAN, E. S. Suicide. In: A. M. Freeman, H. I. Kaplan, and B. J. Sadock (Eds.), *Comprehensive Textbook of Psychiatry*. Baltimore: Williams & Wilkins, 1975.

SHNEIDMAN, E. S. (Ed.). *Suicidology: Contemporary Developments*. New York: Grune & Stratton, 1976.

SHNEIDMAN, E. S. and FARBEROW, N. L. (Eds.). *Clues to Suicide*. New York: McGraw-Hill Book Co., 1957a.

SHNEIDMAN, E. S. and FARBEROW, N. L. Some comparisons between genuine and simulated suicide notes. *Journal of General Psychology*, 1957b, 56:251-256.

SHNEIDMAN, E. S. and FARBEROW, N. L. Suicide and death. In: H. Feifel (Ed.), *The Meaning of Death*. New York: McGraw-Hill Book Co., Inc., Blakiston Division, 1959.

SHNEIDMAN, E. S. and FARBEROW, N. L. *Some Facts About Suicide*. Washington, D.C.: United States Government Printing Office, 1961.

SHNEIDMAN, E. S. and FARBEROW, N. L. Statistical comparison between attempted and committed suicides. In: N. L. Farberow and E. S. Shneidman (Eds.), *The Cry For Help*. New York: McGraw-Hill Book Co., 1961.

SHNEIDMAN, E. S. and FARBEROW, N. L. Sample investigations of equivocal suicidal deaths. In: E. S. Shneidman and N. L. Farberow (Eds.), *The Cry For Help*. New York: McGraw-Hill Book Co., 1961.

SHNEIDMAN, E. S., FARBEROW, N. L., and LITMAN, R. E. A taxonomy of death—a psychological point of view. In: E. S. Shneidman and N. L. Farberow (Eds.), *The Cry For Help*. New York: McGraw-Hill Book Co., 1961a.

SHNEIDMAN, E. S., FARBEROW, N. L., and LITMAN, R. E. The suicide prevention center. In: E. S. Shneidman and N. L. Farberow (Eds.), *The Cry For Help*. New York: McGraw-Hill Book Co., 1961b.

SHNEIDMAN, E. S. et al. In: The management of the pre-suicidal, suicidal and post-suicidal patient. *Annals of Internal Medicine*, 1971, 75:441-458.

SIEGEL, M. Confidentiality. *Clinical Psychologist, Div. 12, American Psychological Association*, Vol. 30, No. 1, 1976.

SIEGMUND, G. *Sein oder Nichtsein, die Frage des Selbstmordes*. (To Be or Not To Be, The Problem of Suicide). Trier: Paulinus Verlag, 1961.

SIEGMUND, G. *Gott*. Bern: Franke, 1963, p. 10-12.

SIFNEOS, P. E., GORE, C., SIFNEOS, A. C. A preliminary psychiatric study of attempted suicides as seen in a general hospital. *American Journal of Psychiatry*, 1956, 112: 883-888.

SIGERIST, H. E. *Civilization and Disease.* Ithaca, New York: Cornell University Press, 1943.

SILVERMAN, C. The epidemiology of depression—a review. *American Journal of Psychiatry,* 1968, 24:883-891.

SILVING, H. Suicide and law. In: E. S. Schneidman and Farberow (Eds.), *Clues to Suicide.* New York: McGraw-Hill Book Co., 1961.

SIMON, H. J. Mortality among medical students. *Journal of Medical Education,* 1966, 41:424-444.

SIMON, W. and LUMRY, G. K. Suicide among physician-patients. *Journal of Nervous and Mental Disease,* 1968, 147:2.

SLAWSON, P. S. et al. In: The management of the pre-suicidal, suicidal and post-suicidal patient. *Annals of Internal Medicine,* 1971, 75:441-458.

SPITZER, R. L. and WILSON, P. T. Nosology and the official psychiatric nomenclature. In: A. M. Freedman, H. I. Kaplan, and B. J. Sadock (Eds.), *Comprehensive Textbook of Psychiatry.* Baltimore: Williams & Wilkins, 1975.

STEKEL, W. In: Paul Friedman (Ed.), *On Suicide.* New York: International Universities Press, 1967. English translation of the minutes of 1910 meeting of the Vienna Psychoanalytic society.

STENGEL, E. Suicide. In: G. W. T. H. Fleming (Ed.), *Recent Progress in Psychiatry,* Vol. 2, 1950, pp. 691-703.

STENGEL, E. Attempted suicide. *British Medical Journal,* 1952a, 1:1130.

STENGEL, E. Enquiries into attempted suicide. *Proceedings of the Royal Society of Medicine, London,* 1952b, 45:613-629.

STENGEL, E. Classification of mental disorders. *Bulletin of the World Health Organization,* 1960, 21:601-663.

STENGEL, E. Recent research into suicide and attempted suicide. *American Journal of Psychiatry,* February, 1962, 118:725-727.

STENGEL, E. *Suicide and Attempted Suicide.* Baltimore: Penguin Books, 1964.

STENGEL, E. The complexity of motivations to suicide attempts. *Bulletin of Suicidology,* December, 1967, 35-40.

STENGEL, E. and COOK, N. *Attempted Suicide: Its Social Significance and Effects.* Maudsley Monograph No. 4. London: Chapman & Hall, Ltd., 1958.

STEPPACHER, R. C. and MAUSNER, J. S. Suicide in male and female physicians. *Journal of American Medical Association,* April 15, 1974, 228:3.

STOLLER, R. J. *Splitting: A Case of Female Masculinity.* New York: Quadrangle Books, 1973.

STONE, A. A. Suicide precipitated by psychotherapy; a clinical contribution. *American Journal of Psychotherapy,* 1971, 25:18-26.

STRECKER, E. A., APPEL, K. E., PALMER, H. D., and BRACELAND, F. J. Psychiatric studies in medical education. *American Journal of Psychiatry,* 1937, 93:1197-1229.

Suicide Prevention Center, Los Angeles, University of Southern California Press, 1960.

SUICIDE PREVENTION TRAINING MANUAL. The American Association of Suicidology and the Health Information Services of Merck, Sharpe and Dohme Division of Merck and Co., Inc., New Jersey, 1978.

SULLIVAN, H. S. *Interpersonal Theory of Psychiatry.* New York: W. W. Norton & Company, Inc., 1953.

SULLIVAN, H. S. *Clinical Studies in Psychiatry.* New York: W. W. Norton & Company, Inc., 1956.

SZASZ, T. *The Myth of Mental Illness.* New York: Harper & Row, 1961.

TABACHNICK, N. D. and FARBEROW, N. L. The assessment of self-destructive potentiality.

In: E. S. Shneidman and N. L. Farberow (Eds.), *The Cry For Help*. New York: McGraw-Hill Book Co., 1961.

TERRY, H. P. Negligence. *Harvard Law Review*, 1975, 29:40-44.

THE FACTS OF LIFE AND DEATH. *Public Health Publication No. 600*, Selected Statistics. Washington, D.C.: U.S. Department of Health Education and Welfare, 1965.

THOMAS, C. B. Suicide among us: Can we learn to prevent it? *Hopkins Medical Journal*, 1969, 125:276-285. Also in *JAMA*, Vol. 228, No. 3, April 15, 1974.

TOYNBEE, A. *Man's Concern With Death*. New York: McGraw-Hill, 1968.

UHLEMAN, M., HEARN, M. T., and EVANS, D. R. *Microcounseling Versus Programmed Learning*. Proceedings Tenth Annual Meeting, American Association of Suicidology, Boston, 1977.

U.S. BUREAU OF CENSUS. *Statistical Abstract of the United States*, 89th ed. Washington, D.C.: U.S. Government Printing Office, 1968.

U.S. Department of Health Education and Welfare revision international classification of disease. ICDA Vol. 1, PHS publication No. 1693. Washington, D.C.: U.S. Government Printing Office.

U.S. VETERANS ADMINISTRATION. Suicide—Evaluation and Treatment of Suicidal Risk Among Schizophrenic Patients in Psychiatric Hospitals. Edited by Edwin S. Shneidman and others. *Medical Bulletin*, MB-8. Washington, D.C.: Veterans Administration, pp. I-II, 1963.

U.S. VETERANS ADMINISTRATION, Department of Medicine and Surgery. Suicide among general medical and surgical hospital patients with malignant neoplasms. Edited by N. L. Farberow and others. *Medical Bulletin*, MB-9. Washington, D.C.: Veterans Administration, 1963, pp. I-II.

VARAH, C. *The Samaritans: To Help Those Tempted To Suicide of Despair*. New York: Macmillan, 1966.

VOLTAIRE. *Of Suicide*. In Works, translated by T. Smolett, 4th Ed. (Dublin, 1772), Vol. XVII, pp. 165.

WAHL, C. W. et al. In: The management of the pre-suicidal, suicidal and post-suicidal patient. *Annals of Internal Medicine*, 1971, 75:441-458.

WEBER, M. *The Methodology of the Social Sciences*. Translated and edited by E. A. Shils and H. A. Finch. Glencoe, Ill.: Free Press, 1939.

WECHSLER, I. *Textbook of Clinical Neurology*. Philadelphia: W. B. Saunders, 1943.

WEISMAN, A. D. *On Dying and Denying*. New York: Behavioral Publications, 1972.

WEISMAN, A. D., et al. Death and self-destructive behaviors. In: H. L. P. Resnik and B. L. Hathorne (Eds.), *Suicide Prevention in the Seventies*. Rockville, Maryland: National Institute of Mental Health, 1973.

WEISMAN, A. D. Thanatology. In: A. M. Freedman, H. I. Kaplan, and B. J. Sadock (Eds.), *Comprehensive Textbook of Psychiatry*. Baltimore, Maryland: Williams & Wilkins, 1975.

WEKSTEIN, L. A classification system as a frame of reference for multidisciplinary communication in a rehabilitation center. *American Association of Clinical Counselors*, Vol. 1, No. 1, 1964.

WESTERMARK, E. *The Origin and Development of the Moral Ideas*. London: MacMillan, 1906.

Why Do People Kill Themselves? *Statistical Bulletin of the Metropolitan Life Insurance Company*, 1945, 26:9-10.

WILKINS, J. Suicidal behavior. *American Sociological Review*, 1967, 32:286-298.

WILKINS, J. A follow-up of those who called a suicide prevention center. *American Journal of Psychiatry*, 1970, 127:155-161.

WILLIAMS, G. L. The prohibition of suicide. In: G. L. Williams (Ed.), *The Sanctity of Life and the Criminal.* New York: Alfred A. Knopf, Inc., 1957.

WINKELSTEIN, W. In: Conditions for Change in the Health Care System (HEW Publ.) (HRA) 78-642. Washington, Department of Health, Education & Welfare, 1977.

WIXEN, J. Lesson in living. *Modern Maturity,* October-November, 1978.

WOLFGANG, M. E. An analysis of homicide-suicide. *Journal of Clinical and Experimental Psychopathology,* 1958, 19:208.

WOLFGANG, M. E. Suicide by means of victim-precipitated homicide. *Journal of Clinical and Experimental Psychopathology,* 1959, 20:355-349.

WOLLERSHEIM, J. P. The assessment of suicide potential via interview methods. *Psychotherapy. Theory, Research and Practice,* Fall, 1974, Vol. II, No. 3.

WORLD HEALTH STATISTICS ANNUALS. Geneva: *World Health Organization,* 1968, Vol. 21, No. 6.

ZILBOORG, G. Some sidelights on the psychology of murder. *Journal of Nervous and Mental Disease,* 1935, 81:422.

ZILBOORG, G. Differential diagnostic types of suicide. *Archives of Neurology and Psychiatry,* 1936a, 35:170-291.

ZILBOORG, G. Suicide among civilized and primitive races. *American Journal of Psychiatry,* 1936b, 92:1347-1369.

ZILBOORG, G. Considerations on suicide with particular reference to that of the young. *American Journal of Orthopsychiatry,* 1937, VIII.

ZILBOORG, G. The sense of immortality. *Psychoanalytic Quarterly,* 1938, 7:171.

ZILBOORG, G. and HENRY, G. W. *A History of Medical Psychology.* New York: Norton, 1941.

ZUBIN, J. Observations on nosological issues in the classification of suicidal behavior. In: A. T. Beck, H. L. P. Resnik, and D. J. Lettieri (Eds.), *The Prediction of Suicide.* Bowie, Maryland: Charles Press, 1974.

INDEX

293